RISE. RECOVER.
THRIVE.

HOW I GOT STRONG, GOT SOBER, AND BUILT A MOVEMENT OF HOPE

SCOTT STRODE

Stand Together Press

**Stand
Together**
Press

*Rise. Recover. Thrive. How I Got Strong, Got Sober,
and Built a Movement of Hope*

For more information, please contact:
Amplify Publishing, an imprint of Amplify Publishing Group
620 Herndon Parkway, Suite 220
Herndon, VA 20170
info@amplifypublishing.com

Library of Congress Control Number: 2024915845

CPSIA Code: PRS0824A

ISBN-13: 979-8-89138-138-4

Printed in the United States

*To anyone who has ever felt like you are not
deserving of love or that you are not enough.
The lessons of the world sometimes teach you that.
But none of that is true. You are a gift to the world,
and expressing that gift can change everything.*

*And to all members of The Phoenix.
This movement to change the country's approach
to addiction to one of empowerment based on a
belief in the strength of all people would be nothing
without the individuals who comprise it.
You are each courageous heroes of your own story,
and you use those stories regularly to help inspire
others toward a place of hope.
You are my friends and my inspiration.*

CONTENTS

PART II: BOSTON

PART III: MOUNTAINTOP MOMENTS

AUTHOR'S NOTE

This book is a memoir with a mission. It is mostly based on my personal memories and research and the recollections of the people closest to me. In deciding which aspects of my life journey to share, I've chosen those that best support the book's main intent, which is to empower anyone struggling with substance use to thrive in sobriety and to offer insights and hope to their loved ones as well. In certain instances, in the absence of a written record, I've recreated events and dialogue that are true to the spirit of what really happened. To maintain privacy and anonymity, where appropriate I have changed the names and identifying characteristics of certain individuals and places in the book.

PROLOGUE: NEPAL

What a man can be, he must be.

ABRAHAM MASLOW, American psychologist

I woke up at 3:00 a.m. in our hotel room in the Thamel District in Kathmandu, Nepal. The faint glow of light from the hallway that had outlined our door when I'd gone to bed had disappeared due to a citywide power outage. An underdeveloped power grid was to blame. The room was pitch-black.

Once my eyes adjusted, I looked across the room at Leo's bed. I could see his eyes were wide open. He was lying on his back, staring up at the cracks in the old plaster ceiling. "Can't sleep?" I asked.

"No, man, I have been up since 2:00 a.m. I don't know if it's jet lag or anxiety about flying up into the mountains today or maybe a little bit of both."

Leo Martinez, my gutsy climbing partner and boxing buddy back in Boston, a five-foot-three flyweight to my six-foot-three heavyweight, never got scared, at least not enough to show it. "Yeah, me too," I said. We lay there quietly in our tiny beds listening to the sounds of the street. Dogs were barking as they ran through the dirt roads of Kathmandu.

In just a few hours, a couple of Nepalese locals would be arriving in their weathered Toyota HiAce vans to take us, along with our climbing guide and all our gear, to the Yeti Airlines terminal at Kathmandu airport. Customers like Leo and I are Thamel's bread and butter, which is why it is also known as the Backpacker District.

Its narrow alleys are teeming with vendors selling deep-fried pani puri and samosas with chutney along with cheap souvenirs and trekking gear to the throngs of visitors coming to Nepal for climbing adventures. We were now part of that throng, about to embark on our first-ever high-altitude mountaineering expedition, up to Island Peak (altitude: 20,305 feet) in the Himalayas.

We'd spent months anticipating this moment. As relative rookie climbers who'd never ascended above 6,288 feet, we knew the weeklong journey ahead posed some dangerous, possibly life-threatening risks. It would be irrational not to feel a healthy dose of fear. But how we had imagined our minds and bodies would react when this adventure started to get real didn't come close to matching the levels of adrenaline and cortisol already surging through our veins.

Looking back, the stomach-churning wait in those predawn hours, as the hands on our alarm clock ticked closer and closer to our departure, was almost more stressful than the climb itself. The nerves, the misgivings, the self-doubt. It felt like unwanted, uninvited demons from the past had started infiltrating every cell in my body. Their goal: to undermine the self-worth I'd worked so hard to develop since a harrowing, cocaine-fueled night back in April 1997, when I made a life-altering choice.

After years of drug and alcohol addiction, I was now two and a half years sober.

On the outside, I looked noticeably better—strong and fit. Like somebody who actually had it together. But on the inside? A whole different deal. I was a mess. Insecure, confused, broken. Still searching. Something was missing; I just didn't know what. I'd come to Kathmandu hoping to find it.

I've chosen to begin my book in this exotic, faraway land because, to be honest, it's a lot more exciting than Lancaster, Pennsylvania, where I grew up. And because in many ways, my story starts here.

* * *

The original plan for this trip was not the Himalayas. Leo and I were supposed to be climbing two mountains in Ecuador—Cotopaxi and Chimborazo. But inconveniently a neighboring volcano, Guagua

Pichincha, had erupted in early October, sending pyroclastic flows into the air and raining ash down on Quito, the city we were scheduled to fly into. "Are you kidding me?" I asked when Leo called with the bad news. We'd spent months obsessively planning for every contingency. "Where on the worst-case scenario checklist did it mention 'volcanic eruption'?"

To be fair, maybe if we'd taken more time to actually decipher the cool topography maps we'd ordered, we'd have realized volcanic activity was a possibility. But we were learning as we went; we'd only been climbing together for about three years, and our adventures were mainly confined to the White Mountains in New Hampshire. As a climbing team, we didn't appear destined for greatness.

Leo was strong and fit—he'd never struggled with addiction—but he wasn't sold on the whole nature thing. I'd always been into outdoorsy stuff. But in the early days of my climbing, I was still buying coke at seedy bars in Boston's Combat Zone and getting blackout drunk a couple nights a week. Let's just say the odds of success weren't stacked in our favor.

I often say we're all in recovery from something, and clearly I'm no exception. I spent my childhood bouncing back and forth between a wealthy workaholic mother (who would later become a U.S. ambassador) and an erratic, emotionally abusive father whose mental illness eventually led him to living on the streets. You can throw in an alcoholic stepfather—whose vodka-fueled insults bordered on cruel—for good measure. In my teens and early twenties, I struggled with suicidal thoughts and near-lethal addiction. I then found joy on a mountaintop.

But it wasn't until I was able to share that joy with others, through The Phoenix, a national sober active community I cofounded in 2006, that I went beyond surviving to truly thriving in sobriety. That's when I realized I didn't need the mountain anymore.

* * *

We all have our stories. If you're reading this, I'll bet you have a bunch that can top mine. What makes my personal journey worth sharing—from my dark days as an angry, morose teen and coke-addicted young adult to a nervous novice climber in Nepal and later a mountaineering guide, triathlete, and leader of a sober empowerment movement—are the powerful principles I learned along the way that transformed my life and provided comfort and a new perspective for my loved ones.

Those principles are the soul of The Phoenix, where we respect the dignity of every person, regardless of their circumstances, and empower our members to achieve their full potential. Whether we are climbing a rock wall, doing yoga together, creating artwork, or helping each other with career goals, at The Phoenix we believe in each other even before we believe in ourselves.

Before we return to my story, here's something you should know: The insights and aha moments I share in this book, which have helped in my recovery, didn't come from traditional drug and alcohol treatment programs or from 12-step meetings, although I've been to plenty of those. My epiphanies came from experiencing and witnessing, through my own frightening, funny, sad, surprising, enlightening, and ultimately joyful voyage of discovery, the remarkable resilience of the human spirit.

Those extraordinary moments shaped me throughout a play with many acts, starting with my childhood in rural Lancaster, struggling with severe dyslexia, my dad's mental illness, and my own budding addictions. Later, it was swabbing decks and reading *The Sea-Wolf* with other learning-disabled teenagers on a two-masted schooner crossing the Atlantic; moving to Boston to work in shipyards rife with alcoholism; and becoming imprisoned in a cycle of drinking, blackouts, and buying crack in dark alleys.

Then came finding hope in Kathmandu, where I first started seeing myself as more than my addictions; losing some of that hope answering drug overdose 911 calls as an emergency medical technician in Boston; barely surviving getting trapped on Denali in a blizzard, which taught me even so-called "healthy" escapes can go too far; moving to Colorado and founding The Phoenix, then returning to Boston as a husband and father. And, most powerful of all, watching people who'd lived in squalor in Boston's open drug market become contributing members of society.

From all these disparate experiences, I discovered a pathway to recovery that was based on embracing an unconventional new mindset unencumbered by the past. Rather than defining myself by my disease, I chose to identify first as the person I had become. So when we meet one day—and I hope we will—I won't introduce myself with "Hi, I'm Scott, and I'm an addict and an alcoholic." Instead, I'll greet you with "Hi, I'm Scott, and I'm in recovery. And I'm so much more than that."

This seemingly subtle shift—away from leading with who we were to focusing on all we can be—lies at the heart of the paradigm shift the Phoenix movement is working to create around how our country views, talks about, and treats addiction.

* * *

After two more hours of tossing and turning on twin beds where the presence of mattresses was debatable, Leo and I finally rose and got dressed. We were standing outside our hotel, too amped up to feel the cold, well before the HiAce vans arrived. The drivers loaded Leo, me, and our climbing guide Bruce Andrews into one van, all our gear in another, and we headed for the Kathmandu airport. The sun was just rising when we got there.

Two weeks earlier, when Guagua Pichincha first erupted, a friend had hooked us up with Bruce, who told us that the Himalayas were "in season" and he was available. So, in an unsettlingly fast and dramatic destination switch from the Andes to the Himalayan giants, here we all were, about to board a twin otter plane bound for Lukla. That's where our climb would begin.

Twin otters are built for short runways and hard-to-reach places, which was our second clue that white knuckles were in our immediate future. Our first clue had been the dour ticket agent who'd told us we could not fly up to Lukla if it was cloudy because it was too dangerous to navigate through the mountains. Yet here we were boarding, and it sure looked cloudy to me.

I also would have bet all my rupees—the official currency of Nepal—that the plane was carrying well over its weight limit. Leo's and my overstuffed black North Face duffel bags alone probably weighed seventy-five pounds each, jammed with climbing gear, their yellow stitching bulging at the seams. Regardless, this was nothing a few rupees could not fix. Corruption and bribes were common; at the time Nepal was the fourth-poorest country in the world.

Our flight boarded almost immediately. We all filed out onto the tarmac into the warm, thick Kathmandu air, still moist from all the monsoon rains. The two pilots standing next to the plane looked like something straight out of *Top Gun*: leather flight jackets, slicked-back hair, and aviator sunglasses. Four or five mechanics working on the engine all seemed a little perplexed by something. There was some head-scratching and wrenching on the engine. They seemed to sort it out and allowed us to board.

The flight attendant greeted us with a smile I didn't buy for a second. "It's all good," she seemed to be signaling as she handed us each a ginger candy, I guess in preparation for turbulence, and two cotton balls to drown out the sound of the engine. Noting my 215-pound frame, she told me to sit in the front. Leo and Bruce sat next to each other in the back.

Suddenly the engine roared to life, and after a short taxi and a quick turn, the captain pushed the throttles forward and the plane skidded down the runway and lifted off into the air. I felt as if I were part of the flight crew. They had seated me just behind the flight deck door, which was missing entirely, with my knees protruding into the cockpit. As we climbed up over the Kathmandu Valley, the crossroads of many ancient Asian civilizations, steeped in history and mythology important to both the Hindu and Buddhist faiths, I thought this might be a good time to pray.

* * *

Legend has it that the visionary Vipassi Buddha dropped a lotus seed in the primordial "Lake of Serpents" where Kathmandu now stands. Later, according to Buddhist scripture, the deity Manjushri came to worship, and in the center of the lake, he saw a radiant golden lotus, symbolizing full enlightenment. With his flaming sword, he cut a gorge at Chobhar Hill to drain the lake so humans could flourish in the sacred Kathmandu Valley.

Manjushri then moved the lotus flower to the top of Swayambhu Hill, northwest of Kathmandu Valley, where in AD 460 the Swayambhunath Temple was built. Now a revered pilgrimage site for Buddhists and Hindus, it is also known as the "Monkey Temple," so called for the hundreds of sacred monkeys that roam its grounds. For centuries it has stood as a symbol of faith and harmony, with Hindu temples and deities sharing space on one of the holiest Buddhist sites in Nepal.

My thoughts drifted back to the visit Leo, Bruce, and I had made to the temple just the day before. While at the time I wasn't a deeply spiritual person, the experience had a profound impact on me. We'd climbed 365 exceedingly steep stone steps to reach the massive white central stupa—a Buddhist shrine used for meditation and to house religious relics—which was encircled by prayer wheels. It happened to be a Hindu holiday, and I noticed Hindu and Buddhist worshippers alike walking clockwise around the stupa, rubbing their prayer beads and spinning the prayer wheels.

It felt foreign to me, and deeply moving, to see two faiths blend so seamlessly like this. In celebration the Hindu worshippers had painted multicolored tilaks in the center of their foreheads and on the foreheads of any willing Buddhists as they decorated their shrines with flowers matching those draped over their animals and automobiles. One couldn't help but feel the presence of their own God or gods here amid the thick whisps of juniper incense that drifted from the small pyres.

After a few minutes spent gazing out at the glory of the Kathmandu Valley below, we joined the eclectic procession of pilgrims and tourists and trekkers who were following the deep grooves worn over the years into the stones around the shrine. Each of us had a turn spinning a prayer wheel; like most climbers do there, we asked for safe travels. But I added my own private prayer: that whatever it was I was looking for, that intangible thing that would help fill the void within me that years of substance use had only deepened, I might find it here.

* * *

Back up at twelve thousand feet, my reverie was broken by the severe air turbulence now buffeting the plane. After we crossed over the foothills of the Himalayas, sheer cliff faces started appearing off our wing tips, with the occasional view of a mountain peak, as we drifted in and out of the clouds. I remember thinking maybe I should have given one of those prayer wheels an extra spin.

I looked back at Bruce and Leo, who both threw me a thumbs-up in sync before going back to peering out their small window. I wasn't sold on their thumbs-up vote because I could see into the cockpit of the plane and we had very poor visibility ahead, only part of which came from the clouds outside the aircraft.

The captain kept taking off his aviator glasses whenever they fogged up, which from where I sat appeared to happen every ten minutes or so. He'd then leisurely wipe them down with a cheap Nepali napkin that looked like wax paper and accomplished nothing. Each time this slightly unnerving exercise took place, the copilot would take over the controls and the plane would slowly drift off course. The captain would then make some large course corrections once his shades were back on.

Shutting my eyes and eating my ginger candy seemed like a good idea at that point; I could imagine myself back at the Monkey Temple preparing mentally for what lay ahead. But at the next lurch, I looked ahead to see a wall of rock mountains and ridges rising up directly in front of us.

There, perched on the edge of a massive cliff under the shadow of a sheer mountain face, was a small village.

It was encouraging to see a runway; I just wished there were a little more of it. It was a small dirt strip that from our height seemed no longer than a city block and looked to slope up and away from where it started on the cliff's edge. The nose of the plane suddenly tipped down, and we dropped with intention toward our destination. The wheels hit the ground just inches from where the runway began, and the plane pushed forward on the uphill dirt path until we turned to the right at the top and came to a stop on a small piece of flat ground. We had arrived in Lukla.

* * *

Small teahouses lined the runway, the odor of yak dung fires wafting from their stovepipes. Teams of massive yaks weighing upward of twelve hundred pounds were being driven by red-cheeked Nepalese yak herders, followed by trekkers and porters, some haggard from long journeys and others, like us, just starting their adventures.

Leo and I climbed our way up the steps of a nearby teahouse and sat at a small table where the owners served us tea and cookies while Bruce went off to haggle with our local guides and porters. It's hard to overstate the wonder I felt in that moment, looking out over the Khumbu Valley, one of three main valleys that form the Everest region, and the anticipation I felt at getting a fresh start on life. I was still at the very beginning of my sobriety journey. But with each passing day, I identified a little more as a climber and a little less as an addict.

With our yaks and porters assembled, we began our way up the trail, staying the first night in a small campsite just below Lukla. It felt good to be in the open air and sleeping in a tent for the first time on our trip. The next morning, we wound our way up the trail to Namche Bazaar, a centuries-old Tibetan trading post. We stayed there for two nights to acclimatize to the altitude (11,280 feet) before continuing to the secluded, tranquil Tengboche Monastery, one of the last stops on the way to the high peaks. If Shangri-La exists, that might be it.

We camped out just below Tengboche, in a small open field. In the morning we climbed back up to the monastery to join the monks' morning meditation ceremonies and to again ask for blessings over our expedition. Whether you're religious or not, the more positive karma you can bring with you when hiking the Himalayas, the better.

Looking down the valley, we caught our first panoramic view of Mount Everest, along with other famous peaks like Lhotse and Ama Dablam. The thought of climbing any of these mountains sent shivers down my spine. They seemed to be out of the reach of human capabilities. But that's exactly why I had come here—to unshackle myself from the sense of worthlessness I'd grown up with and move toward the person I wanted to become.

Inside the monastery, the deep, low, and slow oms of the monks reverberated as one of them walked up and down the aisles on wooden floorboards spreading incense. I was struck by the brilliantly colored paintings on the walls, rich in religious significance. As an important learning center, the monastery also has an extensive library with thousands of rare and valuable manuscripts and books.

Yet in this holy place, in the presence of so much faith, I struggled to find faith in myself, let alone in a higher power. For as far as I'd come, I knew my journey to a truly fulfilling, sober life, one in which I could find and follow my purpose, had only just begun.

*   *   *

I'm sometimes asked why we at The Phoenix call ourselves a movement. Here's my answer: We're a group of people who've come together with shared beliefs about a fundamental human truth—the idea that everybody has intrinsic strength and the ability to rise if they can find a nurturing space to do that.

We are challenging the belief that addiction is a moral failing or that a person doesn't deserve better because of how they've lived their life or due to the pain they've caused their family. Or that some of "those people"—the ones who are living on the streets, still using, having lost everything—are beyond helping.

Because here's the thing: none of that is true.

Who among us doesn't want to rise? Live longer, better, happier? I firmly believe each of us has the ability to do that. Every day I see people who are struggling to survive in Boston's open drug market near where I now work and live. I see the potential in every single one of them. They just don't yet see the potential in themselves.

Self-esteem is a hard thing to hang on to even in the best of times. In the words of my favorite social psychologist, Abraham Maslow, "The story of the human race is the story of men and women selling themselves short." At The Phoenix, our mission is to discourage anyone who joins our community from selling themself short.

Just think how we could flourish as a country if we all started believing in ourselves and in each other. How much more productive we could be if we devoted our energy to lifting each other up rather than pushing each other down. In this moment when we've made a national pastime out of hating on each other, my hope is that the Phoenix ethos can provide a path to healing, not just for people struggling with addiction but for the toxicity afflicting our nation as a whole.

PART I

PENNSYLVANIA

Fire can warm or consume,
water can quench or drown,
wind can caress or cut.
And so it is with human relationships.
We can both create and destroy, nurture and terrorize,
traumatize and heal each other.

BRUCE D. PERRY, psychiatrist and bestselling author
specializing in children's mental health

CHAPTER ONE

CAR TALKS

One of my earliest childhood memories growing up in rural Lancaster, Pennsylvania, is of rolling hills, wispy white clouds, and roadside fruit stands, as seen from the back seat of my dad's silver Mercedes (on loan from the car dealership where he briefly worked) while we careened through the countryside at what felt like one hundred miles per hour.

My big brother Mark, four years my senior, sat in the front passenger seat; I shared the back with my sister Amyla, the middle child. Amyla got straight A's and followed the rules. Even Dad's crazy ones. She probably thought—with good reason—that would keep her safe. By contrast, Mark and I lived life by our own rules. Our dearest wish was to fly under the radar, to not get noticed. To that end, unlike our sister, we both strove for mediocrity. We got an A+ in that.

I remember staring out the window at the green hilltops speckled with white barns; they reminded me of rolling waves topped with whitecaps. Sometimes one of my dad's hunting dogs would come along—I can still smell his wet Chesapeake Bay retriever, who loved to swim. Occasionally we'd stop at a roadside fruit stand and grab a bag of apples for lunch. This might sound like every kid's dream—open road with Dad, fast car, a dog—but for one additional detail: our dad had serious, undiagnosed mental illness.

As kids, we didn't totally understand that. We only knew when we were with him that anything good had the potential to turn bad, fast. We never knew if he'd show up manic or deeply depressed. His erratic moods, accompanied by ongoing threats of suicide, left us ever fearful he'd kill himself and take us with him. For decades I had a recurring nightmare of my dad driving us off the side of a cliff. I was a quiet kid whose troubled thoughts were not my friends. My father intentionally fed those fantasies.

* * *

John King Strode (a.k.a. my dad, mostly known as "Jack"), was a tall (six-foot-two), handsome, deceptively charming man who could flip to scary in an instant. Sunday afternoons were when he returned us to Mom—they'd divorced when I was three—after spending time with us as part of their every-other-weekend custody arrangement. He would use road time for "car talks." We dreaded them.

"You kids know your mom is paying money to a lawyer to keep me from spending time with you, right?" he asked one afternoon as we sped from Kirkwood, Pennsylvania, where he lived, toward the small brick row house on Race Avenue in Lancaster where we lived with Mom. Amyla and I looked out the window as Mark slunk further into his seat. "And I don't have the money to fight back. Do you know how crappy that makes me feel?" As always, none of us answered. Mark's tactic was to disassociate. Amyla would cry and pat Dad's shoulder.

Of the three of us, she was the most enmeshed with Dad and the most sympathetic to his pain. I think that was her way of protecting herself from him. I'd just gaze out the window at the cornfields and let my overly active imagination run wild. How cool would it be to run free in those fields, chasing after the dogs, splashing in the nearby creeks, eating endless ears of sweet Lancaster corn? I wonder how bad I'd get hurt jumping out of the car at this speed? It would be fun to be a farmer's son. I bet I could drive a tractor, no problem.

Then, back to reality. I wondered why Dad hated Mom so much, and what he was going to say next.

"It makes me want to be dead."

There, he'd said it. And not for the first time. By the time we pulled up in Mom's driveway, all of us were sobbing. "Dad, you don't mean that," Mark said, sounding more confident than he felt. "Daddy, we love you," Amyla said. "We love Mom too," I added. "Please don't be mad at her."

Mom came running out to the car—incongruously looking like a million bucks, with her blond Farrah Fawcett hairdo (it was the seventies), wearing faded jeans and a T-shirt—eager as always to get us back. But Dad had other ideas. To intensify the drama, he rolled up the windows and locked the doors.

"Jack, open the door! Let our kids out!" she yelled, loud enough for the neighbors to hear, as she pounded on the driver's side window. "You're insane. Don't take this out on them!" I remember looking around at our neighbors' front doors hoping someone would come out to help us, but no one ever did.

"Stay in the car! Your mom's the one who's insane!" Dad shouted back. "You're my kids too! I'll say when you get out."

"If you don't let them out right now, I'm calling the cops!" Mom screamed back.

This tactic always got to us. "Dad, please let us out," Mark pleaded. From the back seat, kind-hearted Amyla added, "I don't want you to go to jail."

Eventually, he relented. At the sound of the locks popping up, the three of us grabbed our backpacks and scrambled out of the car. We tumbled onto the driveway, and I did what I always did: I ran in the front door of the house, and straight out the back, into the peace and solitude of our small, fenced-in backyard.

And there I waited, under the big pine tree, until I heard the squeal of Dad's tires as he backed out of the driveway, leaving us to the relative calm of Mom's house. Of course, we could never totally relax, knowing it was only a matter of time before we had to deal with Dad again. And Mom, who became my rock in later years, had issues of her own (her "ism" was workaholism), including a pattern of marrying damaged men.

Many years later a therapist explained to me that our body's adrenal system reacts with fight-or-flight hormones when we are confronted with "big *T*" traumas like an attack from a bear. *But what if the bear follows you home?* Those responses don't work so well. It often felt like we lived with the bear.

Our father never abused us physically. But the potential was always there. And the emotional abuse was constant. So did that count as trauma with a big *T* or a little *t*? And did it really matter? In the years to come, I'd find out the hard way.

CHAPTER TWO

GROWING UP FERAL

The year Mom and Dad divorced, the most popular TV show in America was *Happy Days*. Every week more than thirty million Americans tuned in to watch the feel-good adventures of the Cunningham family. Spoiler alert: we were not that family.

On our weekends with Dad, before he married up (for a second time), we lived—or I should say survived—in a dilapidated two-story, unfinished wood and stone structure. The collection of rooms ("house" would be too strong a word) sat on an isolated patch of land near the woods, just south of Quarryville. Dad, a competitive wood-carver, had bought it with some money he made doing carpentry work for people. Unfortunately, he had few repeat customers since a lot of that work went unfinished.

Dad lived squarely in Amish country, surrounded by farms and fields. The view from his front window was deceptively serene and enchanting. His place was nestled in a tranquil little valley. But it was high enough up on one side of the valley that we looked across to the other side, where we could see a natural spring that Dad ended up expanding into a little man-made pond. He could be handy that way.

We would swim across the pond by ourselves, even when I was little and could barely dog-paddle. Nearby there was a culvert with a stream running through it under the road, and we'd splash around in there trying to catch crayfish. Some days we'd help Dad hunt wild rabbits for dinner, then cook them on his single-burner, plug-in hot plate, which sat atop a small cabinet with a piece of plywood over it with a work light clamped to it. That was the dining room.

Other days we'd shoot doves or an unlucky pigeon that flew into the barn. On special occasions, Dad would thaw out a frozen duck, packed in ice inside a white plastic milk jug with the lid cut off, which he'd retrieve from the large, rusted, top-loading freezer in the garage. There were also days we lived on Cokes and boxes of Cheez-Its. I often felt hungry.

On these weekends nobody asked or seemed to care where we were or what we were doing. That's why my brother says we grew up feral. He's not wrong about that.

The ground floor of Dad's house mostly belonged to the hunting dogs. Dad would just throw a bag of dog food on the floor and tear open a corner, and they would eat out of it. Adding to the creepiness, during one manic episode, Dad decided to tear down an exterior wall to build an addition. But he never got around to it, so he covered the gaping hole with plastic. We'd fall asleep upstairs listening to that plastic flapping in the wind.

If, God forbid, we had to use the bathroom in the middle of the night, it meant a scary trip to the outhouse. Dad's property looked haunted in the moonlight. His house cast big, dark shadows on the short hill we had to walk up. The outhouse was even creepier, with no light and a creaky door. Usually we just tried to hold it until morning.

And here's the weirdest thing: all four of us—including Amyla—slept together in one king-size bed, way past when it was appropriate. Today, child services would surely have paid a visit. But I don't recall anyone ever questioning whether we were OK.

"I'm going to renovate this house by Christmas!" I remember Dad telling us the summer after he moved in. "You'll each have your own room." But Christmas turned into Easter, and then it was the Fourth of July, and, well, somehow that work just never got done.

* * *

I recognized early on that two or three personalities were housed in my dad's big, strapping body. He could be charming and gregarious. He was more often mercurial and mean. And, very occasionally, his creative, poetic side would make an appearance.

I remember one fall day when Mark, Amyla, and I were tossing a baseball around in the lower field and Dad came walking down the hill. We didn't usually know where he was during the daytime. But on this day, for some reason he found us. Expecting one of his regular critiques, we stepped up our game. Instead, he sat down in the freshly cut grass by a stream that fed a small pond. The three of us joined him, and we sat together watching the sunset.

Dusk was a magical time in that field as the sky turned pink and purple, the quiet broken only by the nasal, one-syllable honks of geese flying south for the winter. As they got closer, they flew directly overhead in a V-shape before landing on Octoraro Lake just below my dad's farm. In the stillness of twilight, all we could hear was the gentle whoosh of their wings flapping. In that moment Dad said, "I want to call this Wing Song Farm." Perfect, we said. Magical. We love it. I tried hard to believe this peaceful moment could last.

* * *

Unfortunately, at magical Wing Song Farm, we had no heat. Maybe there was an electric space heater in the room where we all slept together. But in the winter, that drafty, uninsulated house got really cold. So Dad empowered whichever kid got up first to go downstairs and start the wood-burning stove.

More often than not, that kid was me. I always liked being the first one up; the quiet morning hours were the time of day I felt most at ease, with Dad's snores signaling I'd have a few hours of calm. But on one ill-fated day, the calm was short-lived.

As always, I threw some logs and sticks into the stove, and after burning the tips of my fingers on a few large kitchen matches that didn't catch, I got a big fire going and partially closed the door. Sitting there in my brother's hand-me-down flannel underwear, watching the flames, I spied a little piece of blue plastic lying on the floor.

Having never been taught fire safety and being too young for Boy Scouts—I'd never even been on a camping trip—I had the bright idea to add it to the kindling. (Most of my knowledge of farm life came from watching *Little House on the Prairie*.) So I opened the door and threw it in. Voila! A beautiful, rainbow-colored flame appeared that turned into thick black smoke at its edges. I was spellbound.

Shortly after that, Dad got up and came downstairs. The minute he thundered into the room, my fight-or-flight response was activated. I couldn't flee, so that left me with one option. "Did you put plastic in the fire?" he yelled.

"No!" I said, my heart racing.

He stared at me hard. It was a mean look, and I knew what was coming. "Are you lying to me?" he asked.

By now I was terrified as his large frame towered over me. He always seemed even taller and bigger when he was angry. "No, I'm not lying to you," I said. My only defense now was to double down on the lie.

At that he grabbed my arm, dragged me across his knee, and spanked me hard. I fought to choke back the tears welling up in my eyes; crying always seemed to make Dad madder. Then he picked up a log and said, "If you *ever* lie to me again, I'll give you an old-fashioned spanking." He waved that log in my face, sending a clear message: one more wrong move, and I'd get a serious beating.

Who knew if he meant it? But the threat was ever present. Then he went about his day, doing whatever it was he did all day at Wing Song Farm, leaving me to wonder how long it would be until his next angry outburst. As it turned out, not long at all.

* * *

Sunday morning was our favorite time of the week because we got to have breakfast with Nanny and Pop-Pop. It was usually a happy occasion. Nanny was our dad's mom, and Pop-Pop was her second husband, our step-grandfather, though we didn't know until years later he wasn't our blood grandfather. He was a solid, funny, caring man whose wrinkled, calloused fingers always smelled like sweet pipe tobacco when he held my hand. He, too, was an expert wood-carver, the one useful skill he'd passed on to my dad.

Nanny usually cooked the same breakfast every Sunday: scrambled eggs and sausage, Thomas' English muffins with guava jelly, and orange juice. It was a noisy occasion, with all of us gathered around a big wooden table alongside the living room, sunlight streaming through the chintz curtains. Then sometimes we'd go to Avondale Presbyterian Church. Going to their house was always a bit of a relief. It felt safe.

One Sunday, though, we were at my dad's house getting ready to go—a ritual that included Dad brushing our hair so hard our scalps nearly bled, so other churchgoers would see he had perfect kids—when we had a memorable mishap with long-lasting repercussions.

At the time we had a dog who had no flea or tick collar. He'd get ticks as large as marbles on him, and our dad made it one of our chores to pick them off. It always turned my stomach. On that day I spotted an especially juicy one. "Whoa, Mark, look at the size of that tick!" I yelled.

Before Mark could stop me, I plucked it off, put it on the porch, and smashed it with a rock. Blood splattered everywhere—including on my clean Sunday shirt. "Oh crap, now we're going to be in *big* trouble," Mark said, alarmed. I didn't have time to change and didn't have another clean shirt to change into anyway.

Sure enough, hearing the ruckus, Dad came bounding out the front door. Upon spotting my mess, he instantly morphed into Big Scary Dad. "What the devil is wrong with you?" he shouted, towering above me in a menacing way. I flinched and, looking down, girded myself as always for a possible strike. But his words always hurt far worse. "You're more trouble than you're worth!" Sadly, I was beginning to believe him.

Compared to tales of serious physical abuse, that incident may sound unremarkable. Yet years later Mark still remembered it and felt responsible for the trouble we got in that day. Since we were totally unmonitored, and he was the oldest, he always lived with the guilt that he couldn't do a better job of protecting my sister and me from Dad's wrath. Another aftereffect of living with the Bear.

* * *

As a kid it was hard for me to make sense of the hurt my dad caused. But as an adult, I came to understand he, too, was damaged by generational trauma. The reason we had Pop-Pop in our life was because years earlier my dad's dad, John Gensmer, had abandoned the family—his wife, his infant son (my dad), and Dad's older sister, my aunt Judy.

Tom Strode had fallen in love with my grandmother while John was still in her life. But by the time Tom got back from World War II, John had disappeared, so Tom married her and adopted her kids. That's when they all became Strodes.

Maybe out of guilt, our grandmother always coddled our dad. She thought he could do no wrong. But I think she and Pop-Pop were a little afraid of him too.

"Nanny, why can't we live with you and Pop-Pop every other week-end instead of with Dad?" I asked once, when I was about eight. "We don't like it there."

Nanny looked up from her ironing and was silent for a minute. "Because he's your dad and he loves you," she said. "He hasn't disappeared." I wondered if she meant that just being in our lives made Dad's emotional abuse forgivable. It was like she read my mind. "He does his best," Nanny said. I never brought it up again.

As an adult, my brother told me one of the few times he ever felt connected to our dad was when he acknowledged some pain at not having known his own father. "I only met my dad twice, and I didn't know until later he was my dad," he told Mark in a rare moment of introspection. Perhaps that man—our biological paternal grandfather, John Gensmer—

had undiagnosed mental illness or childhood trauma as well. Whatever it was, the debris just flowed downhill, overtaking everybody in its path.

Stephi Wagner, founder of the Mother Wound Project, summed it up the best way I've heard: "Pain travels through families until somebody is willing to feel it."

CHAPTER THREE

BORN CURIOUS

Our mom and primary caregiver, Marilyn Ware Strode, came from some money, though you'd never have known that to look at us. In the early days, after she and Dad split, we lived in the modest Race Avenue row house—the scene of the Sunday night driveway battles. The Hamilton Watch Factory was right across the street.

"You were born curious," Mom always told me. "And extremely active."

A standout moment, when I was three, involved getting into a pack of butter and covering myself with it, then running around the house naked, with Mom in pursuit, trying to catch her slippery, buttery toddler. But by elementary school, my exuberance and self-confidence were beginning to fade. Life with Dad was taking a toll. And I was becoming aware I had some kind of learning issue that made me different from other students. I just didn't understand what it was yet.

At times I took solace in playing alone. I especially liked sitting on our front porch, observing the watch factory workers gather on an upstairs balcony to take their smoking breaks. Sometimes they'd wave. I figured they all must be wearing free watches. I still wonder what excuse they gave if they were late. They couldn't very well say they lost track of the time.

* * *

Back in those years, Mom was a reporter for the local newspaper, the *Lancaster New Era*, and later she bought a small local paper in

Quarryville, the *Sun Ledger*. Her passion was campaigning for political candidates. She always had stacks of straw, wide-brimmed campaign hats and gubernatorial campaign posters piled high in our attic.

Her dad, John Ware (my grandpop), was CEO of American Water Works, the country's largest publicly traded water company, and PennFuel Gas. The Ware family, who held a majority stake in American Water Works, was the wealthiest family in Oxford, Pennsylvania, a small, working-class community halfway between Lancaster and Delaware. I was always surprised—and impressed—they stayed in such a small town given the financial opportunity they had.

If you ever find yourself traveling from Philadelphia to Strasburg, Pennsylvania, your GPS will take you down the John Ware Memorial Highway. That's because Grandpop was also a congressman, representing Pennsylvania's Ninth Congressional District in the U.S. House of Representatives. He'd had that highway built during his term to create jobs.

Given his money and influence, I was disappointed he didn't do more to help our mom through her divorce with an emotionally abusive ex-husband. With one call to the judge, he could have helped her protect us in her ongoing, ugly custody battles with my father. But he was never active in our lives. We saw Grandpop and Marmie, our mom's mom, on Christmas, but that was about it.

* * *

Bouncing back and forth between polar-opposite parents felt like hurtling between alternate universes. In one universe, my grandfather served in Congress and my mom took over the family business, became friends with three presidents, and served as the U.S. ambassador to Finland. She was constantly on the phone working or reading the *Wall Street Journal*, snapping her fingers for us to be quiet. Mom always had a project, something to do. Being present with us was hard for her. We had a lot of baby-sitters. And we ate a lot of Swanson TV dinners.

Then weekends would roll around, and we'd be back in that other universe, the one where we hunted wild game for food and had to pick lead bird shot out of our dinner meat. Danger was ever present, from our surroundings—and from Dad. All his goats died in a barn fire, for instance. Years later I wondered whether he'd burned down the barn to collect the insurance money.

Mom loved us. She occasionally tried to cook breakfast or dinner, the latter often supplemented by Hamburger Helper, never very successfully. And she was always up for some holiday magic. "Scott, help me move this sofa away from the wall," she said with a wink one time, when I was too small to be much help.

"It's too heavy!" I protested. "Why do we gotta move furniture?"

She smiled conspiratorially. "Because you said you wanted to wait up to catch Santa. This will give you a place to hide!"

My most special memories with Mom were the trips we took every summer to Avalon, on the Jersey Shore. She'd drive, and we'd all cram into our groovy 1973 Ford LTD station wagon in "burnt orange metallic," along with aunts, uncles, and cousins from her side of the family. I remember sitting on the seat that faced backward, watching the farmers markets roll by, and then somebody would get sick and we'd have to pull over so they could puke.

At the beach Mom would try to do things that were a little beyond her skills, like take us crab fishing in the bay. We'd be eaten alive by mosquitoes. I remember thinking, "This is not such a good idea." But it was nice having her full attention.

On the last night, we'd all have one last seafood dinner and pile back into the car at dusk. I'd be asleep when we got home, and Mom would carry me up to bed. And that was probably the safest I ever felt growing up.

But mostly Mom hid behind her work. We'd see her when we left for school and most days not again until we were in bed. And she had a temper. When the reality of raising three young kids as a single working mom got overwhelming, she would scream at us and throw an occasional shoe.

My father's anger came from a much deeper, darker, unpredictable place. It was a different kind of energy. We could duck Mom's shoe. But we couldn't escape Dad's psychological abuse.

In both universes, during the period of time before both our parents remarried, Mark, Amyla, and I got by pretty much on our own. Mark and I still think it's only a slight exaggeration to say as the years unfolded, we lived life wild, untamed, and, yes, feral.

CHAPTER FOUR

DEALING WITH DYSLEXIA

"**M**ommy, I don't want to read! I hate it!" I was in first grade, and it was always the same meltdown on the rare nights Mom came into my bedroom to read bedtime stories with me. "It's too hard. I can't do it. Please don't make me."

I loved it when Mom read to me. I especially liked *Where the Wild Things Are*. And *Curious George*, whom I could relate to. Like me, his curiosity was always getting him into trouble. But when it was my turn to read, a flood of frustrated tears followed.

Mom was concerned; a battery of tests followed. In first grade, I got a diagnosis: I was severely dyslexic. My brain was not wired to accurately encode letters or numbers into usable information. My case was so bad that I qualified for books on tape created for blind people. That was well before books on tape were common or Audible came along. And I repeated first grade.

Being asked to read aloud in class or write something on the blackboard was excruciating; the more sensitive teachers didn't ask. (Years later, as an adult, that self-consciousness lingers. At AA meetings, which I attend on occasion, when they hand the Big Book around and ask participants to read passages, I sometimes leave the room before it's my turn or awkwardly pass it to the next person.)

The annual spelling bee was even worse. I remember standing in front of the class in fourth grade, the blood rushing to my head, heart pounding, waiting to be called on. "Scott, please spell 'alarm.'" The easiest words came first. I actually knew how to spell it. "*A-l-o-r-m*. Alarm."

Yep, I spelled it wrong—on purpose. My strategy: get out early and cut my losses. I winked at my pals to let them in on the joke.

But nothing about dyslexia was funny. For one thing, I couldn't pass notes back and forth to my friends. "Hey, Scott, why didn't you meet us at the movies?" my friends asked me one day. "We sent you a note." Who knows how many invitations I missed out on in grade school because I couldn't read them or reply. Imagine today being the only kid who couldn't text their friends. (Unlike iPhones, note passing didn't come with spell-check.)

And in every class, I quickly fell behind on required reading. On some days my prognosis looked pretty grim. At one point, after I'd taken a bunch of tests my dad ordered with the help of his new wife Paula—conveniently, she was a psychologist—a clinician delivered some devastating news to my parents.

"Your son's learning disability is so severe he will never function normally as an adult."

My dad pounced on this as proof Mom wasn't doing her job—"You're failing the kids!" he said more than once—and that he should be given more visitation time. I later learned he'd taken me to that clinician in pursuit of evidence I wasn't being taken care of the way I should be. We were pawns in the divorce game, which was heartbreaking as a kid. Imagine knowing you're being used as a tool by one parent to inflict pain on the other.

My grandpop could have intervened. Certainly, at five-foot-eight, carrying herself with the self-confidence that came from her years as a single working woman, Mom commanded respect. But as our family's custody battles dragged on through the late seventies into the early eighties, she pled her case to plenty of misogynistic judges. Even as a kid, I sensed her frustration at feeling powerless to change the visitation. Every other weekend, after our time with Dad, she'd have to repair the emotional aftermath of his erratic and clearly inappropriate behavior. Having had Grandpop in court to help make that case couldn't have hurt.

* * *

I've always been pretty sure there was a direct link between my dyslexia and my addiction. I attended kindergarten and first grade at James Buchanon public elementary school. Then Mom moved us to Lancaster Country Day, a private school where she felt we—and especially I—would get more support. I repeated first grade, and it was not the school's fault, but things kind of went downhill from there. I struggled to keep up with all the reading. And I hated dressing just like all the other kids.

"Why do I have to keep wearing this stupid uniform?" I asked Mom a few years in.

"Because that's the school's rules."

"Well, I don't like those rules."

"Sometimes we have to conform to rules we don't like."

"Even if they're dumb rules?"

This momentarily put her at a loss since she'd always told us to think for ourselves and speak our minds. She opted for a question instead.

"Why do you think they're dumb?"

"Because they don't know what kind of clothes I like. Why should they tell me what to wear? What if I want to express my individuality?" That was a word I'd just learned, and it seemed to fit the occasion.

Lancaster Country Day won that round; the next morning I was back in school, blending in with all my male classmates in our itchy maroon sweaters and awkward corduroy pants.

But looking back I can see my opposition to one-size-fits-all thinking got started at a very early age.

* * *

By middle school my behavioral issues were growing—bad grades, fights—and I was becoming dull-spirited and withdrawn. Turned off by academics, I decided I was too cool for school. At my request, Mom put me back in public school, where I'd have more freedom and could go to school with kids from my own neighborhood. I started out strong: based on my high IQ scores, I started middle school in higher-level classes. By year two, based on my poor grades, I'd been moved to vo-tech (vocational training) to learn how to make aluminum siding.

Don't get me wrong: I have nothing against aluminum siding. It's a respectable career choice. It just wasn't *my* career choice. And it was based on faulty assumptions. I could digest information as fast as or faster than most of my classmates. But because I couldn't read it or write it unless it was dictated, the school assumed my cognitive abilities were impaired. It was just one more assault on my already shaky self-esteem.

To make matters worse, guys like me who ended up in wood or metal shop were viewed as misfits or losers. We were labeled as the intellectually challenged kids the school didn't know what else to do with.

So I helped them out. I started cutting class and getting high by the train tracks. I figured I might as well lower the bar to the level the school expected of me. Granted, a pretty stupid thing to do. But outside of the school walls, and away from my hypercritical dad and my new stepfather—a good guy when he was sober but a bully when he drank—it was one place I could go and not *feel* stupid. In fact, I started feeling pretty fucking cool. Which, at that age, was all I wanted—to be liked and accepted.

So, screw school. The early seeds of my addiction had taken root.

CHAPTER FIVE

FAMILY THEATER

L ittle did Mom know, when she hired the law firm of Hartman, Under-hill & Brubaker to represent her in her divorce from my father, that she'd end up with a twofer: in the process of discarding her current husband, she acquired a new one.

Al Lewis, a colleague of Mom's divorce attorney, was a tall, fit, no-nonsense former district attorney who'd been a college wrestler and who'd successfully prosecuted some high-profile organized crime cases. He was accomplished, fairly well-off, and very responsible. In other words, nothing like my dad. Also relevant: he was quite smitten with my mother. Partly out of self-interest, Al pitched in to make sure Mom didn't get screwed in her divorce. He quickly became her knight in shining armor.

They married soon after Mom and Dad's divorce became final. "Give Al a chance," Mom said when breaking the news to Mark, Amyla, and me that they were engaged. "He might just be the kind of father figure you've always needed."

I was hopeful. Al seemed to genuinely care about us, at one point even offering to legally adopt all of us (we declined), so we were willing to give him the benefit of the doubt.

By then we'd moved from our row house on Race Avenue to a slightly bigger house on Spencer Avenue. That street felt like more of a real neighborhood, with happy little gangs of kids running around playing in backyards and spilling into each other's houses. We'd set off fireworks somebody stole from their dad's Fourth of July stash, race our bikes recklessly down the narrow gravel alleyways that connected our houses, and get chased out of cranky neighbors' trees; it had a bit of a *Stand by Me* feel to it.

Dad had new digs as well. After marrying Paula, he had ditched Wing Song Farm in favor of his wife's brick multilevel townhouse in Wilmington, Delaware. Which, while less remarkable than Dad's place, conveniently had all its walls, along with indoor plumbing. This made our weekend visits slightly more bearable. For a moment in time, life started to feel almost normal. Or at least what counted as normal for us.

Granted, my father's parenting skills were still erratic at best. One weekend Dad and Paula took us to stay on a sailboat she owned that was docked in Havre de Grace, Maryland, on the Chesapeake Bay. Dad quickly tired of entertaining three children on a small boat. "Hey, why don't you kids go out and paddle the rowboat around for a while?" he suggested one afternoon. "Just don't leave the harbor."

It was not a well-thought-out suggestion. But Dad wanted alone time with Paula. You can probably guess what happened next. Three young kids, no boating experience. We immediately left the harbor. It didn't help that a storm was brewing. Ominous dark clouds started forming, and the winds whipped up.

Suddenly our rowboat took on a life of its own, being carried quickly by a strong current toward the Susquehanna River. "Scott, give me the paddles!" Mark yelled, frantic. "Amyla, hold on tight!" Mark took over, paddling furiously against the current, but our little dinghy was no match for the powerful Susquehanna. We kept going downstream. And boy, were we scared.

That's when we saw Dad running along the shoreline. I'm not sure how or when he realized we were in trouble. But he ripped off his shirt and shoes and dove into the water. He'd been a legitimate athlete in college but had to swim with all his might against the strong current. After what felt like forever, he reached us and climbed over the side of the boat, short of breath. "What in God's name were you kids thinking?" he shouted as he rowed us back to shore. He was clearly shaken.

Had we been older and felt more empowered, we'd have asked, "What were *you* thinking?" He'd been brave to come and save us. Heroic, even, in our eyes. But he'd put us in danger to allow for some adult fun with our stepmom. That was the dichotomy of our dad. That day a hero, but a tragic one.

* * *

Soon after Mom married Al, we moved again. This time it was a significant upgrade, to a much bigger house on Conestoga Woods Road, on the banks of the Conestoga River. That's where I met two kids who'd become my close buddies for life, my wingmen through some pretty extreme circumstances, from childhood through the dark days of addiction and into recovery, Danny and Aidan. My brother Mark and Danny, Aidan, and I helped raise each other as men.

In those early years, my buddies and I spent hours playing army and digging foxholes in the backyard and canoeing on the Conestoga River. By high school we'd discovered whose house we could most easily steal liquor from and how many beers we could take from my stepdad's garage refrigerator without him noticing. It was I who led Danny and Aidan to try weed and eventually cocaine. I was now sporting a mohawk and seven earrings. Aidan adopted a mohawk as well, and we got into the punk rock scene. Danny started wearing a trench coat and beret. We were all raging against the establishment.

Like me, Aidan had a home life marred by alcohol. In his case, it was his father who struggled. If anything, that seemed to strengthen his resolve to take a different path. He had clear goals, which he repeated often: "I want to go to college, get a job, and retire by the time I'm fifty!" Danny and I would laugh and shake our heads. That was right about the age we saw ourselves getting serious about life. "Let's have fun while we can" was pretty much the extent of our life plan.

For many years, Danny and Aidan felt more like family than my actual family. Decades later, when my mom died, they both traveled to

Philadelphia for her memorial service. And other than the gray hairs and a slightly deteriorating fitness level, we were just like we were back when we were kids.

The difference between us, back then, was that my life was quietly starting to unravel; their lives were not.

* * *

Early on in their relationship, while Al was still playing the role of Mom's savior from my dad, we'd finally started feeling safe. Al seemed like a decent enough guy, who would have made a good drill sergeant. "Out of bed! Feet on the floor!" was the daily wake-up call we'd get from Al. "And if you don't clean up your room, I'm coming with the green bag." By that he was referring to a reinforced Hefty garbage bag he'd frequently storm through our bedroom with. "Anything that's not cleaned up or not in its place, I'm throwing away!" It's a promise he made good on more than once.

(On a trip home from Boston during my shipyard days, I came across some prized personal possessions that had been confiscated in one of Al's green bag sweeps. When I asked for them back, Al said, "Absolutely not." He still felt the need to drive the message home all those years later.)

But he provided well for us and was, aside from Pop-Pop, the closest thing Mark and I had to a strong male role model.

For all his good qualities, though, Al had a major flaw: he could be an unpredictable, mean drunk. And he was often drunk. We didn't see that side of him at first. But once we moved to the Conestoga Woods Road house, and Mom no longer needed saving, he began drinking more and more. Once his hero role diminished, he didn't know how to be in the family in another way.

Mark and Amyla were now driving and more empowered, so they were out of the house a lot, leaving me to face Al on my own. With fewer dragons to slay, he spent most of his time at home mixing martinis. That's when the bullying and the shaming started.

One minute he'd be talking about excellence, integrity, and how to be exceptional. Then three martinis in, he'd show up at my bedroom door while I was struggling with my homework to blast me for my latest report card, even the ones I was proud of. "I didn't become a big-time lawyer with shitty grades like these," he'd say. "Keep this up, and you've got no future." He didn't seem to realize his biting message was being seriously undercut by the fact he was slurring his words.

Even more unsettling were the nights he'd decide to aggressively relive his glory days as a wrestler at Lehigh University. He'd call Mark, me, and sometimes even Amyla to the living room and start pinning us to the ground, roughly and repeatedly, ostensibly to teach us how to control an opponent using a half nelson and your body weight. We preferred the nights he'd fall asleep reading, next to his empty martini glass.

With both Al and my father, we never knew who was going to show up. Would they be sober or drunk? Manic or depressed? Kind or demeaning? As kids, we were always trying to figure out moment by moment who we should be to be loved. Sometimes it felt like we were living life on the stomach-churning SooperDooperLooper at Hershey Park—the first steel looping roller coaster on the East Coast—only our lives were a lot less fun.

* * *

Al did institute one weekly family outing that served as a bizarre bonding opportunity of sorts. Every Sunday we'd all pile into the family station wagon and drive across the state line into Maryland so Al could buy booze. It was cheaper in Maryland, and unlike in Pennsylvania, they sold it on Sundays. I remember driving along little farm roads, the car noisy with laughter and chatter, everyone happy being together. Then we'd get to an ABC store and Al would load a cardboard box full of handles of vodka into the back of the car and drive us back home.

That's when the party vibe would melt away. We'd usually end the day with a cookout. After a half dozen longneck Yuenglings, angry Al would reemerge. "You didn't put the aluminum foil on the burgers fast enough after taking them off the grill! Now you've ruined dinner for everybody!" he'd explode at whomever had the unlucky job of grilling burgers that night. "Can't you do *anything* right?"

Most kids associate the letters *A*, *B*, and *C* with learning the alphabet. I associated them with Sunday drives to Alcoholic Beverage Control stores and the chaos that inevitably followed. I thought this was how everybody lived. To my siblings and me, it felt like this was what childhood was.

* * *

When it came to get-togethers with Al's crew, Mark and I used to joke it wasn't a family gathering until somebody ended up in the emergency room. And somebody always did.

As it turned out, Mom had married into a family where alcohol was the center of the culture. They would turn any occasion into an excuse to drink—a lot. Mayhem would generally ensue.

Like the time my cousin Tim got hammered and tried to walk around the rim of our above-ground pool, fell off, and broke his ribs. Or the more remarkable incident at a family barbecue where we were making home-made fireworks for the Fourth of July. Inspired by a bunch of beers, my cousin Richard thought it would be a good idea to load a tennis ball with gunpowder and put a firecracker in it as a fuse. But the fuse was too short, so the tennis ball blew up before he could run away. I just remember them loading him into the car to rush him to the emergency room, his eyes and nose caked with burned black gunpowder.

The adults took it to a whole other level. Just as Mom had taken us to Avalon every summer with her family when we were smaller, Al now took us to the Tides Inn on the Chesapeake Bay in Virginia. We always looked forward to going; it was a beautiful resort designed for luxurious family getaways. But ours were always corrupted by the level of dysfunction present.

The focal point of these excursions was, naturally, the hospitality suite—a room reserved for such honored guests as Jim Beam, Tom Collins, and Bloody Mary. The latter beverage was especially popular; I vividly recall my aunts and uncles starting the day with Bloody Marys at breakfast, then continuing their cocktails at the pool. After dinner everyone would head to the hospitality suite, which was really just a fancy name for the designated party room.

I don't know who did the designating. But with Mark now well into his teens, on at least one trip someone decided our room would be a good choice. It was like a ritual: filling the bathtub full of ice, then dumping in bottles and bottles of beer. And of course everyone showed up bearing handles of gin, vodka, and rum. Mark and I couldn't even shower because our tub was full of ice, beer, and booze.

Things always got dangerously rowdy. One night one of my cousins broke his wife's ribs while they were rolling around on the bed in a play-wrestling match while drinking. Our cousins would occasionally get into fistfights or would roughhouse with us in the pool, and it was scary because they'd make us feel like we were drowning.

Being the only sober working adult in the group, Mom would sometimes arrive a day late. This gave Mark and me the opportunity to fully enjoy the hospitality suite. One time Mark got totally wasted before Mom got there, which our stepfamily found hilarious. "Don't say anything to Marilyn!" they joked. "Don't let her know the boys are drinking."

They viewed it all as harmless fun. They were too out of it to realize that anything done in secret is rarely harmless.

CHAPTER SIX

MY FIRST DRINK

Naturally as a young kid, hanging out with a bunch of aunts, uncles, and cousins who liked nothing better than drinking, I wanted to see for myself what all the fuss was about. Pretty much everybody I looked up to at that time stood around a beer keg or had a martini glass in their hand. This was the first time I'd had male figures in my life I could connect to in a more meaningful way, and I wanted to fit in.

One day while we were all out water-skiing, I decided it was time. "Hey, can I have a beer?" I shouted over the roar of the waves and the boat engine. "I'm thirsty."

My cousins laughed. "Oh yeah, you should give him one." Someone threw me an Old Milwaukee. "But if you have one, you've got to drink the whole thing." I was eleven.

A few good swallows in, I was sure I was going to throw up. We were bouncing around the Chesapeake Bay, the day was hot, and the beer was warm. It tasted gross. Most of my cousins were pressuring me to keep drinking. Luckily, one rational cousin grabbed the beer can and poured it over the side.

Allowing my cousins the benefit of the doubt, maybe they'd hoped that by drinking the beer, I'd be disgusted by it and then not want to have another drink. Even if that was not their intention, I *was* disgusted by it. But then an unexpected thing happened.

When I returned home to my friends and told them I'd had a beer, they all lit up and thought it was cool. "What was it like?" Danny asked. They all wanted to know. I'd experienced something unique; nobody my age had yet had a beer. And in that moment, for the first time ever, I felt cool. It elevated me in my peer group.

That's when it sunk in that this was something people admired. It made them want to spend time with me. So the next step was to become a supplier. By age thirteen I was regularly stealing bottles of vodka from the liquor cabinet and beers from the overflow beer fridge in the garage. Then, on the weekends, my friends and I would meet down by the river and drink and have fun. Finally, I was getting the love and acceptance I'd always craved.

I still hated it when Al drank, especially as the toxicity at home became untenable. But drinking helped numb the pain. If my cousins had really been trying to steer me away from alcohol that day on the Chesapeake, their plan badly backfired. As the years progressed, my drug and alcohol addictions put theirs to shame.

CHAPTER SEVEN

WHERE WERE THE GROWN-UPS?

By now you may be wondering: Where were the grown-ups while all this troubling behavior was playing out? Well, even as kids, we were wondering the same thing. At no time in my childhood do I remember an adult stepping in to protect Mark, Amyla, or me from our outrageous circumstances.

I'm not just talking about the most dangerous stuff, like boating with drunk cousins or spending unsupervised weekends with a mentally ill father. I'm also thinking of the many times other people witnessed clearly inappropriate behavior aimed at humiliating us and did nothing to intervene.

One that comes instantly to mind was the time my sister missed a shot during a school basketball game, a commonplace occurrence unless your name is Michael Jordan. But in my dad's opinion, it was unacceptable. "Amyla, get back on the court and try again until you get that shot right!" he commanded, between quarters, as her teammates sat chattering on the sidelines. "I didn't come here to watch you lose!"

Mortified, Amyla walked back to center court, alone. Suddenly, the gym grew silent. All eyes were on her. Mark watched from the stands, feeling helpless. It was a heartbreaking moment because he knew what our sister must be feeling. After an excruciatingly long moment, Amyla made the shot. Mark remembers the "whoosh" as the ball went through the net. The gym let out a collective exhale. Then Amyla stoically walked off the court and rejoined her team. To this day Mark and I wonder: "Why didn't anybody interrupt that? A coach? A referee? A parent?" But nobody did.

It's not surprising, then, that when Dad showed up for Mark's soccer games in high school, Mark's instant reaction was "Oh shit, I wish he wasn't here." I guess because he'd been a great athlete in college, Dad saw this as one area where he could add value to our lives. That might have been true had he not continued to chip away at our self-esteem in the process.

Mark still remembers Dad marching out on the field at halftime to berate him before the rest of the players reached the sidelines. The anxiety that caused left no space for the benefits of youth sports—camaraderie, goal setting, and accomplishment. It took the fun out of the game for Mark. And he wondered, again, "How come no grown-ups stepped up to help me?"

Granted, it was a different era, when people stayed out of each other's business. In fact, the only time I recall somebody else's parent doing something to protect me and my friends from danger, and not very effectively, was when Three Mile Island, a nuclear power plant located just forty-five minutes from Lancaster, partially melted down on March 28, 1979. It was the most serious commercial nuclear power plant accident in U.S. history.

I was at my friend's house, playing with a bunch of kids, when my friend's mom said, "Oh, we've been advised you can't play outside because of the potential radiation." Then she went back to watching the news, and she didn't even close the door. So my friends and I all congregated at the screen door, looking out at the yard, hoping to see some radiation. Clearly, helicopter parenting was not yet a thing.

But years later some of my own trauma work involved acknowledging that part of my pain came from the fact that even our own mom didn't adequately protect us when we were kids. She was the only other adult in our lives, and she didn't shield us from my dad or my stepdad and their emotional abuse.

For years I made excuses for that, some of which were valid: It was a tough time to be a divorced woman raising three kids. And Mom's dad, my dad, my grandpop, didn't protect her either. Later in life, my mother became my business confidante and partner, and we cultivated a deep friendship. But it wasn't until I accepted the fact that her mostly hands-off approach with Dad and Al had contributed to the lasting damage they did to our whole family, and forgave her for that, that I was truly able to heal.

CHAPTER EIGHT

DON'T TREAD ON ME

By the mideighties the hard-core punk rock movement—characterized by the *New York Times* as "young musicians wanting to blow up the world with noise and attitude"—was starting to flame out. But the rebellious nature of it drew me in. It was mosh pits and mohawks and loud, aggressive music, and a bunch of youth who felt disenfranchised in general. To complement my seven earrings, I had a leather jacket that said "Don't Tread on Me." Which, believe it or not, gets you trod on more than you might think.

I went to a school where most of the kids listened to Mötley Crüe and Iron Maiden and had long hair, and I had a mohawk. And I was tall for my age. So after school, when there was going to be a fight, it was usually between me and some jock or metalhead. I always felt othered from my peer groups. Which was partly a self-fulfilling prophecy. In my heart I didn't feel like I belonged. On some primal level, kids picked up on that energy and took advantage of it.

By the time I was thirteen, I'd progressed from beer to hard alcohol. Aidan's dad had a bar in the basement of their house. And we had a whole closet full of booze at mine. Mind you, I said a closet, not a cabinet, because for Al, a cabinet would have been too small. We knew where the key was, so we'd sneak in there and grab a bottle of vodka from the back, then hide it somewhere.

The Conestoga River behind our house offered a convenient refuge. Danny, Aidan, and I would camp down there and invite friends to come over, and we'd all sit around the campfire passing a bottle of vodka around, which we chased with Doritos and family-sized packages of Oreos. If we were feeling really hungry, somebody would grab leftover sloppy joes from home and we'd fight over those.

A river, a fire, lots of sugar, a bunch of drunk, rowdy young teenage boys. What could possibly go wrong? For starters, one of my friends got so sick from alcohol poisoning we had to call an ambulance. Another time a kid I didn't know that well set a nearby field on fire. If our parents suspected what we were doing, they didn't let on.

But in private, and sometimes even in public, I'd begun a serious meltdown. Dealing with two sick dads was taking a toll. I'd started to feel hopeless and desperate. I kept running away, smashing mirrors, cutting myself, drinking to excess, and at one point, I broke my hand punching a wall. I'd even started huffing TV tube cleaner and Wite-Out, which was not fun but provided a quick high. I was failing at everything. By age fifteen I'd reached a point where I didn't want to live.

Adults finally started to take notice. One day in high school, early in my freshman year (I was the oldest kid in my freshman class, having been held back in first grade), I was called out of woodworking class by my school counselor, Mr. Porter. He and I had met earlier, and I'd admitted to having thoughts of hurting myself.

When I got to his office, Mom and Al were sitting there, on wooden school chairs, looking uncomfortable. And bleak. Mr. Porter spoke first. "Scott, as you know, I've been concerned about you. Based on what you shared with me earlier, I called your mother. We want to offer you the support you need."

"Thanks for your concern," I thought to myself. "You're right on time. You guys don't miss a trick."

"Scott, do you really want to harm yourself?" Mom asked. She was never one to beat around the bush. I wasn't sure how to answer. But what was the point in lying now?

"Sometimes."

"You have the option to voluntarily admit yourself to a mental health facility to be evaluated. Would you like that?"

I thought for a minute. I'd seen *One Flew Over the Cuckoo's Nest*. I didn't want to end up like Jack Nicholson. But I was worried about the deep hopelessness I felt. I had a hard time imagining a future with me in it.

"Yeah."

And that was that. Within a few short hours, I'd left school, packed my toothbrush and pajamas, and checked into the mental health ward at the Community Hospital of Lancaster, which has since closed.

At the time, I thought it might be a respite, a place to pause and have some space. Instead, it was just plain scary. I had my own room, as a minor, but all the other patients were adults. There was a padded room where they tied people down who were in crisis. Of course, we were all in crisis; that's why we were there. I remember walking with a nurse down the long, gray, sterile hallway thinking maybe this wasn't such a good idea.

For some reason they let me bring my leather jacket in there, and it had a lot of skull pins and punk band patches on it. A super intimidating-looking guy saw me and walked over. I was scared, not just of him but of the entire unsettling experience. I tried hard not to show it. "Oh cool, can I try on your jacket?" he asked.

I didn't really want him to but figured this wasn't the place to offend anybody. "Oh yeah, sure," I said.

In a flash he responded, "Oh, look at this!" And with that he took one of the pins off and slammed its two sharp prongs into his arm.

I just stared at that skull pin stuck in his arm. And the next morning, I called my mom. "I hate it here. There are really sick people here. I want to come home." I think she was disappointed I hadn't gotten the help I needed, but she drove right over and picked me up.

It was a sobering moment for me in that I had never seen mental illness to that degree. I'd seen it with my father, but this seemed extreme, even compared to him. My own anger, anxiety, and depression seemed minor by comparison. Nothing, I decided, I couldn't handle on my own.

* * *

I did make one friend during my short stay on the ward. Her name was Mariana, and we probably spent an hour together max, but I was scared and lonely and she was the only person who asked how I was doing. After I got out, she became my weed dealer and an odd friend of sorts. I was just fifteen, and she was in her late twenties or early thirties, living with her more hard-edged partner, Gabby—both struggled with addiction—in a tiny first-floor apartment on South Ann Street in a tougher neighborhood in Lancaster.

I didn't have my driver's license, so my friends would drive me and they'd wait down the block at a park while I walked to the house alone. A bunch of people would always be hanging around outside, and I'd go in and talk to my friend for a while and buy the weed.

One day while I was there watching her and some friends cut up bags of coke, she looked up. "Wanna try some?" she asked. She must have sensed my growing curiosity.

"Sure."

She chalked up a small line on a mirror and handed me a rolled-up twenty-dollar bill. I snorted my first line of coke. Then she told me to rub some on my gums.

I'm not going to lie. That first time, it was awesome. But what was more awesome was the reaction of my friends. It was just like when I'd had my first beer at age eleven. My buddies were super impressed. "Dude, can you get us some?"

So the next time I went back, I asked to buy my first bag of coke. "Sure," she said. "I'll hook you up." No matter that I was half her age and on some level she'd come to think of me kind of like a kid brother; she needed the money to feed her addiction. So I bought twenty dollars' worth, which I shared with a few of my buddies who were waiting for me around the corner. And now I was a person who could get people coke.

Every couple of weeks, my friends and I would all pitch in and buy twenty, forty, or eighty dollars' worth, depending on how many of us there were, and I'd go buy it, and we'd all use it together.

By then it's safe to say I wasn't hanging out with the wrong crowd; I *was* the wrong crowd. But just that experience of people wanting to be around me, even though it was for a messed-up reason, felt good. It felt like I was valued. Which is what we all want, right?

It all felt relatively harmless and safe—a kind of innocuous drug dealer place, not threatening or dangerous. Until one day when my friend Matt wanted to meet Mariana and see for himself where to buy coke. I knew that wouldn't fly. So I told him, "Dude, just wait here. I'll be back." And I got out of the car and disappeared around the corner.

Matt didn't listen. While I was with Mariana and Gabby, he pulled around the corner where he'd seen me turn and parked in the middle of the block, very near their apartment. As I started to leave, Gabby noticed the strange car. The vibe instantly changed. She reached out and firmly grabbed my arm. Leaning in close, she said, "Don't ever fucking bring anybody here again." Then she paused long enough to make sure I noticed the gun tucked into her belt.

"All right, cool, got it," I said. And I never hung out with Matt again.

People often ask me what it felt like the first time I ever did coke and why I got hooked. I can't speak for others. But for me it was the escape from anxiety and self-loathing and the uncomfortableness of adolescence and the feeling of worrying whether you belong or don't belong, or are cool or not cool, or whatever. All of a sudden, all of that shit goes away and you feel ten feet tall and strong.

It's a coping mechanism, and damn—that shit works. But as quickly as it starts working, it starts failing you.

CHAPTER NINE

LIFE AT SEA

In late summer 1988, while Danny and Aidan were taking a break from Blockbuster and *Super Mario Bros.* to stock up on spiral notebooks, BIC pens, and protractors at Kmart, I was in my bedroom with The Clash blaring through my headphones, stuffing a duffel bag full with rubber sea boots, Dramamine, and foul weather gear.

Just two weeks earlier, with my freshman year of high school fast approaching, Mom had signed me up for the Watermark Program—two years of school at sea, operating out of Pride's Crossing, Massachusetts. It was run by the Landmark School, which worked specifically with kids with dyslexia. Mom had discovered it while secretly researching boarding schools for kids with learning disabilities; she wanted to get me out of my current environment. And the next thing we knew, we were sitting in the Landmark admissions office talking about boats.

I still had my mohawk and leather jacket with spikes on it, and I took some tests. Then we sat down with the admissions counselor to talk. "If you could do anything, what would you want to do?" she asked.

"Oh, I'd want to just get out of here and go see the world or something."

"Have you ever been on boats?"

My mind flashed back to that terrifying day on the Chesapeake Bay. Other than that, I'd never stepped foot on a boat. "Oh yeah, a little bit."

The counselor smiled. "Well, we have this program on a boat. It's called Watermark, and it's on a 156-foot, two-masted schooner, a traditional rig schooner. And it's in Europe." She had my interest so far.

"There are about thirty students on it. And twenty people on staff—there are twenty or so crew members and teachers combined. It sails around, and you do school while you're on the boat."

The school knew about my detentions, suspensions, and cutting school; it was clear I was one of the more troubled cases academically. They probably felt a boat was the best place to deal with the more extreme sorts of rebellious students like me. It sounded promising. But it was a lot to digest. Mom and I just sat there for a few minutes, across from the admissions counselor, contemplating what to do. "Thank you for your time," Mom finally said. "We'll get back to you."

Headed home, half-asleep, aboard Amtrak's Yankee Clipper from Boston to Philadelphia, I stared out the window as the train rumbled past older cities full of run-down industrial buildings. They looked forlorn and depressing. Mom had bought us hot dogs and cokes from the café car and wanted to talk. But I was worn out. My life seemed like such a confusing mess.

Then suddenly the late afternoon sun was glimmering off the bay outside of Mystic, Connecticut. And it calmed me down, as being out in nature always did. And I made my decision. "I want to go," I said to my mother, looking up from my half-eaten hot dog.

She put down her newspaper and turned to me without showing any emotion. "It's a big step, Scott," she said. "Are you sure?" She wanted me to own this decision.

"Yes," I answered. "Very sure."

* * *

I wasn't as sure as I sounded. I'd be making a transatlantic crossing, thousands of miles from home. Away from my friends and everything familiar. And I couldn't even smoke cigarettes.

But I knew I had to get out of where I was. I feared what my life was becoming, and I wanted to start fresh. That included getting away from

Al, whose bullying had become intolerable. Even my mother had had enough.

My actual dad was becoming less of a factor by then. Mark was now twenty and rarely around; he always had lots of girlfriends. And Amyla would soon see Dad's true colors when he took back the car he'd given her for her sixteenth birthday one day with no explanation; most likely the bank repossessed it due to lack of payment.

But even at the ripe age of fifteen, I was still vulnerable to Dad's manipulative behavior, his not-so-subtle hints that he wasn't long for this earth. One afternoon just a few months before I left for Watermark, he met Mark, Amyla, and me at Jenny's Diner, on the edge of Lancaster, for lunch. This was one of our rare seminormal outings with Dad, squeezing into one of Jenny's ripped red booths beside a greasy jukebox that never worked and ordering burgers and fries.

Before the waitress could deliver our plates, Dad dumped a pocketful of sentimental trinkets on the table and handed a few to each of us. One I still have is a little red soccer ball medal he'd won as a champion athlete on an All-American soccer team. "I want you to have this to remember your old man when you play sports," he told me. "For when I'm not around anymore." That was his way of scaring me into thinking the end could be near.

* * *

So yeah, I was ready to break free of Lancaster and—with a few exceptions—everybody in it. There was an element of fear in the unknown but also hope and possibility. Nike had a brand-new advertising slogan popping up everywhere that became my internal mantra: *Just Do It.*

So I did it. Just a week after our trip to Pride's Crossing, I found myself alone at LaGuardia Airport, boarding a plane for Amsterdam, where I was to meet up with the schooner, the *Te Vega*, which had its own illustrious past and had already set sail.

It's a daunting kickoff to an adventure at age fifteen to get on an international flight by yourself. I was still smoking cigarettes, so I sat in the smoking section, in row 23. It seemed silly to me that rows 22 and forward were magically declared "nonsmoking," considering the wave of smoke wafting through the main cabin from us smokers in the back.

Once we landed in Amsterdam and I cleared customs, I stopped by the frosted doors leading into the terminal to have one last cigarette. I remember feeling very alone, so far from home. Beneath my tough punk façade, I was acutely aware of how really afraid I was. "Fuck it," I thought. I crushed my cigarette into the aluminum ashtray on the wall and stepped into the bustling terminal.

Te Vega's third mate was there to meet me. His name was Steve Jacobusse. "You Scott?" He was friendly, fit, and very tan. "Welcome to Amsterdam! Ready to become a sailor?"

With those words, the enormity of my life change washed over me like a big wave at high tide. "I'll do my best."

He smiled. "We'll toughen you up. You'll do fine."

I hoisted my duffel bag into the trunk of a waiting taxi, and we headed to the commercial dock section of Scheveningen Harbor, about an hour away. It was kind of surreal, being in the Netherlands, watching quaint little towns roll by. Not totally different from scenic drives in Pennsylvania, although none of the signs were in English, and I didn't notice any roadside vegetable stands. I was going to miss sweet Pennsylvania corn. Did they even eat corn over here? Thinking about corn helped calm my nerves.

Pulling up to the harbor where the schooner was docked and boarding that amazing ship, knowing it was my new home, was a crazy moment for me. Walking down the gangway under the sky-high masts and sails, watching crew members and students pitching in to get *Te Vega* ready for the first leg of our voyage, to France, knowing we'd all be facing adversity together, I already felt a bond with the people on this ship, who I didn't even know yet.

I wanted to be part of it. The positive energy and camaraderie and shared sense of purpose sparked something in me. I thought maybe I was finally somewhere I belonged, where I could be useful. And in that moment, a small ember inside of me started burning a little brighter. The glimmer of an idea that maybe I wasn't worthless, that I could contribute to something bigger than myself. It would be well over a decade before that ember got enough oxygen to finally catch fire. But it was a start.

* * *

Life at sea was a combination of the mundane—doing galley duty, standing night watch, cleaning the head, swabbing the decks—and the extraordinary, like the silent splendor of sailing beneath a canopy of celestial bodies so thick that some nights we couldn't pick out individual stars.

Our best education was experiential. In math class, we helped plot our position on nautical charts by taking compass bearings of an ancient lighthouse as we passed by the Cliffs of Dover. English came to life through the seafaring classics—*The Sea-Wolf* and, of course, *Moby Dick*. For history, we made a stop in Granada, Spain, to visit the Alhambra. We had our larger classes in the main salon area, where we also ate our meals—lots of haddock and cod. We'd have a few classes in the deckhouse, toward the stern, and in the bigger cabins below.

If I didn't recognize back then how lucky I was to have a parent who could afford me that kind of education—by then my mom had taken over her family's business—I sure do now.

But the most compelling teacher, we soon learned, was Mother Nature. Captain Wedlock would say, "Be careful going forward in these big swells!" And being rebellious kids, we'd think, "Whatever." Until a massive wave would break on deck, washing our feet out from under us and forcing us to grab the lifelines. And then we'd think, "OK, maybe he had a point there." Instant cause and effect. Nature has the power to teach life lessons in a really profound way.

There was definitely a *Lord of the Flies* feel to the Watermark experience at times. The crew would do their best to lead us all in the right direction. But you get a bunch of adolescent kids together in a confined space, sharing small cabins with eight or ten bunks in them, and it can get dark pretty quick. I don't love the term "broken people," but I could tell many of the students on the ship carried a quiet pain, just as I did. We became a disparate little tribe, realizing we were all in the same boat.

Some of my deepest bonds were with crew members, the professional sailors on board. I had a unique connection with them because I spent so much time working with them. I got detentions a lot, which cost me my shore privileges. I'd have to stay on the boat and paint and take care of the ship while the other kids were on shore. Ironically, that's when the first seeds of transformation were planted.

One seemingly small moment always stuck with me. I had earned privileges to go up into the rigging of the ship and climb up the stays to work aloft. But due to my detentions, those rights had been suspended. Most of the teachers and students were on shore leave, poking around in shops and sneaking cigarettes. I was alone, priming part of the bulkhead for painting, when Steve, the crew member who'd met me at the airport, called my name. "Hey, Strode, grab a harness and come with me."

He knew that losing my privileges aloft had stung. We climbed up in the rigging, and with our feet dangling ninety feet above the deck, we just sat there and talked. I don't remember exactly what about; it doesn't even matter. I just remember being grateful for these little moments that filled some of the spaces a dad never had. Just sitting aloft with a man I respected, shooting the breeze about sailing and what ports lay ahead and the Boston Bruins—and I'm sure Steve threw in a few life lessons as well. I think some of the crew members saw more potential in me at that time than I saw in myself.

I couldn't have known it then, but that feeling of community, of belonging without being judged, of facing adversity together, whether sailing into a storm or putting out an engine room fire or caring for an injured crew member, eventually became a cornerstone of my approach to helping people who struggle with substance use disorder. People who add up to more than their circumstances. People like me.

* * *

The school year culminated in a transatlantic crossing. From the Canary Islands, we sailed to the Caribbean and then onward to New York City. Much to the surprise of no one, I got suspended on the transatlantic trip. At sea we couldn't smoke or drink, so we'd buy and hoard candy, snacks, and sodas. When we got to Antigua, I got kicked off the boat for three weeks for stealing soda and a giant bag of Skittles from some kid's candy stash. Candy was currency for adolescents at sea.

It sounds funny now, but stealing anything on board was a serious offense. The protection of property rights is fundamental to any cooperative, free-enterprise society—especially on a boat where our personal space and possessions were so limited. We had to respect that. A year earlier I wouldn't have cared. But letting down crewmates who expected a higher level of integrity from me landed hard; I felt ashamed.

My timing was good, though. It was spring break, and my family had come to Antigua to meet us. So I ended up sitting on the beach drinking beer with my brother all week while the other kids kept up with their onboard classes. I felt pretty good about that. I made sure to hoist my Red Stripe in their direction when they came ashore for gym class.

A funny thing happened when I got back to Lancaster for summer vacation, though. I came home with a pride and confidence I didn't have when I'd left town nine months before. That summer I quit doing drugs.

"Hey, we have some coke," some kid said to me at a small party shortly after I got back to town. Obviously my reputation preceded me.

"No, I'm good," I said. "I'm all set."

Danny and Aidan, who'd been worried about my increasingly self-destructive behavior, were happy I'd gotten away from Lancaster and understood that at summer's end I'd be headed back to the ship. But the other kids I partied with were confused. "Why are you leaving, dude?" one asked. "I don't get it." One of my party friends had since dropped out of school and was working as a roofer's assistant carrying plywood up a ladder all day long. I didn't know what I wanted out of life, but it wasn't that.

So when I went back to the boat the second year, I was Mr. Sailor. I was head of watch on the ship. I didn't get suspended once. I was really focused on my academics. And I began to cultivate a belief in myself that spread to other parts of my life. Something had changed in me at sea. I'd grown up a little, for one thing. I'd discovered some gifts I didn't know I had, like the ability to lead people to a better place. And I'd shed some of the emotional baggage weighing me down at home.

I wanted to stay on the boat, to keep sailing and studying and working, for life not to change. But, of course, life always does. The year ended, and with it the Watermark Program. Walking down *Te Vega*'s gangway for the last time, waving goodbye to the teachers and students and crew members, I couldn't believe it was over.

My duffel bag was a lot more weathered now. My passport was loaded with stamps from the Netherlands, France, Spain, Italy. I didn't know where my journey would take me next, but I promised myself I would never go back to the life I had before.

CHAPTER TEN

A SIGNAL IN THE FOG

"**M**eet Mark and me tonight in our cabin out back—as usual we have plenty of beer!" I hadn't even unpacked my duffel bag, but I was already on the phone with Danny and Aidan. My trusty wingmen. "Dude, we're glad you're back!" Aidan said. "But don't start going all Captain Ahab on us." To this day, no matter how long it's been, we can always pick up right where we left off.

Two years earlier, before I left for Watermark, Mom and Al had moved us again, this time a little farther away to a farm on Bunker Hill Road in Strasburg. Before she came up with the Watermark idea, Mom had been searching for other solutions to keep me away from bad influences. She still hadn't quite accepted the fact that maybe I was the problem.

At Bunker Hill there was a separate cabin off the main house, which is where Mark, Amyla, and I stayed. Mark was twenty by the time we moved there, but my sister and I were still teenagers. We thought it was great that we got to live in a little house next to Mom and Al's house. Better yet, they let us drink there. They thought that was good parenting, because if we were drinking there, we weren't drinking somewhere else. They'd buy us a twelve-pack of beer, and of course then we'd call all our friends, tell them the brand, and they'd show up with three more cases.

Meanwhile, just a few steps away, in the main house, you could tune in most nights to the alcohol-induced version of the Battle of Bunker Hill. Al's drinking had escalated to the point where everything was fodder for a fight, and Mom was on the verge of filing for divorce. I hoped she'd make good on that.

But I wasn't going to stick around and find out.

* * *

I got a summer job working on the *Spirit of Massachusetts*, another two-masted schooner, doing the same kind of work I did on the *Te Vega*. I'd started to show real skill at working on traditional rigged ships. But when fall came, I returned to Pride's Crossing to start my junior year at the Landmark School, which had run the Watermark Program.

I very quickly fell into a severe depression. For one thing, I felt land-locked, even though my school was located on the northern coast of Massachusetts. I was used to the open seas. Also, thanks to two years away from home, I felt I had become worldly beyond my years. So the Landmark curriculum didn't engage me at all, nor could I relate much to the other students. And some of the protocols just seemed silly.

For example:

> Teacher: "OK, if there's a fire in the dorm, here's where we all meet, by this tree, so we can count to make sure everybody got out of the building."
> Scott: "Can't we just put out the fire?"
> Teacher: "No. That's not what we do."
> Scott: "Well, that's what we did on the boat."
> Teacher: "Does this look like a boat?"

On the *Te Vega*, I was treated with dignity and respect. I was accorded a certain level of equality because I was a contributing member of the crew. I was on fire detail; I'd been trained in how to extinguish a fire in the engine room. I was on the man-overboard rescue crew. I would go out in an actual man-overboard boat to pick up somebody if they went over the side, no matter the weather. I had started to lay the foundation for the person I would become later in life. To again quote Maslow, famous for creating a hierarchy of human needs, "What a man can be, he must be. This need we call self-actualization."

At age seventeen, I'd never heard of Maslow, but subconsciously I'd already been bitten by the self-actualization bug. On some level, I wanted to realize my potential. Or at least not squander it. I had listened to parts of *Walden,* which philosopher Henry David Thoreau had written in Concord, less than an hour from the Landmark School. His famous quote, "Most men lead lives of quiet desperation," had stuck with me. I didn't have clear goals, but I thought I could do better than quiet desperation.

One early morning as I was getting ready for class, I heard the distant baritone blast from a ship's fog bell. I knew it was one of the boats I'd worked on because I'd run into some of the crew a week before in Boston. They'd told me they were going to anchor off Great Misery Island, near the Landmark School, on their way up the coast. I opened my window and looked out to sea. I couldn't see the boat. But the bell was ringing to alert other boats where she was anchored. I longed to be on that boat.

It was only a month or so into the school year. But in that moment, I knew I couldn't stay. This wasn't the right path for me to finish school. I called my mom, and she said I could leave Landmark if I agreed to get my GED. She knew I wasn't feeling fulfilled and was worried I'd fall back to my old lifestyle. So I caught another Amtrak train back to Strasburg and moved back into the cabin at Bunker Hill Road. Mom hired a tutor, and I started studying around the clock.

* * *

To say I was motivated significantly understates the case. Mark was living a town away in Lancaster and would come hang out with me occasionally. Amyla was away at Williams College in Williamstown, Massachusetts, which is where she was when the car Dad had given her was repossessed. (Yet, classic Dad, he randomly met a guy wearing a Williams hat and bought it from him so he could show off that he had a daughter at Williams.)

Meanwhile, Al was desperately trying to argue to Mom that he wasn't an alcoholic so she wouldn't divorce him. "If true, that's an easy thing to prove," I thought. "You just don't drink." Simple as that, right?

To show he could stop, my stepfather had taken to drinking a lot of iced tea. He thought if he could go a whole night without alcohol, it would prove he wasn't an alcoholic. But man, he gripped his iced tea glass so tightly I thought it would break. Then the next night, he'd be back to eight martinis. Mom and Al eventually divorced. And as far as I know, he never did get sober.

I spent October and November hunkered down studying so that I could go back to working on ships. In early December I took my GED exam and passed it. To celebrate, Mom and I did our favorite thing: we got soft-serve ice cream with sprinkles from the Freeze and Frizz along the creek that ran through Strasburg.

Then out came the old duffel bag and rubber sea boots. A couple weeks before Christmas, I flew to Saint Thomas in the U.S. Virgin Islands to rejoin the crew of the *Spirit of Massachusetts*, the ship I'd worked on that summer, whose foghorn had inspired me to quit high school and get my GED. It was working its way down to the Caribbean now that hurricane season had passed. I always joked that I dropped out of school, got my high school diploma, and had a job before my friends finished their junior year.

There's only one flaw to this seemingly happy ending: I was still an active alcoholic. A high-functioning alcoholic, but an alcoholic nonetheless. I was not even close to getting my act together.

The thing I was seeking on boats was not drinking; it was the camaraderie and purpose and self-worth. But while I felt like an adult, I wasn't one. I was ready to travel and party and sample all that life had to offer. Before my twenty-fifth birthday, I would come just a line of cocaine away from losing my life in the process.

PART II

BOSTON

It isn't the mountain ahead to climb that wears you out;
it's the pebble in your shoe.

MUHAMMAD ALI, American boxer and social activist

CHAPTER ELEVEN

CHRISTMAS AT BOMBA'S SHACK

B ack in the days when I was working on boats, I didn't know you put the cap back on a bottle of rum. I thought it just came off and the bottle was open until you finished drinking it.

That sounds funny now, and sometimes I say it to make people laugh. But I don't mean it in jest. As a young adult, I spent plenty of time with sailors (and family members) who'd open a bottle of liquor and just throw the cap over the side of the boat, and that was it. You just passed it around until it was gone. Drinking was part of the culture.

Life at sea was therefore not the ideal setting for an alcoholic. Or it was the perfect setting, depending on your perspective. I'd quit using drugs while I was in the Watermark Program, and I thought that meant I'd gotten my act together, despite my ongoing alcohol dependency. At age seventeen I had a lot of growing up—and sobering up—to do. Only I didn't think so, and that's a bad combination.

Christmas in Tortola, the largest of the British Virgin Islands, is a good case in point. Just a couple weeks after Mom and I enjoyed our celebratory rainbow sprinkle cones in Strasburg, I was back to swabbing decks on the *Spirit of Massachusetts* and helping lead experiential Outward Bound–type charters for students, kind of similar to Watermark, only now I was crew.

Shortly after I came aboard, all the students departed for the holidays. So we felt kind of at loose ends. In a rare act of kindness, our captain—who prided himself on running a tight ship—said he'd stay on board and do anchor watch so we could all have Christmas Day off. In retrospect, that wasn't such a good plan.

After drinking our way through the bars in the capital city of Road Town, the whole crew ended up at Bomba's Surfside Shack in Cappoons Bay on Tortola's north side. The place was famous for its full moon parties because during high tide, waves would wash up into the bar. An enigmatic local named Bomba had built it in 1976 out of driftwood, discarded surfboards, rusted pieces of tin, and other colorful bits of debris he found on the beach. You couldn't come to Tortola and not stop at Bomba's.

Which is how we found ourselves late on Christmas Day in 1990 standing at the bar, ankle-deep in ocean water, knocking back shots and feeling festive. Picking up on our vibe, the bartender asked, "So do you want a piña colada or a Bomba Special?" Of course we all chose the Bomba Special, thinking it had better booze, or more booze, or both. As we started on our third round, the bartender turned the bottle over, and we saw something at the bottom of the rum. That's when I realized the Bomba Special was rum that had been soaking in hallucinogenic mushrooms—for months. All I could think was "Uh oh."

Jason, the first mate, and I were the only two who had ever done magic mushrooms, and we knew that in about forty-five minutes, things were going to get really crazy, perhaps dangerously so. We looked at each other, too impaired already to make a good decision of any kind. "Should we tell them?" Jason asked.

"Let's just see what happens," I said. My budding leadership skills were impotent in the face of the Bomba Special.

The next morning the captain woke up to find a nearly empty boat. Jason and I were the only two who had managed to make it back. The second mate, third mate, engineer, and all the deckhands were unaccounted for. I learned later that one guy had resorted to curling up under a beach umbrella to try to stay warm. Another crew member found himself in a field on a hillside with a bunch of cows. The rest of the crew came trickling in throughout the day. Needless to say, the captain didn't give us another day off for the rest of the voyage.

I don't know about Jason, but afterward I felt very guilty I hadn't gotten everyone back to the boat before it was too late. He and I had known what was coming; we could have mitigated the mayhem. Renowned University of California, Berkeley, rugby coach Jack Clark once said, "Leadership is the ability to make those around you better." In that case I hadn't done that. I was only seventeen, but the memory of my reckless behavior, which negatively impacted my fellow crew members, taught me a lesson that would stay with me for the rest of my life.

CHAPTER TWELVE

A HARD DAY'S NIGHT IN LIVERPOOL

If you're reading this book to better understand someone who struggles with an addiction, it might help you to know we spend a good portion of our waking hours trying to convince ourselves we're not worthless. So when we find moments of joy that don't come out of a bottle, a needle, or a pipe, no matter how fleeting, we cling to those like pieces of flotsam in the sea, hoping we'll eventually get to firmer ground.

For me one of those moments came aboard the *Sea Cloud*, one of the world's largest private sailing yachts—the top of the main mast was 205 feet high, measuring from the water to the top of the rigging. It was originally commissioned by Edward Francis Hutton (cofounder of E. F. Hutton) and his wife, Marjorie Merriweather Post, a businesswoman in her own right who owned General Foods.

The *Sea Cloud* was a beautiful ship, and Daimler-Benz had chartered it for the Barcelona 1992 Summer Olympics. After working my way up to bosun, in charge of all the rigging, after a few more seasons on the *Spirit of Massachusetts*, I'd gotten a job on the *Sea Cloud* as a general crew member, assigned to the foremast, the mast nearest the bow of the ship. My job, besides cleaning and painting, was to go aloft and handle the sails and the rigging. The crew I'd be part of comprised fourteen nationalities.

I joined the voyage in Izmir, Turkey, a city with no shortage of raki, Turkey's national drink, otherwise known as lion's milk. Here's a tip: it's not milk. The next day, my first day on the ship, it was 105 degrees above deck. I was so hungover my only goal was to avoid throwing up on the other crew members. As I recall, they thought it was funny.

One night not too long after that, I was at the wheel of the ship, alone on deck with Antonio, the third mate, under what must have been a full moon, because I can remember looking out at the Aegean Sea and seeing a glow reflecting off the waves. It was like a spotlight was shining on the whitecaps and the deck of the ship.

After a while Antonio took a break to go below in search of candied ginger for an upset stomach, leaving me alone on the bridge of this majestic 360-foot yacht. All I could hear was the creak of the masts as we went up over the whitecaps and came down and the sound of the waves slapping on the side of the ship. Each time they hit, I could feel the rudder kick the wheel a little in my hand. And then a moment later, the spray would come over the rail and land on the deck in an iridescent sheet.

In the distance, two small islands broke the line of the horizon. The sky was exploding with stars because there was no man-made light for as far as I could see. And I had this feeling wash over me that my whole purpose in life was to be here in this moment and to be part of this world in this way.

It left me with the sense that maybe there was a place on earth for me, that I was supposed to be here for some greater good. Even though I was still drinking, trying to fill that void, that insatiable yearning for love and acceptance, I was having these moments that were laying the foundation for a mission that would later change my life.

* * *

En route from Istanbul to Barcelona, we made stops at the lively Greek island of Mykonos and historic Mallorca, a Mediterranean island off the coast of Spain. The nightlife in Mykonos was fun. But seeing as I came from a lineage of woodworkers, and had already developed something of a design eye, I was equally excited to see the Roman and Moorish remains in Mallorca and to at least get a glimpse of La Seu, a medieval Gothic

Roman Catholic cathedral that dominates the skyline of the capital city of Palma.

It's hard to believe, looking back on these profound experiences, that at this point I was still just a teenager. I was incredibly fortunate to have had the opportunity at a very young age to discover my passions and gifts through an astonishing variety of cultures and experiences. I just wish I'd figured out sooner how to use them to give back in a meaningful way.

For as amazing as the *Sea Cloud* experience was, I wanted more. That ship was a chartered yacht rather than a working sail-training ship. The crew would raise the sails for photo ops, which I considered theatrics for paying passengers, mostly wealthy European families. I remember one guy, a dapper Frenchman who clearly enjoyed his croissants, asking if I could take a picture of him climbing one of the masts, *s'il vous plaît?* I don't speak French, but that was an easy one: "Non, Monsieur." Once we lowered the sails, we'd motor to our next destination. I wanted to get back to working on what I thought of as real boats that operated under sail power, not floating hotels.

So when we got to Barcelona, I took a twenty-three-hour bus ride to Liverpool, England, where a large number of sail-training ships were getting ready to cross the Atlantic. I spent several days there walking the docks, trying to get a job on one of them, with no success. I was nearly broke at that point, having squandered most of my *Sea Cloud* earnings on booze and wondering whether quitting had been such a wise idea. I took comfort in thinking the Beatles must have been broke in Liverpool before they got famous. Then again, they had something of value to offer the world, and I didn't.

* * *

The Port of Liverpool was a working-class, blue-collar port with some rough areas around the fringes. One night while out drinking at a pub near the Brunswick Dock, where I was still looking for work, I started talking to a local woman named Marsha who lived nearby with her brother Edwin—or, as he told me later, "Ed to my friends." By midnight I was calling him Ed.

We ended up back at their house, a small, grungy apartment with a kitchen and living room that were pretty much trashed and two bedrooms in the rear, all dimly lit. Despite their grim surroundings, Marsha and Ed were curious and friendly. Both were intrigued by American culture and asked me all sorts of questions about what the U.S. was like. Had I ever seen Madonna in concert? What about Michael Jackson? Had I been to Hollywood? Why do Americans love British accents?

I was doing my best to answer their questions, sitting around their gray, chipped Formica kitchen table drinking bottles of cheap Smithwick's Ale, when Ed said, "Oh, I know a guy who can get us some coke." Without hesitation I chipped in some money, and the next thing you know, after three years of being drug-free, I'm doing lines of coke with Marsha and Ed.

Then the night—by then it was early morning—took a more disturbing turn. I got up to use the bathroom, and on my way, I glanced into Ed's room. His door was partially closed, but I could see he was shooting up; he must have used some of our money to also buy heroin. It was the first time I'd ever seen somebody use any intravenous drug, and the image seared itself into my mind.

It played out like a slow-motion moment, Ed sitting on the bed, looking up at me as he was about to stick the needle into his arm. I remember feeling on the verge of a world darker than I'd experienced before. I experienced a sudden sense of fear, a foreboding.

In active addiction, you have moments of awareness about how bad it's gotten, and they come and go, and they don't always stick with you. But every now and then, you have a moment of perspective where you realize: This is another level. It's deteriorated to a different place. I remember having that feeling in that moment.

Afterward, I felt deeply ashamed and disappointed in myself for what happened that night in Liverpool. Growing up around a family of alcoholics, I thought drinking to excess was still more elevated than using drugs. Through sailing, I was trying to heal some of that residual family stuff and chase those engrossing "flow" moments where I was totally absorbed in something other than substances. I had started to develop pride in who I was. Liverpool was an ominous reminder that this other piece of me was still present and insidious. A warning that the dark side was still there.

* * *

As always, when I was down and out, I called my mother, who invariably seemed to have the answer. She promptly bought me a plane ticket back to Pennsylvania. Mom rarely asked me many questions, other than "Are you OK?" We really didn't talk too much. But maybe we should have. Mom spent a lot of time researching all kinds of ways to help me. She spent less time—if any—looking into counseling or other methods that might help *her*.

It's a catch-22 loving someone struggling with addiction. Try to protect them from hitting bottom, and you're accused of enabling. Distance yourself, and you feel guilty when something bad happens. Either way, you can't win. What I wish my loved ones had done more of was focus on themselves.

Here's what I mean by that. Speaking from personal experience, I know that one of the big challenges, especially for youth, is that when addiction takes hold, it can be so extreme that it necessarily becomes the entire focus of attention of the family. Many times it has to be, in an effort to save that kid's life.

But once any true life-or-death situation stabilizes, the most powerful intervention can often be to broaden the spotlight to include not just the person with the addiction but also their loved ones, caregivers, and peers. Not to cast blame or criticism on others, but to give the person who is the center of attention some space and grace to begin to heal. And to give loved ones some time to do an honest inventory of any unhealthy personal or family dynamics which, if eliminated, might work to everyone's benefit. That's called finding the "why."

I think of the growing addiction crisis in our country as the canary in the coal mine—an early warning of greater trouble to come. Like canaries, whose sensitivity to deadly carbon monoxide gas underground gave miners time to escape, those of us with substance use disorder are highly susceptible to toxic environments. Our negative coping mechanisms (drinking and drugging) are a signal that something around us is wrong.

Coal miners knew a sick canary meant an invisible danger to which they'd soon succumb. So they beat a hasty retreat. By improving the environment (which, granted, back then wasn't possible) they might also have saved the canary.

My mom married an alcoholic after she married a man with untreated mental illness. She buried her own pain under nonstop work. That was healthier and more socially acceptable than drugs and alcohol. But it was an escape just the same. Had she done work to create a less fraught environment—not by working on me, but by working on her—would she have been happier? Probably. Would it have made a difference in my own trajectory? It well may have.

My father carried the pain of his own childhood trauma for a lifetime. His father abandoned him when he was only six years old. If he had addressed the impact that had on his own self-worth early on, might his mental health struggles have become more manageable? Might he have been a better dad? We'll never know, but it would have been worth a shot.

I say that not to excuse my behavior during my years of active addiction but to shed a little light on how a young, developing brain—speaking from my own experience—can misinterpret things. This is significant because so often the seeds of addiction take root at a very young age.

I felt demeaned throughout my childhood. So I self-medicated those self-esteem wounds. Eventually my addiction became hard to ignore. That's when my family decided my "problem" was disrupting our family dynamic and I needed help. Which just made things worse. When the focus became solely on me, it just compounded my belief that I was the reason everything was wrong. The best way to cope with that shame was to use. Getting high will make it go away, you think. And when it doesn't, what do you do? Use more.

To anyone weighed down by the complexity of life with someone active in their addiction, trying to help keep them alive while preventing everyone else in the family from going over a cliff, the idea of taking time out for deep self-reflective work might sound ludicrous. I get it. And we can't rewrite the past. But we can change our approach moving forward. There are things each of us can do individually and together to heal. And that extends to society as a whole.

That's why I use the canary example when talking about the addiction epidemic in this country. It's not just unhealthy family dynamics or early childhood traumas that foster addiction; it can be societal toxins as well. So when addiction and overdose deaths reach an all-time high, it may be time to ask: What is it about today's toxic culture that is causing so many deaths of despair? What's out there killing the canaries that will eventually take down the rest of us too?

* * *

After the Liverpool misadventure, I returned briefly to the cabin on Bunker Hill Road and got a job at Builder's Square, a home improvement retailer similar to Home Depot, Menards, and Lowe's, loading construction materials into trucks. I wasn't happy with myself; being back in Strasburg felt like a giant step backward.

Danny and Aidan were away at college; Mark had voluntarily left the navy shortly after testing positive on a random drug test and was back in Strasburg doing construction work. At a girlfriend's behest, he'd quit drinking. But when we found ourselves in Amsterdam at the same time during Mark's sober stint—he was traveling with Amyla and a friend—I, in my infinite wisdom, had persuaded him that drugs were the problem, not alcohol.

He needed very little arm-twisting, given that Amsterdam has bars and beer at every turn. So thanks to me, at a famous Amsterdam establishment called The Bulldog, he fell off the wagon. I then had the audacity a few years later to accuse him of having a drinking problem. "Dude, you're an alcoholic," I told him one night on the phone, shortly after I got sober. If he didn't hang up on me, he should have.

But back in the fall of 1992, Mark and I were both in Pennsylvania, still drinking, while Mom stayed busy—as always—running American Water Works Company. Al was still in the picture; he, too, was still drinking. None of us was doing anything that didn't begin with the word "still."

I wanted to return to the only other world I knew—ships and shipyards—as fast as possible. By September I was back on the Yankee Clipper, headed for Boston, memories of Liverpool receding, buoyed by thoughts of leaving Pennsylvania behind, for good. But I was nagged by the old cliché: "Wherever you go, there you are."

CHAPTER THIRTEEN

SHIPYARD SHENANIGANS

Perhaps not surprisingly, it wasn't an adult who saw through the hypocrisy of my sober-by-day, trashed-by-night lifestyle, but a fourteen-year-old, street-smart kid named Marcus.

The New England Historic Sea Port in Charlestown, separated by the Charles and Mystic Rivers from the rest of Boston, became my next home. It offered a shore-based experiential education program for at-risk kids at a place called the Boston Boat Shop. It utilized the power of the ocean and the craftsmanship of boatbuilding to help boost their self-esteem and instill good values while teaching teamwork within a positive support network. Given my prior experience on the ship, I got invited to join as an instructor.

It was similar to the Watermark Program, but instead of living at sea, we'd build boats with the students, most of them from nearby housing projects, and then take them out sailing on the vessels they'd worked on. I lived on the decommissioned U.S. lightship *Nantucket*, a national historic landmark that was part of the program. I worked with one other instructor, a nice guy from England named James White.

James did his best, I think, to lead by example. He walked the walk. Which made me feel even more like a fraud. I'd spend the day telling these kids how to live their lives. "Don't hang out with kids who drink or do drugs," I'd say. "They're on a path to nowhere. Find people who are living the life you want and do what they do." And I meant it. Then at 4:45 p.m. sharp, I'd clock out and walk with some other crew members to Store 24 and we'd buy a twelve-pack. It was the nightly routine.

Then I'd get dinner somewhere and spend the rest of the night drinking alone at a bar.

My drinking got so bad that I would sometimes blackout drink and go back to using. During these times, despite never imagining I'd use coke again, I'd be so out of it—in a state of alcohol-induced amnesia—I'd sometimes even end up smoking crack. The next day I'd be overcome with shame. My job was to teach kids how to lead a good and principled life. Meanwhile I was partying so hard I often had to call in sick. How were others supposed to live by my example when I wasn't following my own advice?

And those kids had it rough. Several clearly had fetal alcohol syndrome. A few had parents in jail. Many lived in foster homes. And then there was Marcus. He was fourteen. He'd been stabbed, and his brother had been killed, mistakenly, by a gang of kids who'd thought he was Marcus. That's trauma at a level I can't even imagine.

Marcus could see right through all my bullshit; because of his upbringing, he pegged me instantly as an alcoholic and an addict. He knew everything I said was hollow because of how I was living. He never called me on it, but he knew, and I knew he knew. And he knew that too.

* * *

My twenty-first birthday, which happened while I was still living on the *Nantucket*, working at the Boat Shop, was anticlimactic, in a way. It's not like I was going out for my first drink. Or doing anything I'd never done before. Of course I did indeed drink, all night long, back home in Strasburg with my brother. We hit as many bars as we could find around Lancaster in a single night. He was my best drinking buddy in terms of being able to go the distance.

Mark was still struggling with his own issues related to a childhood spent walking on eggshells—an ever-present feeling that now might be a happy moment, but the next moment might not be—and like me, he used substances as an escape.

He remembers one night we went out drinking with some teachers we knew. "You guys are lightweights!" we ribbed them, comparing their drinking ability with our own. "To abandon your beer on the bar without drinking it—we consider *that* alcohol abuse." Everybody laughed. Then Mark and I proceeded to get trashed. The following night one of the teachers ran into Mark. "Wow, you guys drank a lot last night," she said, "and you didn't really seem like you were that drunk."

This should have triggered an alarm for both of us. "I was in a black-out for most of the night," my brother admitted, "but I was functioning to the point they thought I wasn't even drunk." This might explain why it took our friends and family so long to realize we had a problem.

* * *

Back in Boston, I'd found a true alcoholics bar, the kind of bar that nobody goes to but the regulars you find sitting on the same barstools every single night. I didn't really know anyone in Boston, so I would walk across the Charlestown Bridge into the city every night after work and sit at that bar drinking with a bunch of forty-year-old alcoholics. Increasingly, I'd come back to the *Nantucket* blackout drunk.

One morning after such a night, I woke up and noticed a hole in the front of my shirt. "How'd that happen?" I wondered. As I was changing into a clean T-shirt, I was startled to see a cigarette burn on my chest; I'd fallen asleep with a lit cigarette burning into my skin, and it hadn't even woken me up.

Once on deck, I encountered a supremely pissed-off coworker in the form of the ship's caretaker, Alex, a gruff, gray-bearded German guy who'd worked with me previously on the *Spirit of Massachusetts*. It turns out in addition to incinerating myself, I'd also somehow burned a bunch of holes in the awning that covered the ship's deck. "Get it together, man" was all he said.

"Yep," I said, "no problem." But I knew in that moment it was time to move on. I was ready to take my demons to a new locale.

People often ask me what causes somebody struggling with addiction to finally "hit bottom." Or to get to a place where they "want recovery." I wish I had a definitive answer. Barring that—and not to get too lofty—I'll share an observation by famed economist and sociologist Ludwig Von Mises that might be useful. He argued there are three conditions that motivate humans to act: 1) unhappiness with their current situation 2) a vision for how things could be better, and 3) *a belief there's a path to get there.* Given that the millions of us with a substance use disorder also qualify as humans—despite what some people seem to think—there's a good chance this logic applies to us as well.

One thing we know: For every person, that moment of clarity, or of agency—the realization that you're ready and able to change—is different. It can be something major, like a scrape with death. Or something seemingly more minor, like looking at yourself in the mirror and realizing you once took pride in your appearance and now don't recognize the person looking back.

The whole concept of "hitting bottom" can be dangerous, though. The phrase has become such common parlance in the recovery industry lexicon that it has taken on the gravitas of one of the 12 steps, as if it's a necessary precursor to beginning recovery. Loved ones are too often told there's nothing they can do until the person struggling with addiction wants to change and it may take hitting bottom for that to happen. That myth is killing too many people.

My dream today, as a fifty-one-year-old adult with twenty-seven years of sobriety, is to work relentlessly to build and grow a sober active community—The Phoenix—that helps get more people into recovery by helping them imagine a better future. And then offering them a path to get there. But back then, at age twenty-one, I had not yet found mine.

CHAPTER FOURTEEN

MOVING TO BACK BAY

One thing I knew: I'd burned myself out trying to help kids become the kind of person I couldn't be. The shame was ever present. In an effort to change my path, I decided to switch from nonprofit training programs to the commercial side of shipbuilding, where I could make use of what seemed to be an innate knack for woodworking.

So late in 1994, I started doing repair and reconstruction on ships drydocked at Fairhaven Shipyard & Marina, which was just across from New Bedford, a historic New England working port just off of Buzzards Bay. Bill Clinton had been president for nearly two years, but the lyrics of his Fleetwood Mac campaign song had stuck in my head: "Don't stop thinking about tomorrow." I especially liked the refrain, "*Yesterday's gone, yesterday's gone!*" I had a lot of yesterdays I never wanted to see again. I was clear on that. Tomorrow was murkier.

In terms of lifestyle, Fairhaven wasn't exactly an upgrade. We'd pull a boat out of the water, upfit it, fix and repair things, and then put the boat back in. We usually worked under intense three-month contracts, normally during the frigid winter months. Laboring outside in New England from December through February is punishingly hard work.

To this day, after all my mountaineering adventures, I have never been as bitterly cold as I was working outside on the scaffolding surrounding those ships, with nor'easter storms blowing the cold, damp sea air through my heavy-duty Carhartt dungarees and vests. A group of tougher men I have not met. You would often split your finger open while driving a trunnel into a three-inch oak plank swinging a nine-pound sledge with one hand, and your buddy next to you would just wrap it in duct tape for you so you could get back to work.

My haphazard sleeping arrangements did nothing to compensate for the long, laborious days. I was living in crew housing—in this case a drafty, split-level, 1950s-era Cape Cod house with fourteen guys sharing space. I thought it was a big deal when I got to upgrade my bedroom, my bedroom being my sleeping bag, wedged in between two other guys' sleeping bags, in the living room.

When one crew member left, I was able to move my sleeping bag behind the sofa, which I moved out from the wall about three feet. In that house, this was what came closest to privacy. But there was a dude sleeping on that sofa, and there were dudes on the floor in front of the sofa. The Ritz it was not.

I called Mark. "You should come join me in Boston," I said. "All the shipyards need crew. We could get an apartment. You need to get out of Lancaster." I had an ulterior motive. Beyond just wanting Mark around—he was my best friend—I figured that between the two of us, we could afford to rent a place together. My shipyard earnings didn't go far, especially since I spent most of them on booze.

"OK," he said. "If I can find work up there, I'm in."

We both were pumped. The idea of living together somewhere other than in the cabin on Bunker Hill Road sounded like fun. Mark started calling Boston-area shipyards while I looked for an affordable rental apartment. I found a cheap two-bedroom that backed up to the Massachusetts Turnpike in Back Bay and signed my first lease. Despite its location in a desirable part of town, our place was nothing special. We could almost touch the brick wall of the building behind us, which blocked the sun for all but twenty minutes a day, the period we called our "sun time." If we opened the back bedroom window, soot from the turnpike coated the whole apartment. But it was a significant upgrade from crew housing, which I still had to endure during the week.

Move-in day was a non-event. Having lived a vagabond lifestyle since age fifteen, living on ships and in shipyards, I hadn't acquired much in the way of material possessions. I just walked in and dropped my seabag on the floor, and that was it. I had no furniture, nor much in the way of clothes. I immediately splurged on a bed with a comfortable mattress. When Mark arrived a month or so later, we hit a cheap furniture outlet and bought a couch, a table, lamps, and a bed for Mark.

Honestly, between working long days at the shipyards and partying most nights, Mark and I probably only clocked a few hours each day in that apartment. And they were the wee hours. I would live in the fourteen-man crew house during the week and drive back to Boston on the weekends, and sometimes even on weeknights, go out drinking with my brother, then drive back. I still thought I had my act together, or at least together enough that I felt no need to change.

* * *

Mom started calling more often, worried that she could never reach me in the evenings. "Don't worry," I told her. "I never drink and drive." Yet I would stay out drinking until 3:00 a.m. and then wake up to drive to the Fairhaven shipyard at 5:00 a.m., just as the sun was coming up. I'd slept for just two hours. How silly—and unsafe—to think I was sober enough to drive.

By now, even my fellow crewmembers were growing alarmed. Which is saying something coming from a group that commonly enhanced their workday coffee breaks by adding rum. "Hey, Strode, I'm worried about you," a fellow ship worker, Pat, said one morning while we were toiling away, side by side.

"Why?" I asked, surprised.

"Because you smell like booze, man. You actually smell like booze, and it's eight in the morning." I was drinking so much that my body reeked of alcohol.

Despite that significant deficit, I was one of the most productive guys on the ship. At the worst of my addiction, I never lacked for work ethic. I remember one day the captain was walking on the starboard side, talking to the guys who were planking—that is, putting the wooden planks on that side of the ship. "Hey, how's it going?" he asked them. "When do you think you'll be finished?"

I heard one guy reply, "We're going as fast as we can, sir. Probably another week or so."

Then he walked down our side of the ship, where Pat and I were planking the port side. "Wow, you guys are going pretty fast," he said. "How long till you're going to be done?" And we told him. Then he walked right around to the starboard side again. "Wrap it up, guys," he ordered. "You're fired."

Within three days, Pat and I could start planking the other side, and we were the faster crew. It was just that kind of work.

We got the message. "Man, we better keep working," Pat said. "We want to keep our job." But *did* I want to keep my job? I was beginning to wonder. I needed money to pay the rent. And I had to cover my nightly bar tabs, which could total more than $1,000 in any given week. But the nomadic, work-hard, drink-just-as-hard lifestyle of boats was starting to weigh on me, and the ninety-minute drive between Boston and the Fairhaven shipyard was taking a toll.

In fact, I was spent. I'd earn near minimum wage doing grueling labor all day, then give a hefty portion of that money to bartenders and drug dealers at night, in the relentless pursuit of . . . what? I didn't know. Every night was the same: drink for hours with Mark at The Last Drop, our favorite neighborhood pub, then hit an after-hours club, usually The Glass Slipper.

Once everyone else went home, I'd find an after-after-party, and on my worst nights—which were becoming more frequent—end up in a blackout, smoking crack with strangers. I'd wake up feeling sick, exhausted, and disgusted with myself. A day would pass, and after work

I'd be back at Marlboro Market on Mass Avenue grabbing a twelve-pack of Rolling Rock. And the cycle would repeat.

* * *

Fortuitously, it was about this time that my mother finally shared with Mark, Amyla, and me that we had access to some trust money from our grandpop—the illustrious but elusive Senator Ware—who had passed. It was intended to be used for our health, education, and well-being. I'm not sure what Amyla did with her money—she probably spent it to further her education—but Mom presented the money to Mark and me as an opportunity to buy a decent apartment.

Implausible as it seems, until this point I had no awareness of the level of financial opportunity that would become available to me in the future, thanks to our mom's family's business interests. I knew the Ware family had significant financial assets that many other families didn't, thanks to their substantial ownership shares of American Water Works, the company they'd built from the ground up. But I didn't know the extent of it at this point. I think my mom intentionally was trying to hide some of that from us, given that Mark and I had been actively struggling with addiction.

As kids, we had not grown up thinking we were rich. Our father came from modest means. His dad sold mushroom spores to local mushroom houses in and around Avondale, Pennsylvania. His mom owned a small women's clothing store.

And while our mother came from wealth, she didn't act like it. She didn't take us to coming out parties; we didn't belong to the country club. That wasn't a life we knew. Mark and I both gravitated to work that was anything but glamorous. Amyla got her master's degree and pursued a career in inner family systems therapy and energy healing. In retrospect it might have been Mom's greatest gift to us, because we all developed a strong work ethic and a desire to help others as a result. Which, given the trauma we all experienced, might have been the thing that eventually saved us.

But it wasn't work ethic that explained how Mark and I suddenly ended up owning clean, sunny apartments within a few blocks of each other, with fancy Back Bay addresses. It was all thanks to Grandpop, whose presence we felt more in death than in life.

For those who don't know Boston, Back Bay is an affluent shopping and dining destination with a coveted zip code. For Mark and me it felt surreal, suddenly living like privileged yuppies. We hadn't earned it. We knew financially we'd won the birth lottery, born into a family of self-made millionaires.

In fact, in the blue-collar world where Mark and I were pursuing our chosen career path, having money was viewed as a sign you were soft—that things came easily for you. It was a fast way to lose the respect of the guy next to you in the shipyard. So it was something we tried to hide.

But for anyone who thinks wealthy addicts hit a cushier bottom than addicts who are less well off, here's another thing I've learned: addiction doesn't give a shit about your zip code. A fat bank account only gives you the means to kill yourself faster. And I seemed hell-bent on trying.

CHAPTER FIFTEEN

DARTS, DARKNESS, AND THE LAST DROP

One of my favorite TV shows in the early nineties was *Cheers*, the hit series about the staff and patrons at a fictional bar set in Boston. I liked it for all the reasons tens of millions of Americans did (nearly 40 percent of the U.S. population tuned in for the series finale)—it was funny, with a brilliant ensemble cast who brought to life characters you really cared about.

But what drew me in more than anything was the feeling of community it evoked. I loved the idea of a place where this cast of misfits could gather and find friendship, camaraderie, support, and even love. It's what I'd been seeking all my life.

At The Last Drop, I found it. It was, and still is, a cozy, crowded, garden-level pub (meaning it was below street level, with windows offering a scenic view of people's feet walking by) with lots of brick and no shortage of brass. Conveniently, it was located at the corner of Marlborough Street and Massachusetts Avenue in Back Bay, just a couple of blocks from where Mark and I rented our first apartment. We found it shortly after moving in, while wandering around in search of a good neighborhood bar.

The front door of The Last Drop, which has since been renamed the Corner Tavern, is on a side street, down several steps, so we almost missed it. Once we walked inside, sampled the impressive beer menu, and got drawn into a competitive game of darts in the back, we became regulars on the spot. "Hey, Marty!" we'd yell to one of our favorite bartenders and hold up four fingers. Magically, four beers would appear. Our friends in Cambridge would ask us to meet them there sometimes, but it felt like a real bother to go across the bridge to other bars where we'd have to wait in line for a drink.

Through all the madness, The Last Drop became my mainstay. This was before cell phones became popular, so when Mom couldn't reach Mark or me at home, that's where she'd call. Marty loved to jerk our chains about it. "Hey, Scott!" he'd shout in his thick Irish brogue. "Yer mam's on the phone fer ya!" He made sure everybody sitting at the bar heard him.

We soon became enthusiastic members of The Last Drop's Tuesday night dart team, where we went on to win several area-wide championships. I've joked it was probably the high point of my athletic prowess, even counting the Ironman triathlons that would follow. My brother thought it was hilarious when we got interviewed by a local news station, talking about darts as a sport, wearing our matching forest green "Last Drop Dart Team" polo shirts, mine with a huge Guinness stain down the front. And Mark smoking a cigarette. But we were in it solely for the camaraderie.

To Mark's way of telling it, we were for the most part "happy drunks"—big tippers, raucous jokesters, the kind of guys who were frequently saying, "Hey, let's buy a round for all our friends." Meaning we usually racked up a doozy of a tab, which we'd then be too drunk to pay. The next time we'd go in, the bartender would just say, "Another banner night!" and give us a two-hundred-dollar bill. "Don't sweat it, boys," he'd say. "Your bar tabs are putting my kids through college."

* * *

That was the fun side of The Last Drop. But for me, there was a dark side as well. And there was nothing fun about it. At midnight or so, I'd depart for my evening's next chapter, a stop at The Glass Slipper, a strip club in a run-down part of town famously known as the Combat Zone. In the seventies it had been a lawless part of the city, festering with drugs, crime, and prostitution. It wasn't quite as rough in the nineties, but it was still a seedier section of Boston.

Mark came along sometimes. But he generally preferred staying at The Last Drop, hoping the girl he'd met playing darts might turn out to be the woman of his dreams. My only real relationship at that time was with booze and drugs. And since one of my coke dealers was a regular patron of The Glass Slipper, I became one as well.

This is where my story starts becoming uglier, grimmer, and dark-alley dangerous. In case anyone reading thinks my early life sounds self-indulgent and glamorous—and I can understand how it might—I want to set the record straight: it was a miserable existence, and I hated myself for being trapped in it.

On a good night, I'd start out with friends at The Last Drop. Eventually, they'd all go home, and I'd go to The Glass Slipper, where I'd score some coke and head to an after-party somewhere. Eventually those folks would also go home. I'd then go back to my apartment alone and keep drinking until I passed out around 4:00 a.m. The alarm would go off at 6:00 a.m.; I'd wake up looking and feeling like hell, force myself to get into the shower, and start the whole routine all over again.

That was on a good night. On the more disturbing nights, particularly toward the end of my usage, I'd get so drunk I couldn't even smoke crack. I was too drunk to get high. I remember being in an alley in Boston trying to smoke crack and not being able to light it because I was literally blind drunk. And let me tell you, late-stage hangovers are excruciating to the point you'd almost rather be dead.

I used to say I might as well have just one bottle of beer and break the other twenty-three on the back of my head, the pain was so agonizing. Yet I continued to drink and use. You could argue that should have been my bottom. But there's always so much further one can go before hitting the ultimate bottom, which is death.

* * *

Why didn't friends and family intervene at this point? The honest truth is, they didn't know. I had turned into three people living parallel lives: Scott the worker by day; Scott the happy drunk at The Last Drop; and Scott who at midnight turned back into a hardcore addict, buying crack at a dingy hellhole of an apartment in East Boston with graffiti on the walls and paint flakes peeling off the ceiling, guarded by a huge pit bull, as the sun was coming up.

Even my brother rarely saw that third Scott; by 3:00 a.m. all but the most hardcore partiers were home in bed. They assumed I was too. They didn't know I was so brutally hungover or sick from using cocaine for twenty-four hours straight that I couldn't go to work on Monday. I still hadn't recovered from the previous Friday night.

If you haven't struggled with addiction, it can be incomprehensible that someone who seemingly has everything going for them would choose to stay on such a self-destructive path. Looking back at those years, it seems insane to me too. But the disease grinds you down; the disease wants you dead.

I'm often asked what triggers addiction. Is it nature? Or is it nurture? A therapist who became a dear friend once put it this way: "Nature loads the gun, and nurture decides whether the trigger gets pulled." That's where, in my opinion, early childhood trauma, or unresolved trauma from any time of life, can have a role to play.

In a TEDxMileHigh talk I gave in 2016, I called trauma the number-one public health crisis in our country. I wasn't just talking about life-threatening trauma like growing up in a combat zone, enduring physical or sexual abuse, or being the victim of a violent crime. I was also referring to smaller traumas, like your parents getting divorced or being bullied in school or facing rejection by a friend group. Even though these traumas don't leave a wound that we can see, they affect how we see the world.

My trauma history wasn't nearly as horrific as a lot of people's—I'm in awe of how many of my close friends in the Phoenix community survived unimaginable trauma—but it was deeply impactful to me. Nor was my drinking and drug use as extreme as a lot of people's. I wasn't experiencing homelessness or using intravenous drugs or drinking Listerine out of a bottle under a train bridge. Yet it very nearly killed me just the same.

I don't present any of this as an excuse. But for anyone struggling to understand the scary, selfish, self-sabotaging stranger their loved one has become, keep this in mind: nobody ever dreams they're going to grow up to be an addict.

CHAPTER SIXTEEN

SCOOPED UP WITH LOVE AT A BOXING GYM

S oon after I moved into my own five-hundred-square-foot apartment on Beacon Street, while still working on ships in Fairhaven, I'd used some of Grandpop's money, earmarked for education, to enroll in classes at the North Bennet Street School, a trade school in Boston that offered everything from bookbinding to locksmithing to jewelry making. I chose cabinet- and furniture making. I thought if I could refine my skills, maybe I could work on higher-end boats and make more money.

So once the boat I was working on went back in the water, I quit the shipyards to become a full-time student. (I use the term "full-time" loosely.) Mark followed suit with classes in historic home preservation. We'd hatched the idea of starting a woodworking company together, which was not a bad idea, if only we could show up for classes and work. It seemed we had both inherited the woodworking gene, and we were excited at the prospect of building our own business. But drinking and throwing darts at The Last Drop took a lot less effort.

After school I'd normally get some beers with my fellow students, then grab a burger and crash. But for every half-dozen days like that, there'd be one where I'd end up drinking a whole bottle of Stoli vodka. I'd come to hours later pushing a straw or rolled-up dollar bill down a line of coke on a glass table, a CD case, or even on a metal toilet paper holder in the bathroom stall of a bar or club.

On those days I felt well enough, I'd show up for class. I somehow managed to not get kicked out—all those hours carving chipmunks and mallards under the patient tutelage of Pop-Pop plus many years working on ships had paid off in some strong woodworking and design skills—but my life was continuing to unravel.

At this point, I'd developed something of a reputation among my friends' girlfriends and parents for being a bad influence—a label that I, with my fantastical mindset, perceived as unfair. The enthusiasm I now apply to growing The Phoenix, back then I put into drinking and partying. Mark and I would walk around the bar with a tray of shots, handing them out to all willing takers. It was part of my hospitality skill set.

One day I invited a friend from woodworking school to join Mark and me for a few beers after class. As usual we started out at The Last Drop, and frankly I'm not sure what happened after that. At three in the morning, my phone rang. "Where's Toby?" his wife asked, sounding both annoyed and concerned. She assumed he was with me.

"I don't know where he is," I said, feeling groggy and grumpy. "Why should I know where he is?"

That was the wrong answer. "He went out with *you*, and he hasn't come home!" She had every right to be upset. It turns out Toby had drunk so much he'd passed out on the "T," our regional transit system, and woken up to find himself locked in a car in the train yard. To get out, he had to hit the emergency switch to open the door, walk through the train yard and climb over a fence, then figure out how to get home. I added him to the list of friends who weren't allowed to hang out with me anymore.

* * *

Given my track record, it's ironic that it was the roommate of Mark's girlfriend Alexandra who introduced me to the thing that would, in time, set me on the path to sobriety.

Eve was a Golden Gloves boxer. One night while I was tearing into my bread bowl of creamy clam chowder with extra oyster crackers at

Legal Seafood, I couldn't help but notice Eve's whitefish accompanied by steamed broccoli. "I'm trying to make weight for an upcoming fight," she explained. Then she started sharing boxing stories with Mark, Alexandra, and me.

"Wow, that is just wild," I said. "I could get into that." It struck me that I could use a healthy hobby. Or at least one a little healthier than my current pastimes.

She knew a likely recruit when she saw one. "Well, Scott," she said in what sounded like a challenge, "you should come to the gym sometime."

Mark and I both flinched. A recent outing to the gym hadn't gone so well.

I'd always been intrigued with fitness. But shipyard work was so physically demanding I was too tired to go bench-press after work. Once I started school, though, it seemed like a good time to start a fitness routine. So Mark and I hired a personal trainer. His name was Rudy. He sounded nice over the phone. We didn't expect him to look like Arnold Schwarzenegger.

We showed up for the training session psyched to get in shape; all the beer was taking a toll. Then we spotted the stretch marks on Rudy's pecs and biceps. Loads of them, on full display around his very tight, white tank top. What the hell were we in for? All I could think was "This guy looks like a killer."

He gave Mark and me the once-over. "Ready to do some bicep curls and bench presses?" he asked. Mark and I looked at each other and thought to ourselves, "We've made worse decisions together." So we said yes. He proceeded to destroy us.

The next day I was so sore I couldn't even wash my own hair. (Yes, I once had hair.) I had to squirt shampoo in my hand and turn my head upside down to rub the soap around because I couldn't lift my arms above my head. That's how torn up I was after just one session. I felt like a jellyfish. I told Mark, "No way am I going back to a gym like that."

But for some reason, Eve's depiction of the boxing gym intrigued me. I was still smoking, drinking, and doing drugs. So I wasn't exactly boxing ring ready. But something inside me—that pilot light flickering in anybody with a pulse—was beginning to burn just slightly brighter as I transitioned into what I thought of as "seeking mode." Almost subconsciously I'd gone from "This is who I am, this party persona" to "I'm really unhappy in this place, and I'm losing me." And I didn't even know who "me" was. So I began seeking. And as I was seeking, I said yes to boxing.

* * *

Eve was doing some personal training, so I signed up for some sessions with her and she started teaching me how to box. I went alone at first. Mark and I were going through similar moments in life, and he eventually took up boxing as well. In the early days, though, it was just me facing Eve in a gym full of cauliflower-eared, flat-nosed men. Who could all—like Eve—kick my ass. And plenty of them did.

But they did it with love. From the moment I set foot in City Gym in Kenmore Square, temptingly located above Store 24 where I was still buying twelve-packs after work, I felt a fellowship. Nobody judged me. That's why I always say I was scooped up with as much love as you can find at a boxing gym. Some of the toughest people you could imagine were the people who began to help me heal.

To me, the boxing community felt like a society within a society, with City Gym at the heart of it. The owner, John, had carved out a little room for boxers in the back, behind the aerobics workout room; from the window you could see the lights of Fenway Park. It wasn't too far from my Back Bay apartment. So I'd walk home past The Last Drop, which until I got sober wasn't helpful to my training regimen.

I was starting to hit harder and was progressing as a heavyweight. At that point Eve, being really tiny, couldn't hold the punch mitts for me anymore. So City Gym's boxing coach, Dave "Sully" Sullivan, started coaching me. Sully was a well-known local pro whom people came from around the city to train with. It helped that Dave was sober, which reinforced the path I was on. Part of me wanted to be sober, even if I wasn't fully there yet.

Back then Sully was building a cool little community of boxers, which I became a part of. Eventually, I got invited to join a half-dozen guys every Saturday to spar at other gyms throughout New England. We'd go to Murphy's Gym in the Boston suburb of Woburn once a week; the next weekend we'd drive thirty miles north to the Lowell West End Gym, the first place I actually got into the ring.

Lowell has been, since 1945, the site of the New England Golden Gloves, the most highly regarded amateur boxing tournament in the U.S. So it attracts a lot of up-and-coming boxers. But back then the drive into town was extremely depressing. We were brushing up against a much darker time in America in regard to crack cocaine usage, and Lowell was an epicenter of it. With its vacant factories and run-down neighborhoods, it had the air of a town that had given up on itself.

If you saw the 2011 Oscar-nominated movie *The Fighter,* you know what I mean. It tells the story of a promising boxer named Dicky Eklund (portrayed in the film by actor Christian Bale), who was for a time known as "the Pride of Lowell," until he succumbed to a crack cocaine addiction. Dicky's story also became the subject of an HBO documentary, *High on Crack Street: Lost Lives in Lowell.* He later got into recovery and trained his half brother, Micky Ward (portrayed by Boston's own Mark Wahlberg), who went on to become a champion boxer known for his brutal "liver punch."

Both men were training at the West End Gym at the time I was there. Sully himself was from boxing lineage, having trained with Dicky and Micky, and with the coach who trained Joe Frazier. (To this day my lower ribs still hurt from the legacy of that liver punch.) *The Fighter* resonated with me because at that time, Dicky and I were on the same self-destructive path.

What struck me most about the guys I boxed with, though, was their mindset: these were guys—and apart from Eve and a few other women, it was mostly guys—who'd rather get up at five in the morning to hop in a car and go spar with other boxers than stay out until five in the morning. They were disciplined and focused on their training because they were all trying to cut weight and make their weight classes for upcoming fights. A few were in recovery. And over time I started to feel like I had a place where I belonged more than in a bar.

CHAPTER SEVENTEEN

SOBER SATURDAYS

There's no doubt I owe my first serious steps toward sobriety to a Gore-Tex winter jacket and a tough, determined flyweight boxer named Leo Martinez. The jacket because it serendipitously introduced me to an utterly foreign new world, one that would change my life. And Leo because he was willing to suffer along with me as I attempted to conquer that death-defying—but life-affirming—new world. I couldn't have hoped for a braver, steadier partner during the arduous climbs in the wilderness I embarked upon after barely surviving the next and darkest chapters of my life.

But we're still in this chapter, so we'll focus on the jacket.

Between making furniture at the North Bennet Street School, sparring on weekends, and partying a lot in between, I was busy. But I still felt a void. Mark and I were making a half-hearted attempt at building our woodworking business. But I found it really lonely. On boats and in shipyards, I'd been around a crew. Or with fourteen guys in a house. But when we had our own woodshop, we were in there alone all day building stuff. The work was meaningful. But I realized what had always been more meaningful for me than work was the people I shared it with.

This was another seedling that would later take root in my triathlons and mountain climbing and in building the Phoenix community. It's not about the finish line or the mountaintop. It's the people you're sharing the journey with.

At the same time, I started feeling a drive to become more "outdoorsy." As a kid, the one time I bonded at all with my father was in nature. Being out in the woods with him, Mark, and Amyla in a quiet, beautiful place was an occasional respite from the peaks and valleys of my dad's mania. Likewise, one of my best memories of my stepdad was in a sporting goods store, buying gear for a camping trip he was going to take us on. The trip got rained out. But I never forgot the thrill I felt getting ready for it. Again, a seed had been planted.

You never know when those seeds will start to sprout. They might lie dormant for years. But if you're one of the many humans struggling to recover from something, or if you love someone who is, never doubt that those seeds are there.

So one day I found myself over at Eastern Mountain Sports (EMS) and told one of the employees I planned to start doing some hiking. "What do I need to start getting outdoorsy?" I asked him. His recommendation: "You should probably start with a Gore-Tex jacket." Which turned out to be good—albeit expensive—advice; I left the store with a two-hundred-dollar jacket. It would cost six hundred dollars today.

But that was the best two hundred dollars I ever spent, because on my way out I saw a black-and-white brochure for the EMS Climbing School, with a picture of a guy in a helmet ice climbing on the front. He was on a vertical climb, his ice ax and feet stuck in the ice, and he was looking upward. I was blown away; it was like nothing I'd ever seen. I picked up the brochure and returned to the checkout counter. "What is ice climbing?" I asked.

"It's when you climb on ice," the cashier answered, with what looked to me like a smirk. "We have beginner's lessons. Are you interested?"

The next weekend, I drove two and a half hours to North Conway, New Hampshire, with my Gore-Tex jacket and all the warm clothes I owned. I had to borrow boots and a helmet, and they gave me different gloves. I also borrowed crampons (spikes that attach to boots for traction on ice) and ice axes. And yes, I was nervous.

They took us out to a cliff that was only about twenty feet high and taught us how to swing the ice ax and kick our feet in with the crampons.

As the guide talked, he climbed effortlessly, looking down over his shoulder and teaching us as he climbed. I was thinking, "Oh wow, that's cool. It can't be that hard." And then it was my turn.

In mere minutes, memories of my agony at the hands of Rudy the trainer flooded my head. How could I be this stupid twice? I struggled my way up, sweating profusely, feet falling off the side of the cliff, arms above my head hanging on for dear life. My shirt was riding up so my belly was against the ice, and snow was falling on top of me, into my face. Let's just say I suffered every moment of my way up that cliff. The experience felt analogous to my life. I was suffering through everything, and it had gotten really hard.

But as I watched how the teacher moved with ease, I thought, "Someday I want to climb like that." I had no idea what that would entail. But again, it planted a seed and became one more thing that anchored me to the light instead of the dark.

* * *

Back in Boston, I kept boxing and going to school for woodworking. As often as I could fit it in, I'd go up to New Hampshire and take another lesson from the climbing school. I'd stay sober Friday nights so I could climb on Saturdays. Not drinking on Friday nights was a big deal for me. Until ice climbing school, I don't think I'd had many sober Friday nights since I was fourteen or fifteen, other than maybe when I had the flu. And even then I could count on cough medicine with codeine.

Pretty soon I realized I could climb on Sunday too if I stayed sober both nights. So I started climbing more regularly. I was doing harder climbs under the guidance of the EMS teachers. And I was still going to woodworking school, where I was designing a captain's desk I hoped would be chosen for display in their spring gallery showing on Newbury Street. All in all, things were looking up.

Then the holidays hit.

CHAPTER EIGHTEEN

MY VERSION OF A WHITE CHRISTMAS

On December 13, 1996, two blockbuster movies were released: *Mars Attacks!*, a sci-fi comedy starring Jack Nicholson in the hilarious role of U.S. president during a surprise attack by Martians, and *Jerry Maguire*, a romantic comedy starring Tom Cruise as an ambitious sports agent who couldn't sustain a relationship even though he detested being alone.

The first is relevant only to disclose I love dumb action movies. As in, the dumber the better. I know I'm no longer the target demo; Hollywood makes these films for people ages eighteen to twenty-four. But I never grew out of them. My wife Kait teases me because I'll get home from an intense day at work and watch the silliest movie I can find on Netflix just to shut my brain down.

Jerry Maguire is another story. That movie actually made me a little uncomfortable, especially since I saw it with a date. It just hit a little too close to home. The film had nothing to do with addiction. But it had everything to do with love avoidance (a phrase I learned later in therapy), which my disastrous romance track record made clear was a problem. Of course, the term "track record" would imply I had something to track, which when it came to relationships I did not.

I wanted a serious girlfriend. But many of the women I tried to date found it tough to keep up with my drinking. On top of that, I felt unworthy of anyone I was attracted to. Rather than wondering what she liked to do for fun or what kind of food she liked to eat, my first question was always "I wonder how long until she dumps me?" I never stuck around long enough to find out.

That may seem at odds with my aversion to being alone. I learned years later in trauma therapy that it was all part of the same sad pattern of craving love and acceptance and then, out of fear of rejection, pushing it away. But more on that later. At this stage of my life, I wasn't asking those kinds of questions. I just wanted to surround myself with so many people and parties—so much noise—that I didn't have to worry about actually feeling anything.

Which brings us to Christmas. Which I celebrated in Strasburg. Which was my first mistake.

Returning to the Lancaster area was always a trigger for me. Back to the same friends, the same routines, the same family dynamics. Mom still lived with a phone in one hand—now a state-of-the-art Motorola flip phone—which she used to simultaneously wave us off while inviting us in. (Love avoidance?) Al was planted in his favorite armchair, drinking his martinis, though given my heavyweight stature, he now stifled his snide comments.

Dad and Paula had divorced, and he'd moved back in with Nanny and Pop-Pop, who were now at the receiving end of his emotional manipulation. I had no interest in seeing him. Nor did Mark, who had recently refused Dad's request to visit him in Boston. That had prompted an angry call to me. "I hope you never have to hear your own son talk to you the way Mark just talked to me," he said.

"If Mark talked to you that way, you probably deserved it," I replied. That was an empowering moment for my brother and me—an assertion of our escape from Dad's shaming abuse.

Mom's house looked and smelled festive, as always. A fresh Pennsylvania pine tree was decorated in the living room, with piles of brightly colored packages beneath. Tree lights twinkled in the window. Mom had bought roast beef and green bean casserole to cook on Christmas Day. It's too bad most of us weren't present enough to enjoy any of it.

I'd promised myself I was going to refrain from drinking over the Christmas holiday; after all, I was managing to stay sober in order to climb most weekends. But the minute I returned home, I was right back in it. Danny and Aidan called on Christmas Eve. There was a party; did I want to come? Does a chicken have wings?

So we went out drinking, and I ran into an old friend who hooked us up with a bunch of coke. I remember somebody joking, "It's gonna be a white Christmas after all!" Then we gathered in a high school friend's basement, where we proceeded to get wasted. At one point while doing a line of coke I saw a kid smoking a cigarette, watching me, who looked like he was barely out of middle school. I showed him how to scoop some coke up with a straw and dump it into the end of a cigarette, then twist the end shut.

"What's your name?" I asked him. Even in my messed-up state, I was sickened by the thought this young kid might end up like me.

"Johnny Armstrong," he said as he lit up the cigarette.

With that, I went to another time and place altogether. Suddenly I was back in school, being tutored by a kind and patient woman who spent hours helping me function better with my dyslexia. Her name was Mrs. Armstrong, and she always had her young son with her, usually asleep in his stroller. His name was Johnny. And tonight I was teaching him how to smoke coke.

My shame was so great I had to leave the party. I'll never forget the horror of that. If I had a moment of true self-loathing, that was it. My buddies and I had a lot of drugs left over, and I had to get rid of those since the next day was Christmas and we all had to go home. I was so hungover and sick with withdrawals the next day I couldn't even celebrate Christmas. I missed the whole day. I despised myself for that too.

I remember Mom knocking on the door of the Bunker Hill cabin that Mark, Amyla, and I still stayed in when we visited, hoping I was going to join the family for Christmas dinner. I knew she was disappointed—and initially pretty scared—that I was a no-show. Amyla, on break from graduate studies at Duke, checked in on me too. But once they determined

I was suffering from another horrific hangover that was likely not life-threatening, they left me alone for the rest of the day. The next day I apologized, opened my gifts, thanked and hugged my mom, and life went back to "normal." As it always did.

Because here's what happens to people who have close relationships with folks battling addiction: you keep resetting your expectations of them and of what they can bring to the relationship as their addiction and alcoholism get progressively worse. For example, in our family it just became a fact we could never plan anything before eleven in the morning because Al and Mark and I were all alcoholics. And then it was noon, and eventually it got to the point where I missed Christmas and nobody was all that surprised.

That lowering of expectations doesn't happen overnight. If you belong to a family like mine, you are likely vulnerable to what's known as the "boiling frog" syndrome: that's an allegory that says if a frog is put into boiling water, it will jump out, but if it's put in lukewarm water that is brought to a boil slowly, it won't realize how hot things are getting and will be cooked to death.

Scientists have since disproven that premise, at the expense of some frogs. But as a metaphor for families dealing with substance use disorder, it has some value. As the person in your life who is struggling with substance use starts lowering the bar on their baseline behavior, you just keep readjusting to a new normal. It can happen so gradually you don't realize you're doing it. Until one day you realize things are falling apart in the family to the point you are all in crisis.

If there's a silver lining to drug and alcohol addiction, it's that the warning bells generally get loud enough that you have to listen to them—whether those alarms are sounding within you or for a loved one—more so than you would with seemingly healthier coping mechanisms, like workaholism or getting fanatic about exercise, or extreme sports, which can also kill you. And I think that's a blessing of sorts.

In the weeks and months leading up to that abysmal Christmas holiday, I *had* started listening to what my body and soul were screaming at me. It was hard to ignore. I'd gotten to that point in my addiction where I'd shed all the layers of normalcy that characterize substance use for most people, and each layer you get to is a little more messed up until you get to that place where it's just you by yourself using. (Actually the layer just before that—where you're still seeking comfort in a group setting—is in some ways even worse, because there's nothing more lonely than a room full of addicts using together.)

The irony is that the joy I was seeking from drinking and drugs, starting from the age of eleven—the camaraderie, love, and acceptance I was chasing, the void I kept hoping to fill from a beer keg or a fifth of vodka or a twenty-dollar bag of coke—turned out to be every bit as elusive as the magic of Wing Song Farm.

CHAPTER NINETEEN

HITTING ROCK BOTTOM

For anyone still not fully convinced that the disease of addiction causes otherwise sane people to do insane things, what I share next might open your mind to the possibility. Not because my final chaotic, uncontrollable, dismal days of drinking and using were so unique, but because they weren't. Right now as you're reading this, according to the latest statistics, more than forty million Americans are in the place where I was nearly thirty years ago, some having their dreams stripped away by their relationship with substances, and others on a path that will ultimately end their life.

After the disaster that was Christmas Eve, I didn't even bother to make any New Year's resolutions. I figured that was just setting myself up for more failure and self-hatred. Instead, I did what I do best: I planned a party. I headed back to my Back Bay apartment right after Christmas. Not wanting to be alone on New Year's Eve, I invited Danny, Aidan, and the rest of the Lancaster crew to come to Boston to ring in 1997. They said yes.

No surprise, I got blackout drunk. By then I'd started sleepwalking, in my case a scary side effect of later-stage alcoholism. On New Year's Day, I woke up on my sofa totally naked, with a maroon sheet covering me. The thing is, I didn't own any maroon sheets. Once I became fully conscious, I realized it was my shower curtain. I'd apparently gotten out of bed in the middle of the night, ripped the shower curtain down, and covered myself with it to keep warm on the couch. I was just totally on drunk autopilot.

From there I pretty much went into an uncontrolled nosedive. Which any pilot will tell you can be extremely difficult to pull out of. I'd started drinking and using on weekends again; on one of them, I woke up to find I'd torn one whole leg of my jeans wide open to pull my work boot out and had passed out with both boots still on. I'd gone to a party for a friend, and the last thing I remember is doing a shot of tequila with him. The next morning I woke up on my sofa with shredded jeans. I would just lose whole periods of the night. That's terrifying, in retrospect. It was getting scarier in the moment too.

By the end of St. Patrick's Day, even my die-hard party pals had had enough. A group always came up for that holiday for obvious reasons. Boston at its craziest. But this year it reached new levels of wild, at least for me. I remember we went to see the parade in Southie, as the locals call South Boston, and that's about all I remember. I blacked out after that. Which is super alarming because it was two in the afternoon.

We went to three other bars later that night, or so I'm told. The last one was The Glass Slipper, where I connected with my supplier. Then we returned to my Beacon Street apartment, where I went into my room, chalked up a bunch of lines on a CD case, and passed out. I was too drunk to even do the coke. A few hours later, I walked naked into the living room, where one of my buddies was sleeping on the sofa, grabbed him, and threw him onto the floor.

The next morning, I woke up on the sofa, surrounded by a bunch of friends who were sleeping on the floor and on the other sofa. "What the fuck happened?" I asked. This felt different than my usual morning-after chaos. Nobody was smiling. One of them said, "Walk into the other room." My friend whom I'd pushed off the sofa had gone to sleep in my bed, not even realizing he was sleeping next to a CD case with a bunch of lines of coke on it. "What's wrong with you, man?" he asked when he saw me. It was a rhetorical question. But I could see in his face he was genuinely worried about me. Unlike after past incidents, which I normally blew off as funny, I was now worried about me too.

For him it must have been like the Liverpool moment when I saw the girl's brother shooting up. This guy had just come to Boston to drink some beers. He was a pretty normal kid. And suddenly he's getting pushed off the sofa by a naked dude and waking up next to lines of cocaine on a CD case. He'd gotten sucked unwittingly into my helter-skelter, crazy-making, substance-seeking vortex. I had that effect on people. Close friends like Danny and Aidan drank a lot less after I got sober.

* * *

April 7, 1997, was a big day for me. The North Bennet Street School had an exhibit of student work opening on famed Newbury Street, and they'd chosen the captain's desk I'd designed and built for display in the front window. I didn't have much to feel good about back then. But I was very proud of having my work on display on such a prominent street in Boston.

I remember standing on the sidewalk staring at that desk, wishing my family could be there to see it. Mark came, of course, but nobody else could make it. Somewhere in my heart, I would have liked my father there, despite the pain he'd caused, because of his background in woodworking and his love of carving. He was a hard man to have as a father, but I never stopped loving him.

The opening was on a Tuesday, which meant Mark and I had another obligation once we'd made an appearance on Newbury—it was dart league night. So we had a few beers with friends after the show and then headed to The Last Drop to meet the dart team. I can't remember if we had a home game or an away game that night; every other week, we traveled to a different bar in the league and represented the Drop.

Either way, the evening started off with 2 or 3 pints of Guinness that turned into 10 or 15, augmented by 6 or 7 shots of whatever was put in front of me. This was a typical night out in those days. The challenge was not getting too drunk to play darts. Then, armed with a small leather case filled with spare flights and shafts and three nickel darts tucked in my back pocket, it was "Game on!"

Even inebriated, I occasionally scored what's known (appropriately in my case) as a "Champagne Finish," with at least two bull's-eyes in rapid succession. For me, the hardest part about playing darts while drunk was doing the math. Then it was back to the bar for more shots and beers and some good-natured gloating.

This night was different, though. I was feeling particularly full of myself after watching pedestrians stop to look at my captain's desk in the window on Newbury Street a few hours earlier. And darts always revved me up. My two aptitudes on display, back-to-back. I was flying high.

* * *

After a stop at another bar, just before last call at 2:00 a.m., I ended up at The Glass Slipper, its harsh yellow neon sign promising all manner of debauchery within. Sometimes I brought friends. But on this pivotal evening, I was alone.

It was very dark inside, the better to shield people's identities. I walked past the three-quarters empty bar on the right toward the stage area in the back where you could sit in a small booth and shell out big bucks to buy a cheap drink for one of the dancers. For one hundred dollars, she would sit and pretend to be interested in your life, and you'd want to believe that she was.

At the bar near the edge of the stage, a few men sat thinking they had the power—because look what these women would do for them for a few dollars. And on the stage the women thought they had the power—because look how easy it was to get these men to hand over their money. The truth is everyone in there was either just trying to make ends meet or to escape significant pain in their life.

I fell into the latter category. But hell, tonight I was celebrating, right? Rocky the bartender (nobody used their real names) sent me over a bottle of crappy champagne, which I worked my way through to the last drop while attempting a rambling, increasingly slurred conversation with a stripper whose fake name I didn't even know. An hour or so later, the man I'd come to see finally walked in. I'd met him through a friend who worked there; she gave me the signal, and we met in the men's room (sometimes it was his car), where he left with my money and I left with my bag of coke.

One particularly dangerous aspect of my addiction at this stage was I had more than enough money to feed it. When I was younger, I was always broke. But now, after years of working plus having inherited the money from my mom's father, I had ample spending money. I wish every human being on planet Earth had that good fortune. But it's a bad situation for someone in active addiction.

I was no longer content with buying half a gram of cocaine; I'd graduated to eight balls. Each of these snow-white, powdery balls weighs one-eighth of an ounce—hence the name—which is equivalent to 3.5 grams of cocaine. So on any given night, I was ingesting at least 700 percent more cocaine than when I'd started using, in a futile attempt to satisfy my constant craving for more.

The instant euphoria I'd experienced the first time I'd used, if I felt it now at all, was quickly overshadowed by the intense, drug-induced anxiety, paranoia, and depression that followed. Some nights I'd jump into a car with a few strippers and use cocaine until the sun rose. On this night, though, I was crashing early, having woken up at 6:00 a.m., been hyped-up all day in anticipation of the exhibit opening, and then having consumed copious amounts of alcohol and coke after the dart league.

Normally I'd be riding home through the Ted Williams Tunnel, in the back of a cab I had no recollection of hailing, just as the sun was coming up. Tonight I couldn't wait to get back to Beacon Street, though. I was feeling paranoid in the extreme; God knows what kind of garbled guff I gave the cabbie. I don't remember him picking me up or dropping me off.

Did I pass out on the cab ride home? Did he have to jolt me awake? Who knows?

All I know for sure is where I ended up that night—locked in my apartment with all the lights off, huddled on my bathroom floor with a flashlight, doing lines of coke off a CD case. In my drug-induced paranoia, I was convinced my neighbors could hear me and would call the cops. I turned some music on, just loud enough so that anyone standing outside my front door would not be able to hear me snorting lines. My heart was pounding so uncontrollably it felt like it was going to explode in my chest. I'd now been doing coke nearly nonstop since the night before. I knew that's how I was going to die.

I could hear the city coming to life—I was acutely aware of the garbage truck arriving, the intermittent rush of traffic down my quiet street, a door slamming, a horn or two beeping in the distance. I knew if I looked out my window, I'd see students rowing crew on the Charles River as early-morning joggers ran and bikers rode along its banks; I had a great view in the winter and early spring when the trees were bare.

But as the sun rose over Back Bay that morning, casting golden rays of light through my living room windows, do you know what I thought of? I thought of my mom. I thought somebody was going to have to tell her that her son died on a bathroom floor from a cocaine overdose.

And that's the last time I ever used.

April 8, 1997, is my sobriety date. Instead of dying, that's the day Scott Andrew Strode was born.

PART III

MOUNTAINTOP MOMENTS

*It's transformative to stand on top of a mountain.
From those heights you can see something in yourself you can't
see from down here. But over time you realize you don't need
the mountain anymore—that what you need is in your heart.
That's when you can walk away from who you are as an addict.
And you can walk away proud.*

SCOTT STRODE

CHAPTER TWENTY

WAKING UP SOBER:
A BREAKFAST OF GRIT AND GRATITUDE

I woke up on April 9, 1997, shivering. I was in my own bed, covered by a green blanket, not a maroon shower curtain. I was even clothed—I was wearing an old, faded *Sea Cloud* T-shirt. But I still felt chilled. Which was weird, since I was detoxing, which causes me to sweat profusely. As it turned out, that happened to be the coldest morning in April that year, the only day when the high in Boston dipped to near freezing. Two days earlier, the day of the North Bennet Street School gallery opening, it had been seventy-five and sunny, so I'd turned off the heat. I was twenty-four-hours sober.

Rising briefly to turn up the thermostat, I could hear the sound of slush splashing from under the tires of cars on Storrow Drive as people started their day. On April Fool's Day, a blizzard had dumped twenty-five inches of snow, along with some rain and sleet, on Boston in the space of several early morning hours. The weather that month was as mercurial as my mood. Paranoia, depression, euphoria, terror, anxiety, loneliness, anger, regret—a blizzard of emotions raged inside my soul in the days leading up to and following my decision to get sober. And even, just faintly, the stirrings of hope.

But mostly I just felt wretchedly ill. The nausea and sweats—which did come, once the heat kicked in—were so bad my first instinct was to grab a beer from the fridge. "Hair of the dog that bit me," I used to say. But the fridge was empty except for an old pizza box from Captain Nemo's. Instead, I just toughed it out in my apartment. Alcohol is one of the most dangerous drugs to detox from. Even with medical supervision, it can be life-threatening.

Which is why this chapter should come with the warning label: "Don't try this at home." Unless of course you absolutely have to. But when you're truly ready to get sober, regardless of your age or your circumstances, you will. One way or another. You will find your inner grit.

I'd been through detox before, so I knew what to expect. This time was no different from the others, but for the addition of one crucial emotion I'd never had before: resolve. This time I didn't waver in my intention to give up drugs and alcohol for good.

I've talked about seeds being planted throughout my life—on boats, in shipyards, in the boxing gym or on the side of a mountain, and with teachers and mentors who believed in me—that were waiting for the right moment to take root and grow. For me, that time was now. I don't know why. At the time, I was too sick to care. But in those miserable, scary, lonely early days of sobriety, the other thing I felt, improbably, was gratitude.

If you talk to friends or loved ones who've gotten sober after a long struggle with substance use disorder, you might be surprised—and skeptical—to hear them say they wouldn't change a thing about their past. I sometimes tell people the same thing. I know it sounds inconceivable, not to mention selfish, given the hurt and damage we've caused ourselves and others. We wouldn't wish to repeat that. But we know our journey led us to this place, a better place, thanks to the mistakes we've made, the people who've helped, and the experiences we've had along the way.

So in addition to owing many amends, there are so many people to whom I owe thanks. And it's those people I thought about for strength and inspiration as I sweated and vomited and swore and boxed and climbed my way through the process of clearing my body of years' worth of toxins.

One of those people was a stripper at The Glass Slipper who called herself Onix. She was roughly my age and struggling to get by herself, yet somehow had compassion and insight to share, even in that dark time and place. We formed a connection; I'd go to buy drugs, and we'd talk, and I'd counsel her about changing her life and doing something more substantial than being a stripper. She'd listen and share how she dreamed of going to school or about the career she hoped to have. Then she'd ask how I was doing and seemed to really want to hear the answer.

One late night—actually it was early morning, around two—I was sipping a beer to wash down a shot of Stoli and expounding on all the things Onix should do to make her life better when she stopped me cold. "Scott," she said, "have you ever considered that you're an alcoholic? Have you thought about quitting drinking?"

Have I ever considered that I'm an alcoholic? I was shocked. Here I was in a strip club in the Combat Zone and a stripper was calling me an alcoholic? At the time I thought, "Who is she to judge me?" Then again, who was I to judge her? The last thing either of us needed was judgment. But she'd asked me the question because she cared about me. And deep down I knew that. So it began to ruin drinking for me. In retrospect, it was one of the final seeds that got me seriously thinking about recovery.

I wish I could find her and thank her. But since Onix was her stage name, I have no way of tracking her down. I hope she's well and happy. And if she happens to be reading this book, I'd tell her this: in a moment of honesty one night, in a place I least expected to hear it, but at a time I most needed to, you helped save my life.

CHAPTER TWENTY-ONE

LEO THE LION-HEARTED

You'll recall a few chapters back I gave shout-outs to a Gore-Tex winter jacket and a flyweight boxer at my gym named Leo Martinez. Both were instrumental to my recovery journey. The jacket because it led me to discover mountain climbing. And Leo because when I asked him to be my climbing partner, he said yes.

To combat the loneliness of early sobriety, when most of my friends and even my brother were still heavy partiers, I immersed myself in boxing, climbing, and outdoor stuff. Anything I could do to stay busy and not think about drugs and alcohol. I needed to replace the time, thought, and effort I was applying to drinking and using with something more positive.

Mountain climbing had become my passion, but I was at a transition point. The leader of EMS Climbing School was a guy named Dave Kelly, who had become a friend and mentor. One day I showed up for another lesson and asked Dave what he saw as the next step in my growth as a climber. "Scott, there's not much more we can teach you at this point," he answered. "You need to get out and have your own experiences. Get into some stuff a little bit over your head, have some adventures, but come back safely."

And by the way, he added, "You need to find a climbing partner."

I quickly ticked through the friends I had in Boston who might be up for some wilderness adventures and then made a mental note of who'd be worth calling. I landed on two options: "Mark" and "Nobody."

Knowing Mark my whole life, I was pretty sure he wouldn't want to hang off an ice cliff all day. And he was still drinking. I went with "Nobody."

Meanwhile, City Gym had become my refuge. I'd go there on a Saturday and not leave until it closed. If anyone needed me to hold punch mitts for them, I'd do that. If Sully was available for a training session, I'd jump at the chance. Trash needed picking up? I was your guy. Then I'd go straight home.

Around the time I got sober, a new guy who'd trained with Sully elsewhere started coming to the gym, a kid fresh out of Boston College who was a couple years younger than me, nearly a foot shorter, and about one hundred pounds lighter. His name was Leo Martinez. Aptly named, with the heart and soul of a lion—independent, self-sufficient, fearless, and amazingly strong. When we goofed around with our boxing gloves on, it was almost farcical watching me with my Goliath stature trying to match Leo's blinding hand speed, given he was literally half my size.

Leo joined our group of guys who sparred around the state on weekends. We were a gang of six, a small, tight-knit community of pugilists, and when we weren't sparring or working, we began hanging out. It brought back memories of my Bunker Hill posse meeting up by the creek, but minus the drugs and alcohol. This new, more crooked-nosed crew preferred dressing up and going out for a nice dinner in Boston or coming to my place for pizza and a movie. Occasionally we would do a road trip to the Mohegan Sun Casino and Resort in Connecticut to catch some fights or to Atlantic City to watch Micky Ward face off against Arturo Gatti.

Beyond boxing, we didn't have a whole lot in common. Leo was born in Mexico City, came to America as a young boy, and grew up in working-class Watertown, Massachusetts, six miles northwest of Boston on the Charles River. Some people would embellish that story to flaunt their self-made, rags-to-riches image, but not Leo. When asked about it, he'd simply say, "That's just a small part of who I am. There's not much to tell."

Then there was Jake, a roofer from Woburn, Massachusetts, whom we'd met at Murphy's gym and the first guy I got in the ring with. He was a welterweight fifty pounds lighter than me. But he was a formidable sparring partner—Sully always joked that "Jake's so ripped, he has muscles on his eyelids." And his forearms looked equal in size to his thighs. We loved to razz him about his Boston accent—he called me Squawtty (his version of Scotty), and my brother was "Mahk." He even laughed with a Boston accent. Seriously. Instead of "ha ha," it came out as "haw haw."

I remember riding with Jake in the car one night and him looking slightly uncomfortable. "Dude, I hate these kinds of roads," he said.

"What do you mean?" I asked.

"These ones without lights," he replied. "They're so freaking dahk."

I realized he was so city-bred that he had never been on streets without streetlights.

Our differences didn't matter, though. We bonded initially through boxing, and those bonds grew into friendship; we had each other's backs. For me, having that support and fellowship in early sobriety was crucial. As was the physical activity: smashing the heavy bag until my hands were sore somehow helped me feel better. Our shared goal of becoming better athletes connected us even more. I didn't realize it at the time, but being part of that little gang showed me how good it felt to be part of a strong, albeit small, sober active community.

I was, however, beginning to see the downsides of boxing. It was destructive. Mark was feeling it too. Now, instead of waking up feeling like we'd been punched in the head, we actually *had* been punched in the head. And it was clear to both of us that we did not have an illustrious career ahead in boxing. "If you're not waking up every morning wanting to win the Golden Gloves, it's likely the guy you're fighting is," Sully told us. "So take up tennis or something."

I certainly didn't wake up thinking about boxing—and me on a tennis court is just plain funny—but I was always daydreaming about the mountains. The trouble was, I still needed a climbing partner. Mark went climbing with me a few times in New Hampshire but preferred snow-boarding. Which is why I'm eternally grateful to Leo.

Despite considering himself "more of a city person, not a nature guy," interested in books, music, and art, Leo was the only one in our group who expressed interest in climbing and exploring pursuits other than boxing. He had an adventurous spirit and a desire to try what I called, in air quotes, "outdoorsy-ness." (I was pretty sure serious mountain climbers didn't use that term.) He'd also read *Into Thin Air: A Personal Account of the Mt. Everest Disaster*, by Jon Krakauer. I took that as a sign he was drawn to adventure.

So I asked him if he'd be up for driving to the White Mountains in New Hampshire to climb Mount Washington with me. It was a big ask, given it was the highest peak in the Northeastern U.S., at 6,288 feet, and notorious for its erratic weather, with hurricane-force winds. But Leo being Leo, he said yes. I immediately lent him some crampons and ice axes, threw additional gear and a couple sleeping bags in my pickup truck, and promised to show him the ropes.

That weekend we were off to the White Mountains for Leo's first lesson with EMS Climbing School. I stayed by Leo's side to give him pointers. At the bottom of the mountain, which looks deceptively easy to climb, it was a balmy forty degrees, with a slight breeze. The group was pumped. By the time we hit six thousand feet, the winds were blowing at sixty miles per hour, with windchill in the teens. The enthusiasm level of the class was rapidly waning. A few students bailed. Leo thought it was "awesome." An unlikely climbing partnership was born.

* * *

From our first day climbing together, I always felt safe with Leo. He was the kind of partner and friend everyone should be so lucky to have, not just on mountainsides but in life. Someone who, no matter what happens, is still thinking of you on the other end of the rope, determined to keep you from falling.

He proved that on a couple of our outings in the White Mountains. On one early climb, our guide was teaching us about "top-down" belays where one climbing partner, the "belayer" (in this case Leo), lowers the other from the top of the cliff, with the rope running from the belayer's harness up through a carabiner and down to the climber (me) being lowered off the face of the mountain.

This gave me pause. (You can imagine me, a 210-pound guy, falling off a cliff and flyweight Leo being the counterbalance on the other side of the rope expected to stop my fall.) "Hey, do you think this is a good idea?" I asked our instructor.

"Sure," he said with a slight smirk. "What's the worst that can happen?"

We soon found out. The sudden force of my weight on the rope pulled Leo off his feet and dragged him toward the carabiner, the metal clip connecting the two of us to an anchor. Leo resolutely kept his white-knuckled brake hand on the rope and slammed up against the carabiner and anchor—and he didn't drop me. Whenever I bought a new carabiner after that, I'd jokingly hold it up to Leo to make sure it was smaller than he was so I wouldn't suck him through it as I fell off a cliff.

Another time some fellow climbers knocked a massive chunk of ice off a nearby cliff. When this happens, climbers yell, "Ice!" to warn others nearby. (Kind of like golfers yelling "Fore!") The louder the cry, the greater the danger. It's not much of an exaggeration to say the cry that day echoed off the mountain walls, causing birds to take flight.

As it fell down the cliff, the rock-hard chunk of frozen snow shattered into icy shards, most of which flowed over Leo. I found him on the ground in the fetal position to protect himself from the mini avalanche that had buried him—still with his brake hand locked off. It's no wonder Sully used to always say of Leo, "There ain't no quit in him."

I was so convinced of Leo's potential for climbing after his very first lesson in New Hampshire that a few days later Mark and I stopped by

EMS and bought him a present—a waterproof winter shell jacket for mountaineering. One night when we met up at Mark's place to go out to dinner, the two of us presented it to him. "Anyone who tackles Mount Washington on their first climb deserves the proper gear," I told Leo with a smile. "I want my new climbing partner to stay warm and happy."

Leo was so touched he didn't know quite how to respond. "You guys shouldn't have done this," he said. "This is incredibly generous. I don't know what to say. Thank you."

My brother has a thousand-watt smile, and he turned it on Leo. "From what I hear, you earned it, dude," he said.

I added a thumbs-up. "Try it on!"

It fit perfectly and went on to accompany Leo through peaks and valleys all over the world, including the Himalayas. That well-worn jacket could write its own book by now.

Later Leo said he'd been caught by surprise that night because it was a caring gesture he hadn't encountered with other friends in our age group. I figured most of his friends were probably just out of college, like Leo, with limited means. Mark and I were just grateful we had the financial wherewithal to be able to do something nice for someone who truly deserved it.

* * *

Which brings us back briefly to the issue of wealth. And, more specifically, my family's wealth. And how it impacted my sobriety.

When we first met, Leo recalled thinking Mark and I were "just normal guys who wore jeans and T-shirts and hiking boots." Then he noticed some people being weirdly deferential around us a few times, and he learned we'd inherited some money, and it put him off a bit. He'd worked his way through high school and college at his uncle's restaurant, Sol Azteca, in Boston. It was a hot spot frequented by celebrities, politicians, and rich college students. He'd seen some bad behavior, up close and personal. He was not a fan of dilettantes.

He came to learn my brother and I were anything but. We did live in nice apartments we could not have otherwise afforded at that age. And we had the ability to travel. But we didn't drive fancy cars or wear designer clothes or otherwise flaunt our financial good fortune. We were both still pursuing woodworking, following many years of hard labor on boats and in shipyards.

Beyond the basics, most of my disposable income now went toward quality climbing equipment—purchases Leo came to appreciate because it taught him how to shop for products based on excellence in crafting, design, and tradition. I'd tell him, "Just because it's expensive doesn't mean it's good."

I bring this up for anyone reading this who might feel you can't relate to my recovery journey—either because you don't have the financial freedom or just plain lack the desire to travel the country (much less the world) scaling mountains. That's understandable. Most people don't get a generous family inheritance. I'm guessing even fewer share my passion for ice climbing. Luckily, neither is a prerequisite for conquering addiction. Getting sober is enough of a mountain to climb.

CHAPTER TWENTY-TWO

MARK GETS SOBER

Memorial Day that year was uncharacteristically low-key for me. No drinks, no drugs, no drama. I spent the long weekend helping Sully at the gym, riding my bike around the Charles River, and researching future climbing trips. To avoid the temptation that packed bars presented that weekend, I picked up some hot dogs and steaks at the corner market one afternoon and invited Mark, Leo, Jake, and the rest of the gym gang over to watch sports and chew the fat. It was the first holiday weekend in years I could remember in its entirety.

My brother couldn't say the same. He was still a heavy partier, so I'd been trying to keep my distance. But on Saturday night, he and I both got invited to a party in Cambridge, and I figured I'd go along as the designated driver. I was worried about Mark, and I'd told him so. But given I'd been the one to knock him off the wagon several years earlier when we were both in Amsterdam, my credibility as an addiction expert was pretty much zero.

So I drove Mark to the party. I spent the next couple of hours nursing a club soda, moving from group to group telling skeptical friends that "Yes, I really *have* been sober for going on two months."

This led to a few raised eyebrows. "Not even beer or wine?" they'd ask.

"That's right," I'd reply. "Not even beer or wine."

Meanwhile, across the room my brother was doing what I'd been doing a couple months earlier—drinking beers and doing shots and quickly becoming the life of the party. I might have been envious if not for all my firsthand experience in where his night would lead.

I dropped Mark off at his front door later in the evening, and I can't say for certain what happened after that. Nor can Mark. He vaguely remembers me getting him home, at which point he moved on to The Last Drop for drinks. The last thing he remembers about that night is heading out from The Last Drop for a party across the street. He woke up the next morning to find his apartment a complete mess. He'd thrown up something resembling charcoal. Worst of all, his wallet was gone.

Later that day Mark's phone rang, and there was a strange woman on the other end. "I found the contents of your wallet," she said. "If you want to come pick them up, I'm going to drop them off at the gym where I go." She gave him the name and address of the gym; he thanked her, said he'd get to the gym as soon as possible, and hung up. And that was the moment that triggered my brother's recovery.

He later explained to me why. "I was so worried about what I might have done in that blackout, I had so much shame, that I didn't even ask the woman where or how she found it," Mark told me. "Even going to pick it up, I was nervous. I kept thinking, 'What if this woman's watching and waiting for me to pick this up? What if she works here? Did we have some encounter that I don't remember?'"

That was the day Mark said, "I just can't do this anymore."

One phrase you hear a lot in the recovery community is "sick and tired of being sick and tired." Mark says now he was just tired of being hungover and not remembering large blocks of time and having to worry that he did horrible things during those blackouts. His phone call to me on May 25, 1997, marked a turning point for us both. "Hey, Scott, I'm ready to get sober," he said. "Do you know anybody who's done that recently who could give me some tips?" I laughed. Even in life's darkest moments, he could find the funny.

And then I cried. I was a recovering addict. But I also knew the pain and helplessness that comes with loving an addict. My brother was my best friend. Since getting sober, I'd been praying for the day he'd join me on the journey. But I knew it would have to be his decision, not mine. That it happened so quickly after I got into recovery was a blessing.

"You still there?" Mark asked. "I'm going to need your support." He knew how emotional I could get.

"My man," I said, "you have come to the right place."

* * *

As we had growing up and as younger adults, Mark and I now leaned heavily on each other as we navigated the highs and lows of early sobriety. To fight loneliness and cravings, we went out for coffee and dessert a lot. And tried to stay grateful. It was September of 1997. Princess Diana's death had me thinking about mortality and my new lease on life. Mark later told me that if I'd started drinking again, he probably would have too. In hindsight, I think on some level I knew that, and it helped keep me sober. Not too many years later that principle—that by helping others I could also help myself—became part of my motivation for starting The Phoenix.

Mark and I both got sober the hard way, without the support of a robust sober community and without any therapy. Both of those later became crucial to our long-term sobriety. But for now we were struggling along, clueless, with a lot of underlying, unresolved pain. Most of our friends, it turned out, had just been drinking buddies; take away the alcohol and cocaine, and we had nothing else in common. We'd go to a movie, and then they'd want to go drink. Now that we were sober, it was eye-opening to see how we must have appeared to others for so many years: we hadn't been so funny and witty and charming after all. We'd just been loud and obnoxious and annoying.

It would be years before Mark and I found the courage to dig deep into the emotional pain we'd been running from. But I want to mention here an intense therapeutic experience Mark had, when he'd been sober for more than a decade, that validated for me the belief that early childhood trauma is real and, left untreated, can cause lasting damage.

In the third week of his stay at The Meadows, an inpatient trauma and addiction treatment center he checked into when his first marriage was falling apart, Mark participated in what's known as "Survivor's Week," which deals with childhood trauma—events that happened through age seventeen. For Mark, all that came to mind was being robbed at gunpoint once, but that was a drug deal gone bad, which he decided didn't count. When it came to big-time trauma, like sexual or physical abuse, he had nothing to share.

Then he tried something called somatic experiencing. A therapist, let's call her Ally, put him in a dreamlike meditative state (not hypnosis) and had him talk about what was coming up for him. After a few minutes, Mark started to feel a tightness in his chest and it became harder to breathe.

"What's happening?" Ally asked.

"It's just after my parents got divorced. I'm around seven," he said. "My brother and sister and I are playing in the backyard of the house where my parents used to live together."

"Can you see the house?"

"I can see the house."

"Can you go in the house?"

"I don't think I can go in the house."

"Why can't you go in the house?"

"I don't know. My parents are in there."

"OK, well, can you see if you can go in the house?"

In his mind, Mark entered our old house. "My parents are in their bedroom, but I can't go down there. The hallway is black, like I'm stuck."

"Why do you think you can't go down there?"

"I don't know. I really want to go down there, but I can't. For whatever reason, I just can't."

* * *

Fast-forward to the following week, Family Week at The Meadows, when my mom and I joined Mark to talk through a lot of stuff. It helped all of us. One day Mark and Mom were sitting in chairs across from each other, with Mark listening to Mom talk about life with our dad and their divorce. Without any prompting, she started recalling a day shortly after they'd split when we'd gone back to the house to get some of our belongings.

Mom walked into the master bedroom to find our father in there with two loaded guns on the bed. "Jack, what are you doing?" she asked, frightened. She was used to Dad's emotional manipulation, but now he was playing for broke.

"You can't leave me, Marilyn," he said. "If you don't come back to me, I'm going to use one of these on myself."

Mark was floored. Goose bumps washed over him. "As soon as she told me that story, I could feel it happening," Mark said later. "I was overcome with emotion. And I realized that's why I couldn't go down that hall. I somehow knew that was happening, that trauma was happening. I don't think I ever saw it, but I somehow knew." That might not have counted as "big T" trauma. But it was trauma just the same.

For Mark, that experience marked the beginning of a deeper recovery, and it remains one of the most impactful moments, or series of moments, he's ever had. It also made him more open to spiritual occurrences in his life he might earlier have dismissed. Mark is positive by nature; the trauma work actually strengthened—or maybe fully unleashed—his upbeat, open-minded, life-is-good attitude, which has been reinforcing for me as well.

"I think like anything, if you're looking for something, positive or negative, you'll find evidence for it," he says. "If you want to think the world is a horrible place and people are miserable, you'll find a lot of that. But if you want to think there are good people out there and people are helping each other, you'll find that too."

CHAPTER TWENTY-THREE

LEO'S EPIPHANY ON CATHEDRAL LEDGE

If Mark was my "always got your back, but preferably within Boston city limits" blood brother, for the next five years Leo became my trusty "go anywhere, do anything" mountain brother. After Leo's trial by fire on Mount Washington, we returned to the White Mountains to climb every weekend we possibly could during that winter and the following spring.

To do that, Leo, who worked for an energy trading company—the same one he works at today—would use his two weeks of vacation one day at a time, on Fridays throughout the winter, which gave us a bunch of three-day weekends to go camping and climbing in New Hampshire. For my part, I was now directing all the passion I'd had for partying into outdoor exercise. I saw it as added insurance that my recovery would stick.

Leo would drag all his equipment to the office on Thursdays, and on Thursday nights I'd load my pickup truck with ice axes and climbing ropes and crampons and sleeping bags. Then I'd drive to the financial district and double park outside Leo's office building. He'd come down in his work clothes, hop in the truck, and throw on jeans and a T-shirt as we started the long drive to New Hampshire.

After grabbing foot-long subs—meatball with American cheese for me, turkey and mayo for Leo—plus Doritos and large cokes at a Subway near the edge of town, we'd settle in for a quiet drive on dark country roads, not talking much, mostly listening to music. Leo always said those drives were magical, leaving the city hustle and bustle behind and heading into the purified air and starlit skies of the mountains.

Once we got near the mountain, we'd pull into the parking lot of a large EMS store and find a deserted spot to change into our camping gear for the night. That meant undressing outside on some bitterly cold nights. We'd then set out to find a spot at the camping grounds to pitch our tent—in those days, before ice climbing became a thing, we'd often be the only ones there—and get some sleep. Leo said being out in the chilly night air under the stars heightened all the senses. I couldn't disagree. For me, it was the first time in years, maybe ever, that I'd felt fully alive.

* * *

We'd climb all day Saturday, then head back to the truck and put our climbing boots on the dashboard and let our socks, Gore-Tex, and fleece dry while draped across the truck's defroster as we drove into town for dinner. (As an aside, I feel like I owe an amends to whoever the second owner of that smelly, well-worn truck was.) A favorite spot was Delaney's Hole in the Wall on White Mountain Highway in North Conway, where we'd ravenously consume five thousand calories worth of cheesy garlic bread, fried green beans, baby back ribs, and slaw. Then we'd head back to our campsite, jump into our sleeping bags, and pass out. The next day we'd climb again before heading back to the city in the late afternoon.

We were fully committed to developing into seasoned climbers. And to protecting each other. Leo still remembers our trip from hell to the Catskills one holiday weekend. We'd gotten a late start—my fault—and then sat in bumper-to-bumper traffic in Boston for a couple hours. We finally made it to the Catskills at around 10:30 p.m. and then had to hike an hour or more to our campsite. It was pitch black, with noises everywhere. Was that a moose? Was it a bear? I'll agree with Leo: it was a scary night. But I remember him saying, "Whatever happens, happens, man. If something comes out and tries to get you, it'll have to get me as well."

Real or imagined midnight moose encounters aside, Leo and I loved wilderness treks of all kinds. But the trip that really sealed the deal for

Leo was in the spring of 1998, our first rock climbing adventure, at Cathedral Ledge, a five-hundred-foot granite wall that towers over North Conway. He and I joined an EMS rock climbing class, and because the teachers knew us well from our winter ice climbs, I think they decided to torture us a little bit.

The guide would go up first and then bring us up to the anchor, which in this case was our first hanging belay. What that means is you are hanging from the anchor with your feet suspended in air. Then one of us belayed the guide as he led off on the next section or "pitch." Hanging belays rarely happen in ice climbing given how ice forms by dripping down the cliff. So this was a foreign world to us, and we silently started to freak out.

We were used to kicking our crampons in and having our ice axes hammered into the ice, so just simply relying on the friction of our climbing shoes holding on to little nubbins of rock seemed like an impossible way to get up the climb. I remember the guide saying, "Grab that little nubbin there, and press your foot into that little flake of rock." And I thought to myself, "What the heck is he talking about?" Even though at this point Leo and I identified as mountaineers, we desperately wished to get off that cliff.

Once we got to the top, though, we were in another world. There were ledges to sit on, no more than two feet wide, with birds soaring in the breeze just in front of us, and nothing below but air. As Leo succinctly put it, "If you fall, you fall." I remember sitting there in the quiet, looking down at the pine trees and North Conway, my fingers raw from the granite. I had recently completed my first year of sobriety. And it was another one of those "awe" moments.

Leo and I didn't talk much while hiking down the descent trail; we were both reflecting on this latest accomplishment and how rewarding it felt. But once we were back in the truck, he asked me a question that caught me by surprise. "Scott, what is it that makes you so hungry for life? I've never known anyone with your insatiable appetite for experiences." I didn't have a good answer; I'd never thought of myself in that way. "After today I'm officially sold on climbing," Leo went on. "Before, I thought it was a cool thing to do, but now I'm a convert. So whatever adventures you have in mind, I'm in! Let's see how far we can take it. I want the same kind of fire for life you have."

At times like that, it took me a minute to realize maybe I was different from how I viewed myself based on experiences from my childhood and adolescent years. When I heard things like that, it was hard to imagine somebody was actually saying that about me. But the more I heard it from people like Leo, whom I admired and respected so much, the more I started to believe just maybe it was true.

CHAPTER TWENTY-FOUR

THE VIEW FROM 18,500 FEET

So I took Leo at his word and started taking steps to up our game. First stop, learn how to rock climb. Second stop, Ecuador. Which, as I mentioned briefly at the beginning of this book, didn't work out so well. Leo and I had spent months planning a trip to the Cotopaxi Mountains in the Andes, hiking and training every weekend with huge backpacks in the White Mountains. We'd even ordered a few "topo-maps," thinking we'd get quickly up to speed on the topography of that section of the Andes just south of Quito. The maps were indecipherable. They drove Leo nuts. Mountaineering 101: you don't get quickly up to speed on anything.

A few weeks before we were to depart, I got a call from Leo. "Houston, we have a problem," he said, sounding uncharacteristically glum. I figured we'd made more miscalculations on our climbing route.

"Just throw out that damn topo-map!" I told him with a laugh.

"Will that shut down a volcanic event?" he asked. "A mountain near the ones we're climbing appears to be erupting."

That mountain was Guagua Pichincha, a neighboring volcano that had begun spewing ash and pyroclastic flows down on Quito, the city we were scheduled to fly into. About two weeks before we were due to leave, we got the news that the airports were closing due to the danger that the ash would clog the airplane engines. We hadn't prepared for *that*.

In the old days, I'd have gone to The Last Drop and told funny volcano stories and drowned my disappointment in lots of shots of whiskey. But that was not an option. Instead, I called my friend Sue, who was a climbing guide. "Hey, a buddy of mine just went through a divorce," she said. "His name is Bruce Andrews, and he's a Himalayan Mountain guide. I'm sure there's nothing he would want more right now than to get out of town for a while and clear his head."

So I called Bruce. "There's a big volcano erupting in Ecuador," I told him. "Is there anywhere else in the world we can go to climb a big peak?"

He didn't miss a beat. "The Himalayas are just coming into season now. Do you want to go to Nepal?"

* * *

Two weeks later, Leo and I met up with Bruce at Los Angeles International Airport, and we were all off to Kathmandu by way of Osaka, Japan. It was late, or very early, when we landed in Osaka, and Leo and I were beat. We'd spent the flight resenting the guy next to us because he slept the whole way and we couldn't sleep at all. My body and an airline coach seat are an incongruous matchup.

My pre-climb adrenaline had already started flowing, so it was hard to sit still. I was still missing the edginess and the thrill-seeking element I got from my addiction. I was still hunting that. I wasn't comfortable just being me, in a quiet place; I had to have distraction and adventure and the kinds of extreme sports goals I was now striving for to give me a sense of self-worth. Because I was still badly injured and hurting inside.

Landing in Kathmandu gave us a second wind. As Leo later said to me, "Once we were in Nepal, everything was self-actualizing in every way." Night skies were darker, stars were brighter, silences were more comforting and expansive. And sounds were definitely louder—especially in Kathmandu's airport, where everything, including how much weight a plane could bear, was a negotiation. In a debate with a ticket agent over whether our duffel bags were too heavy for our final flight to Lukla, rupees carried the day.

We'd come to Kathmandu to climb Imja Tse—"Island Peak"—a twenty-thousand-foot mountain that stood fourteen thousand feet taller than the highest peaks of the White Mountains. Still, compared to Mount Everest and the other Himalayan giants, it's just a baby. And—spoiler alert—we never even made it to base camp. Leo got sick, plus the days we'd lost on the long trip to the Himalayas didn't allow enough time to acclimatize sufficiently for the hike to Island Peak's summit. But it was transformative nonetheless, proving that whatever one's goals in life, there are as many rewards in the journey as in the destination itself.

* * *

Having survived what is best described as a death-defying, over-booked, understaffed flight on a twin-engine Otter to Lukla (as described in the prologue), Leo and I tucked into one of the many teahouses that lined Lukla's small (and to my untrained eye hazardous) runway to get something to eat. The floor was black from years of muddy climbing boots. It was partially covered with worn tapestries to sit on to stay warm, and a wood stove burned with dried yak dung in the corner.

The family who owned the teahouse kept peeking out from the kitchen as new climbers entered; their cheery smiles and warm laughter, characteristic of the Sherpa people, kept us toastier than the yak-dung-fueled fire. Outside, Bruce was haggling with another noisy bunch of porters and yak drivers and Sherpas-for-hire. We felt like we'd been air-dropped into an alternate universe.

Sipping on a mug of steaming hot brew—influenced by British expeditions, they still served afternoon tea and biscuits—with the majesty of the Himalayas on the horizon, I reflected on the paradox of this strange new world. We were in awe of its beauty but taken aback by the difficult working conditions, with kids in flip-flops carrying backbreaking duffel bags up and down mountains while men and women made cement by hand and used it to slowly and laboriously construct a new structure on the runway. It's where I first came to fully appreciate the intrinsic strength in all people, which would inspire all my future work.

Bruce's voice broke my reverie. "Come on, guys, tea time's over," he said, poking his head into the teahouse. "We've got a lot of ground to cover." Bruce was a kind soul whose love of life was infectious. He was a superior guide who also became my friend. Tragically, he later died in a plane crash on his way to a climb in Alaska.

Late that afternoon we set out on a three-day trek toward Island Peak's base camp by way of Namche Bazaar, gateway to the High Himalayas, not far from the Teng Boche monastery, where I had an unforgettable experience I shared in this book's opening pages. (To get into the spirit, now might be a good time to reread those pages with some tea and biscuits.)

Pretty much every climbing expedition coming up the Khumbu Valley from Lukla will make a stop in Namche. It is a bustling town full of tourists, climbers, trekkers, and Sherpas, and an exotic mix of merchants selling all kinds of knickknacks and trinkets. A mountain pass that connects Namche and Tibet runs by Cho Oyu base camp. At 26,864 feet, Cho Oyu is the sixth-highest mountain in the world. It topped my list of high-mountain dream destinations.

Even though we took things slow to acclimatize, on our long hike from Namche toward Island Peak base camp, Leo started feeling the effects of altitude sickness. (The accompanying headaches are unparalleled.) He'd never complain, and he'd be the last one to cut the trip short. But Bruce made the decision that given the time it would take for additional acclimatization, Island Peak would be out of the question. Our new summit destination should be Kala Patthar. Though it wasn't as high as Island Peak (20,226 feet), at 18,500 feet, Kala Patthar was still much taller than any mountain in the continental U.S. except for Denali in Alaska, which rises 20,310 feet above sea level.

It turned out to be the pinnacle of our expedition, literally and figuratively. Everything up until then had been trekking, and this was going up to a summit. It was a snowy day, and the snow was under our boots, and it felt good to be climbing. Once you get to the top of Kala Patthar, because it's a climatization peak for so many mountaineers before they go up to a base camp and other mountains, you see loads of old Buddhist prayer flags that have been left behind by climbers and Sherpas.

The idea behind the prayer flags is that the words written on them are whisked away by the wind and carried across the valley and eventually the mountain peaks. Standing there looking across the valley, you can see almost the whole route up Everest. That experience of looking at Mount Everest and the other Himalayan giants, like Lhotse and Ama Dablam (which we called "I Want My Mom" because it was a really scary-looking mountain), was life-changing for me. It was in those moments that I truly got bitten by the high-altitude mountaineering bug.

It was nearly inconceivable to me that just eighteen months earlier I'd been standing in an alley in the Combat Zone in Boston, too drunk to light my crack pipe. And now I felt like I was on top of the world. Mind you, I was in recovery, but I was not recovered; I was still more broken than I could have imagined. Even so, it's transformative to stand on top of a mountain. From those heights you can see something in yourself you might not see from down here. Until eventually you don't need the mountain anymore.

So as we began our trek back down the valley to head home, I immediately started to figure out how I could get back to the Himalayas. Back to Cho Oyu.

CHAPTER TWENTY-FIVE

MY NEXT PEAK EXPERIENCE

B ack in Boston, while I continued to hone my climbing skills in the White Mountains, I decided it would be a good idea to get some kind of wilderness first aid training. You can't always count on having an emergency medical technician (EMT) available on the top of a mountain, especially in the Himalayas. I found a wilderness EMT course, but to take it I had to be certified as an EMT or a first responder.

So I enrolled in a semester-long course in the evenings, which I found extremely challenging due to my dyslexia. But I felt driven. If I was going to climb mountains, I was going to be the best damn mountain climber I could be.

Like so many folks with substance use disorder, there could be a compulsiveness to my behavior. For instance, I had terrible sugar cravings as I was detoxing, and I also had process addiction issues (being addicted to certain behaviors or actions) that kept popping up. So I'd go to the store and buy Chips Ahoy! cookies, and I had to eat the whole sleeve. If somebody took one cookie, it would mess me up; I'd have to take a cookie from the other sleeve. If I'd get a pint of ice cream, I'd have to eat the whole pint; nobody could even have a bite of it. I was really untethered in how I could soothe myself. Being in nature helped, but even there I probably overdid it.

So after months of lectures and hands-on practice and lots of Starbucks-fueled late nights trying to get through the printouts and the textbook, and with some help from a kind fellow student named Kelly, I passed the final exam and got my certification. I felt really proud of myself.

Once I had my EMT certificate, I headed to Maine for a five-day course to become a wilderness EMT. I stayed in a big house with a bunch of outdoor leaders who led us through all kinds of wilderness scenarios. It was all in an effort to be a better climbing partner and to prepare for mountain expeditions—in particular my planned return to the Himalayas the following year.

But once I finished that class, I realized I now had a certification in emergency medicine but absolutely no experience applying it. "If something actually happens, I'll probably freeze and have no idea what to do, even though I'm trained," I told Leo one day as we trekked into a remote climb in the White Mountains. In retrospect maybe not the best time to share self-doubts with my climbing partner.

Leo was unfazed, though. "You should get a part-time job as an EMT to actually put your skills to use."

And that's just what I did. For the next several years, between climbs, I worked at the Cataldo Ambulance Service in Somerville, along with my friend Kelly and my partner, Scott Ryan, both of whom became, for a period of time, very significant people in my life, especially Kelly. That job gave me a disturbing firsthand view of the opioid crisis that was rapidly emerging thanks to aggressive sales of prescription opiates. It was one more experience that helped me discover and develop the gifts I'd eventually use to contribute to society in a meaningful way.

For now, though, it was time for my next big climb. I was finally headed to Cho Oyu. I was pumped. "Hey, Sharon, I need four weeks off," I told my supervisor prior to my next shift. "I'm headed back to the Himalayas."

Sharon seemed a lot less pumped. "There's no way that's possible," she said.

"All right, but I'm going anyway," I said. "I've been planning this trip for eighteen months." Then I played my ace. "Will you have any midnight shifts I can pick up when I return?"

She didn't have to answer. We both knew my willingness to man the graveyard shift always got me hired back.

* * *

If you Google "Easiest 8,000-meter peak to climb," Cho Oyu comes up. But that's relative. It's like asking, "Which is the best alligator to wrestle?" or "Which is the best shark species to catch by hand?"

Despite its intimidating height, Cho Oyu has relatively moderate slopes. And it's easy to access: you can drive all the way from Lhasa or Kathmandu to Chinese base camp, which is where the climb begins. So it's often the first of the true giants that people climb. Given my experience level, I figured I should start with the least worst to test my ability to scale a really big peak.

But I chose Cho Oyu for another reason as well: From reading *Into Thin Air*, I'd learned of a popular expedition group called Mountain Madness that was now owned by Christine Boskoff, one of the most revered female mountaineers of that era. As luck would have it, she had a trip planned to Cho Oyu. And while it was higher than they thought I should go—my previous high point, Kala Patthar, was the same height as Cho Oyu's base camp—they decided to let me join. I was thrilled. And nervous as hell.

The flight from Kathmandu to Lhasa (the traditional seat of the Dalai Lama in the Tibet Autonomous Region in Southwest China) was breathtaking. Looking out the windows of our small plane, I could see Everest and Lhotse and Cho Oyu. I got goose bumps knowing that's where I was headed. When I'd first started talking about climbing the Himalayas, just months into my sobriety, my friends no doubt thought I had my head in the clouds. I smiled to think that in a few days' time, I actually would.

The next part of the journey brought me back down to Earth. From Lhasa we had to drive three days to the base camp on a road that was maybe one-tenth paved. We were in old Toyota Land Cruisers. At one point our driver decided that driving through the riverbed—it actually had a river in it—was a better route than the road itself.

We'd drive in the river for a hundred yards until the road got better. If the road was too washed out to get through, we'd have to unload all of our stuff and carry it so the driver could navigate over the washed-out part. For what it's worth, all of this was happening on the side of a two-thousand-foot cliff. (I want to take a minute to retract my earlier statement about Cho Oyu being easy to access.)

With me in the back of the Land Cruiser, chatting and getting to know each other, were Matt Mooney, a tell-it-like-it-is guy who worked in finance in Manhattan; Julio, a cardiologist from the Midwest; and Dan, a sturdy Midwesterner who reminded me of the plain-spoken Pennsylvanians I'd grown up around. (Leo couldn't make this trip.) Matt and I hit it off from the start.

We'd been out of the airport maybe thirty minutes when the driver lit a cigarette. "No, man, that's not going to work," Matt said. "You're going to have to throw that thing out." Then he turned to me and said, "There's no way I'm going to sit in here with him driving over high-altitude passes smoking cigarettes for the next three days." And I thought, "Oh, I kind of like this guy." The driver looked at Matt, seemingly sizing him up, and threw the cigarette out the window.

Matt and I soon started talking about what had brought us to climbing; I found out he was sober, and we bonded immediately. Both of us were about the same age, making big changes in our lives, looking for ways to give our lives purpose and meaning. We ended up chatting for pretty much the rest of the expedition.

Several hours into this delightful road trip, we'd all noticed the driver would occasionally seem uneasy and start to sweat. Whenever this happened, he would pop in a cassette tape of monks praying. We came to recognize this as a signal the road ahead was about to get treacherous. That led to some extensive but inconclusive debates on whether wearing a seat belt would be helpful if the Land Cruiser plummeted down the two-thousand-foot cliff. By the end of the drive, we too had adopted the ritual of getting anxious, sweating, and enjoying the tape of monks praying.

After driving three days to cover what would have taken a few hours at home, the trucks dropped us off at Chinese base camp. From there we climbed with yaks and porters to advanced base camp, which at 18,530 feet is the highest base camp of any of the world's 8,000-meter peaks. We spent several days there acclimatizing. Then we set out for camp one, camp two, and high camp. From there you climb to the summit. So from camp one, we'd climb up and leave sleeping bags, a tent, and food at camp two, then come back down to the lower camp and let our bodies adjust to the altitude. A few days later, we'd move up and sleep at camp two—same drill, adjust to the altitude, and then climb to high camp.

It was at camp one where I had what Abraham Maslow would call a "peak experience," a moment of intense happiness and fulfillment. In this case a "peak" experience is exactly what it was. It was late one night, and nature was calling. I also wanted to escape the snoring of the three other climbers I was sharing a tent with. So I stepped outside while everyone was sleeping. By then we were at twenty thousand feet at least; I could see in the distance the pass running between Nepal and Tibet. Blue glacial ice pools below me glittered like diamonds.

I just stood there for a few minutes, bare chested, looking at the moonlight cascading over the fluted ridges and saddles between the mountain peaks, with the crisp, cold air shocking my lungs and biting my skin, reminding me I had a limited amount of time to enjoy this moment. The awe was so powerful it kept me there until the shivers forced me to crawl back into my sleeping bag.

I was taken back to a similar moment I'd had on the *Sea Cloud*, which I described earlier, in the middle of the Aegean Sea. Alone on deck watching the moonlight reflecting off the waves, I felt like there was a reason I was in that place at that moment. And that I had inherent value as a person that

I could share with others. I was still chasing that sense of self-worth and purpose and belonging that had been so elusive my whole life.

But it was on Cho Oyu, alone on a moonlit mountaintop, that it first dawned on me: If I could use all the things I'd learned and experienced on my road to sobriety and share these unique gifts with others, that might finally fill the void. That would be the magic.

* * *

We never made it to high camp. Matt and I made that decision based on the weather forecast, despite our head guide, Thomas, encouraging us to keep climbing. He was determined to chalk up his first eight-thousand-meter peak. "Go up," he instructed our group, which that day comprised just me and my three jeepmates, Matt, Julio, and Dan. Matt and I thought that was a bad call. We could tell high winds were picking up on the summit because we could see a ribbon of snow being ripped off the peak. It just didn't feel right. "We're going down," we said. "Anybody else coming?"

The rest of the group kept climbing. They got trapped by weather as soon as they reached high camp. We'd been right about the winds: the one-hundred-plus-mile-per-hour gusts from the jet stream blasting snow off the summit plateau left them badly beat-up in their tents, battling dehydration, frostbite, and some altitude sickness. Thomas had to be injected with dexamethasone to treat the onset of high-altitude cerebral edema (swelling of the brain from a buildup of fluid) and brought back to base camp.

I was disappointed I hadn't made it to the summit. But it was also a catalytic moment for me, in terms of my developing identity as a climber. Making the right call on Cho Oyu, despite the challenge from a professional guide, left me feeling empowered. I was reminded of the ancient maxim "when the student becomes the master." Not that I was so cocky as to believe I had mastered mountaineering. But I felt I could now hold my own with some of the guides who'd trained me initially. I no longer felt shy about calling myself a climber. And with that simple identity shift, I became a little bit less an "addict."

As fate would have it, by heading back down when we did, we were in the right place at the right time to save a man's life. A German climber had also developed high-altitude cerebral edema. So obviously he wasn't thinking clearly. When we found him, he was trying to rappel off a cliff. His fingertips were black with frostbite and barely functioning; his harness was around his ankles. I looked at Matt and said, "We've got to help him."

Because of the swelling in his brain, he felt like we were impeding him from getting down, so he kept sitting in the snow, wanting to stop. But Matt's no-nonsense New Yorker kicked in. "Uh-uh, no way, this isn't happening," he'd bark. "Get up, keep moving." And we basically force-marched the guy back down to a lower camp. He'd surely have fallen four thousand feet to his death had we not been there.

* * *

Revelatory and self-congratulatory moments aside, I also present this chapter as a serious cautionary tale. Replacing drugs and alcohol with other, so-called healthier pursuits (especially something as tied to the fickle hands of fate as mountain climbing), if done carelessly or to an obsessive degree, can be nearly as detrimental and deadly as substance use. Any activity taken to an extreme can be dangerous. If you continue to pursue it despite that, perhaps you, too, are hoping to fill a void in your heart the same way I was. It's something to consider.

Unlike Matt and me, Thomas wasn't using mountaineering as a replacement for drug or alcohol addiction. Nonetheless, his drive to summit an eight-thousand-meter peak took him—and those depending on his experience and wisdom—to a life-threatening place. British mountaineer Joe Simpson, who survived several events that should have meant certain death, grappled with the whimsy of mountain climbing in his book *This Game of Ghosts*. Was it luck or choices, he wondered, that led so many fellow climbers to lose their lives climbing?

I believe it's a bit of both. While we were still hiking to Cho Oyu base camp, which was brutal for me given I had little experience at such high altitudes, my climbing team ran into a famous climber named Charlie Fowler, who was on his way down. He kindly brought me tea and cookies and sat with me, and we talked for a while. He and Christine Boskoff, whom I'd befriended on this expedition and whose climbing continued to inspire me over the years, would later die together on a first ascent on an unclimbed peak in China. Christine had aspired to be the first woman to climb all fourteen of the eight-thousand-meter peaks.

After Cho Oyu, Matt and I developed an enduring friendship, and he later became a big fan of The Phoenix. One of my climbing mentors, Dave Kelly, used to say, "There are old climbers and bold climbers. But there are no old, bold climbers." Sadly, Matt never made it to old. One day in August ten years ago, I got the devastating news he'd suffered a fatal fall on a solo climb in the Eastern Sierra. I miss his contagious laughter and calming presence to this day.

My realization that certain passions have the potential to become destructive influenced me when I was building a sober active community with The Phoenix. Climbing had been a great way to achieve self-efficacy and self-actualization. But it could also be a selfish pursuit.

Similarly, racing triathlons taught me how to draw on intrinsic strength I didn't know I had. But I realized the all-consuming nature of it could start coming at the cost of the people I loved if I prioritized my obsessive training and expeditions over spending time with them. How was that any different from my mom disappearing into her work? Activities we think of as respectable and character-building can be an escape the same way drugs and alcohol are.

CHAPTER TWENTY-SIX

REAL-LIFE RESCUE 911

Back in Boston, I settled back into my routine of climbing, wood-working, and working as an EMT. (All the Cataldo rescue office said when I returned home was "Night shift, buddy.") I'd also started dating Kelly, the woman I'd gone through EMT training with. She had a big heart, liked to hike and climb, and she seemed to like me despite my obvious drawbacks, starting with my miserable dating track record. I figured if she was brave enough to be an EMT, she might have the courage to give me a chance. Our joint shifts on A-41 (Ambulance 41) always passed quickly.

We saw all levels of human suffering. Some people become an EMT or first responder out of a desire to kick in doors and save lives. This happens from time to time. But EMTs spend 90 percent of their time bearing witness to the hardest moments in people's lives—when they lose a loved one, fear their own mortality, or experience immense pain.

At Cataldo, we worked across five greater metro Boston suburbs. All night long, we'd hear dozens of emergency calls going out across the city. Heart attacks, falls, domestic abuse, drug overdoses. That would stick with me when my shift ended. I'd drive home thinking, "This is just one radio and one ambulance across five cities; imagine the volume of pain and trauma and accidental injuries and violence happening in every city in America." If you take that to scale in your mind, it's overwhelming.

One of my early EMT instructors must have picked up on my sensitive nature, because one night he pulled me aside and shared one of the most profound pieces of advice I've ever received. "Scott, it will help you later in your career to realize something: Every single one of your patients is going to die. So it's just a question of 'Do they die when they're with you, or do they die years later of old age and something else?'" He gave me a moment to let that sink in. "Understanding that will help rightsize your thinking about what you can actually do to change their life in the period of time you're with them."

What that taught me, which I carry with me to this day, was that every time I was with a patient, I should try to make their life a little bit better. Sometimes that meant breathing for them and doing chest compressions to keep them alive. Other times that just meant sitting with them on their way to a dialysis appointment and learning a little bit about their story and their life—being an interested witness and listener.

There's a simplicity to trying to make everyone's life we touch a little bit better, even if we can't ultimately change and control all the outcomes. That's a philosophy that has helped me immensely at The Phoenix.

* * *

One particular call my ambulance partner Scott and I responded to haunts me to this day. We'd been called to the parking lot of a dying strip mall that was home to a Dollar Store, Kmart, and a few other failing businesses just across from the Mystic River. We jumped out of the ambulance with our first-aid bags and oxygen, but we could feel in our guts the moment for us had passed. We noticed a late-model sedan parked off by itself with a few Somerville police officers standing around it. "No rush, guys," one of them said as we walked up.

One look inside the car told the story. It was obvious the car had been there for several weeks. One of the tires was almost flat, and the sandy dirt of the parking lot had blown into small cones around each tire. We could see remnants of black dirt and residue on the old, rutted blacktop, where a snowplow must have shoved snow and debris around the car after a recent winter storm. The back seat and passenger side were full of fast-food wrappers, cigarette packs, and empty Styrofoam Dunkin' Donuts cups.

The driver's side window was cracked about an inch and a half; inside, a lifeless young man slumped down in the cream-colored vinyl driver's seat. His head was turned ever so slightly toward the window, with his chin slightly lifted, as if he were sniffing the fresh sea air that would blow up the Mystic River from Boston Harbor. More likely he'd cracked it to ash his cigarette, seeing as cigarette butts were strewn about the car and overflowing from the ashtray.

His skin was gray; gravity had long since pulled his blood into his extremities. This is known as dependent lividity. What startled me most were his hollowed eyes, which had sunk back into his skull deeper than I had ever seen, almost what you'd expect to see with mummification. Here in the middle of a Kmart parking lot, this struggling soul must have lived out his last days before succumbing to his addiction. I envisioned all the parking spaces filling and emptying and filling and emptying. Meanwhile, this guy's dying in his car and goes unnoticed.

I wished deaths like his would serve as a wake-up call to our country that we need a new approach to addiction.

Maybe the nation was not changed by the passing of this one man, but I certainly was. Working as an EMT in early recovery allowed me to see the other side of addiction. In the late nineties and early 2000s, heroin and "club drugs" like ecstasy were back on the upswing and we'd started hearing reports about the occasional CVS pharmacy being robbed for Oxy-Contin. Sadly, nonprescription opioids like heroin had been a problem in poorer, more diverse neighborhoods for generations. The issue only began to get attention as it spread into more affluent white communities.

It just sat with me. How many deaths does it take before we start to make a change? If the loss of loved ones from coast to coast was not enough of a catalyst for change, what would be? Who would lead the charge? As I wrestled with those questions, the thought entered my mind: Could it be me?

CHAPTER TWENTY-SEVEN

STIGMATIZED

This will be a fairly short chapter, because Alcoholics Anonymous (AA) teaches you not to hold on to resentments, and I agree with that. Of course the fact that I'm including this chapter at all, about a decades-old snub that still bugs me a little, tells you maybe I need a little more growth in that area. Trauma therapy and working a 12-step program several years after I got sober helped me release a lot of pent-up anger and darkness, particularly related to my dad and stepdad. But it's an ongoing process. So let's go with this: I'm still working on it.

Before I get to the perceived snub, I think it's appropriate to say a few words about my relationship with AA. I know it's unusual to get sober without the help of rehab, AA, or both. Early in my recovery, I went to an AA meeting that happened to be a pretty rough crowd, made up mostly of people older than me. So I walked out. I later realized those guys and I were more alike than I could have imagined. But I didn't give AA's recommended 12 steps of recovery another try until after I started The Phoenix, where I'd made a lot of friends who were in the 12-step community.

I thought it would be cathartic to work the steps. So I got a sponsor. His name was Michael, and he was also an early member of The Phoenix. Michael was a kind and grounded person from Hell's Kitchen in New York City, a fitting address given he'd been to hell and back while struggling with addiction. He worked the steps with me, and I'm grateful for that experience; I think everybody could benefit from working a 12-step program at some point in their life.

Michael sponsored me until he passed, and we'd become close. He'd beaten up his body so badly in his addiction it finally gave out. His death hit me hard, and I didn't go to many meetings after that.

In hindsight, my brother and I agree that not having a community of recovery early on made staying sober more difficult than it had to be. Once his first marriage broke up, around the same time he went to The Meadows for trauma therapy, Mark got involved with 12-step fellowship. He wishes he'd found it sooner; he considers 12-step and exercise his two biggest recovery assets.

I craved community too. But AA wasn't the right fit for me. In the national sober active community I went on to create, I lead with "I'm Scott, and I'm in recovery." I understand that many people in the 12-step community identify themselves first as an alcoholic or an addict; that is their choice. But I feel our disease is just a part of us, not all of who we are. Indeed, even though I've spent my whole adult life talking about my recovery journey, I see that as just one of many facets of my life. I'm Scott, and I'm a husband, father, brother, nonprofit business leader, rock climber, Phoenix member, and a person in recovery.

* * *

There was one moment in my life when being honest about having a history of addiction *did* come back to bite me. At least I think it did. You be the judge.

When I was an EMT working for Cataldo, my partner Scott and I both decided to apply for Boston Emergency Medical Services, which was the most prestigious job you could get as an EMT. They had 200 applicants in the written exam. We both made it through that. They had 100 applicants in the physical exam. We made it through that. They then chose 11 finalists for interviews; we made the cut. Following those interviews, 10 finalists were hired. Guess who the one guy was who didn't make the cut? Yep, yours truly. And here's where just the smallest smidgeon of resentment still lingers: I think it's because I told them I was sober and in recovery.

During the in-person interview, they'd asked, "What's something major you've overcome in life?"

And part of my brain was wondering, "Would a lie of omission be so bad?" But I told them the truth. "I've been in recovery for three years, and my life has been totally transformed through my sobriety. I think it gives me a unique perspective to do this job."

Apparently they didn't agree. Back then addiction was less understood and more of a stigma in society than it is today. But still I was surprised and super disappointed. If I had it to do again, would I still come clean? I'd like to think so. Honesty has been integral to my sobriety journey. But it's something that stings to this day.

CHAPTER TWENTY-EIGHT

FUTURE TRIPPING

T he Boston Emergency Medical Services disappointment aside, I sometimes overcompensated for my lifelong lack of self-esteem by inflating
what I thought I deserved or was capable of at a given point in time. That
sometimes-magical thinking did not apply to women. I went into every
relationship (and there were only a few that rose to a level you could call
a "relationship") on the premise that the odds of it working out were on
par with those of Boston's "Big Dig" ever being completed.

(As it turned out, that notorious $24.3 billion highway project,
described on Massachusetts' official website as the most challenging in
the history of the U.S., finally wrapped up after twenty-five years, on
December 31, 2007. By way of comparison, it would be another ten years
before I finally had a relationship work out.)

Here's how attempts at finding a life partner played out on more than
one occasion: I'd meet a woman, she'd be better than I thought I deserved,
miraculously she'd fall for me and I for her, we'd marry and have kids,
she'd see me for who I truly was and divorce me, and we'd put our kids
through the same pain I went through as a kid. Many lives would be
shattered. Then the waiter would break my reverie. "Would you care for
an appetizer, sir?" And the woman, whom I'd only just met, would be
staring at me, wondering where this guy she was on a first date with had
gone for the past few minutes.

It's called "future tripping," and it's a form of anticipatory anxiety. I
suffered from it a lot. I'd create a foregone conclusion in my mind of how
something was going to end, and it would become a self-fulfilling

prophecy. Over the course of many years as a clueless single guy looking for love and belonging in all the wrong places (and sabotaging anything that looked promising), I hurt a lot of people, starting with myself. I couldn't get out of my own way.

* * *

Low self-esteem and unresolved trauma can be relationship killers—or lead you to exactly the wrong person. During the years people typically fall in love and get married, I was still hampered by both. If I began to have feelings for someone, I couldn't let them in. I figured I wasn't deserving or worthy of love, and if I showed how I felt, I was opening myself up for rejection. My main goal was to avoid getting hurt or hurting somebody else. When I was lucky enough to find someone who'd stay with me while I worked through these fears, it just made me feel more vulnerable. So I'd leave her before she could leave me—an outcome that in my distorted view was inevitable.

I learned later in trauma therapy that's called "love avoidance." Because I had a deep desire to be loved, I would try to pull people toward me. But then when they would get close, I'd push them away. That caused a lot of pain for a lot of people, and to those I hurt, I'm deeply sorry.

I was fortunate to be able to go to The Meadows, where Mark had gone, for Survivor's Week, which explores the origins of self-defeating behaviors such as addiction and falling into a pattern of unhealthy relationships. The workshop is based on the work of Pia Mellody, a pioneer in the field of recovery. If you're interested but not able to spend time at The Meadows, I recommend Mellody's book *Facing Codependence* and her online worksheets.

For someone who's love avoidant, like I was, the worst possible dynamic is to end up with someone who's a love addict. You'll trigger each other incessantly. When I read that during Survivor's Week, it stopped me cold. I knew what that was. I'd been enmeshed in a relationship with a sweet and caring woman named Sabrina who was wired to give—and receive—an overwhelming amount of love. I learned in therapy she was likely a love addict.

She came to my workplace once (by then I was running The Phoenix) and convinced folks to let her into my office so she could decorate it for my birthday. That included putting pictures of her and me together, and her kids, and Happy Birthday streamers all over everything. When I came in, she was waiting with a cake she'd made for me. And we weren't even really dating at that time.

But her thinking was "Maybe the more I pour love into you, the more you'll start to love me." And of course I was thinking, "The more you pour love into me, the more I want to push you away." But the sick part of the love-avoidant mindset is that I *did* want to be loved, and that stuff *did* feel good.

To a love-avoidant person, a love addict is like ice cream—you crave it until you get too much. But after a while, you want more. So Sabrina found herself constantly in this middle ground where I'd push her away but then want her to be close. And she just kept running back and forth in that place as aggressively as she could. And for too long, I'm ashamed to say, I let her.

CHAPTER TWENTY-NINE

"DAMN, THAT LADY CAN CLIMB!"

Romantic ruminations aside, I feel deeply blessed by the strong, very special women who have made my life immeasurably better. My mom Marilyn, my sister Amyla, and my wife Kait would of course top that list, along with my maternal grandmother, "Marme," whom I grew very close to late in her life. I hope my daughter Alice will grow up as strong, principled, and courageous as each of them.

But there's another very significant woman in my life. She was there in the early days of my sobriety. She was with me on a climbing trip in Canada on the first New Year's Eve I didn't think about drinking or using. She encouraged me to move to Colorado to pursue my dream of starting a sober active community. And later she joined me there to help make it happen. Her name is Jacki Hillios, and she's deputy executive director and cofounder of The Phoenix. I'm proud to call her my business partner and dear friend.

We met at the Boston Rock Gym—no shocker there—a climbing gym in Woburn. It was after Leo and I had started climbing together. I remember watching her scale a difficult rock wall with such agility and grace and thinking, "Damn, that lady can climb!" So I introduced myself to her, and we struck up a friendship.

Jacki had recently moved to Massachusetts from California and was going to the Rock Gym five nights a week to "stay sane" and meet people. It was her happy place. So we had that in common. We were also both at a crossroads. Jacki had been working as a clinical social worker for about fifteen years and was thinking of going to graduate school. I was in my late twenties and still wasn't sure what I wanted to be when I grew up. I had a strong hunch it involved using my unique combination of life experiences to help others. I just hadn't yet figured out exactly how.

We started meeting regularly at the gym to climb. We'd generally meet late in the day and climb until eight or nine at night, at which point we'd be famished. We'd often grab dinner after, and we started sharing our stories. It turned out Jacki, who had never misused substances, wasn't a big fan of adult addicts. Her mom had struggled with alcohol since Jacki was a kid, leaving her daughter very angry about the oversized, unhealthy role alcohol had played in her life. "I'm *pissed*," she said. I understood where she was coming from. I'd felt the same way about Al.

When I shared with Jacki that I was in recovery, she didn't seem to give it much thought. By then we'd started climbing outdoors together. So I figured maybe she hadn't heard me or was distracted by the more pressing priority of keeping her footing on the side of Cathedral Ledge. She explained later that at the time she really didn't understand what "being in recovery" meant. She'd picked up a lot of biases while studying to be a social worker. One of them was that anything that wasn't clinical was dangerous—that it involved people trying to be clinicians without the proper training.

Jacki's relationship with the addiction recovery industry shifted significantly over time as she rejected those learned biases and came to understand how many destructive coping mechanisms, like her mom's alcoholism, result from trauma. When Jacki and I first met, I was still trying to sort all that out myself. In the absence of clear-cut answers, as we both sought greater meaning in our lives, we sweated out a lot of unresolved anger and angst in the mountains.

Jacki jokes now she spent half of that first year of our friendship tied to trees to keep me from falling over a ledge. As Leo had learned, when your climbing partner is twice your size, you have to tie yourself down. Over time Jacki became a trusted anchor, in more ways than one.

* * *

The only time I saw anything close to fear in Jacki, or I guess it was pure terror, was the day I took her ice climbing for the first time. "I'm a face-your-fears kind of person," she had told me. So I thought I'd help her face one of them.

"Hey, I'm headed to Frankenstein Cliff this weekend," I said one night at the Rock Gym. "Are you ready to learn how to ice climb?"

Frankenstein was a famous ice climbing cliff you could see from the porch of the 1930s railway engineer's log cabin I'd purchased in Crawford Notch, New Hampshire. By now I'd moved in and out of a few apartments in Boston, flipping each for a good profit. I used that money to fund my climbing trips and to pay for the cabin. The address was 0 Camp Onion Road. In retrospect Jacki must have wondered if she was about to become part of a chilling Stephen King novel. But she said yes.

We'd done a lot of rock climbing together by then. We often met up at Quincy Quarries, where the mob reportedly dumped dead bodies back in the days when local crime boss Whitey Bulger ran Boston's infamous Winter Hill Gang. But Jacki had never climbed ice, which is a whole different deal.

Leo kindly offered to lend her his new one-piece Gore-Tex yellow and black climbing suit. Not just the suit, but mask, gloves, and ice axes—the whole nine yards. The net effect, in Jacki's opinion, was she looked like a bumblebee. What made it even funnier was that I had almost the same climbing suit. Jacki thought I looked like a *giant* bumblebee. Not the look Leo and I had been going for, but OK.

I think Jacki's amused reaction to the bumblebee suits was the last smile—or words—I got out of her for the rest of the day. She was used to being prepared and being in control. And here she was on a sheer wall of ice doing something she'd never done before, at the mercy of a guy she hadn't known for more than a few months. It threw her sideways a little bit.

But here's the remarkable thing: she loved it. "Ice climbing was a very freeing experience," she later said. "I was 100 percent terrified. But there's something about the way you swing your ice ax and it hits the ice and sinks in—it's a feeling of transcendence and perfection, like nothing you've ever experienced before. It's quiet and still. I couldn't get enough of it."

And when I heard that, it was another aha moment. Maybe I really *could* share my knowledge and love of outdoor adventure sports in a way that transformed the lives of others. It had certainly transformed mine.

* * *

I love being on a bike, turning the pedals, the sounds of the gears changing, and especially the feeling in your legs when you stand up out of the saddle and you're rolling through a canyon or down an open road, or into the woods, and you can hear the creek running next to you. Everything just kind of melts away, and it's just you and the bike, surrounded by nature. For me it's always had the same therapeutic effects as climbing or running or swimming.

So one day when I was climbing with Leo and someone mentioned they knew a professional triathlete, my ears perked up. "Maybe I could do a triathlon someday," I thought. It just seemed like a natural progression for me. Leo was up for the challenge as well. Scott and Leo's next excellent adventure.

Once again we faced a steep learning curve, though I flew my "novice" flag higher than he did. For instance, the first bike I bought to train for triathlons I got secondhand from a guy who was a triathlete. That seemed like a sensible decision. What I didn't understand is that bikes are sized to the person. So envision a huge guy riding a tiny triathlon bike. My elbows would hit my knees when I'd pedal.

At my first triathlon, one of my friends asked if I was nervous. "Yes, I am," I admitted. "How can you tell?"

My friend pointed to my front-facing zipper. "Because your wet suit's on backward."

OK, so maybe I wasn't a natural at transitioning to new sports. But I'll let you in on a little secret—no one really is. Everybody you see out there doing extreme fitness pursuits started somewhere. Don't let the intimidating nature of anything keep you from trying it. It was by testing some uncharted waters that a few years into my sobriety, I was zeroing in, little by little, on what I was meant to be doing with my life.

In the early summer of 2001, a group of us were training for a race called the Monster Challenge, a sprint triathlon in Boston Harbor. We had to swim in the harbor, then do a bike ride around Memorial Drive, past Cambridge, and finish up with a run through South Boston. We'd started an email list of folks that would swim and ride and run together to get ready for that race. It was fun sharing our learnings and adventures with each other. After the race was over, I emailed the group and asked, "Is there anybody who wants to keep training together? If so, let me know, and I'll drop everybody else off the email thread." A dozen or so people said yes.

Jacki, Leo, and I cultivated that list into a group we called Team Mercury Multisport, named after the Roman god of speed. We would climb, ride, bike, and run together. Or just walk, talk, have meals, and hang out. You didn't have to be training for a triathlon to join. It was basically a free social club with a great group of people who came together to help each other grow. We shared knowledge, helped sharpen each other's skills, and inspired each other. At our peak, we had about sixty members.

What I didn't know then, but know now, was that Team Mercury Multisport would be the analog for The Phoenix. I'd started to realize we each had unique gifts we could contribute in a meaningful way to help others. There were people in there who had raced Ironman. I had never raced Ironman. They inspired me. There were people who had done mountain bike races. They taught me how to master a mountain bike. Mostly, though, we gave each other a sense of supportive community.

* * *

My Crawford Notch cabin became a popular weekend getaway for Team Mercury members. It had a loft and one bedroom, and everybody else would sleep on futons or in sleeping bags. In the winter, we'd have to snowshoe in sometimes because it was hard to keep the road open. It was a special place shared with special people. I'd never been to college, but weekends there felt like what I imagined college must have felt like, only without the booze.

One of my friends was an engineer, so he built a sled ramp. He was pumped to put it to the test. "My back-of-the-napkin calculations tell me we can jump over eight people," he explained when it was finished. "But we need somebody who's really big on the sled, so they go fast." Suddenly all eyes were on me.

This seemed like a terrible idea, having the biggest person in the group be the one that crashes on top of everybody else. Yet the next thing you know, I was on a sled soaring over Team Mercury. Not necessarily a group growth experience, I'll grant you. (For the record, no humans were harmed in this experiment.) But we filled each other's lives with a lot of joy. For years I'd searched for meaningful friendships at the bottom of beer mugs and vodka bottles. But it was here, sober on a frozen hillside in New Hampshire flying through the air, that I actually found them.

I don't think I was alone in my search. I think we're all looking for connection with others. Maybe we just need to change the places where we're searching.

* * *

It was roughly around that time in my life that Jacki and I and a bunch of friends went ice climbing at Pont Rouge in southern Quebec over the New Year. It was grueling. We'd get up at 5:00 a.m. to hike to vertical ice columns so steep our arms would burn just looking at them. We'd climb so hard each day we had trouble eating our food at night; our arms were too sore to pick up our utensils. We'd eat fast, dispensing with all table manners, and then just crash.

And that's how it was that New Year's came and went and didn't even register for me. Which was significant given that New Year's Eve had been such a triggering holiday in my early recovery. I was still early in my recovery journey, so there was something very special about having that holiday come and go with no power over me. I attributed that to being with people who had a genuine love of life and each other.

That's when I started more seriously asking myself, "What if I could share my active lifestyle with others who want not just to survive but to thrive in sobriety?" And that's when the earliest seeds of a sober active community were born.

CHAPTER THIRTY

NEAR DEATH ON DENALI

I am respectful of death and the dangers inherent in extreme sports like mountain climbing and ice climbing. Too many of my friends and climbing partners died early deaths. But despite the precarious nature of the life I led, I never expected to get so close to death myself.

That I'm alive to tell the story of how I survived a three-day blizzard on Denali I owe in large part to my well-prepared New Hampshire climbing partners, Brett and his wife Andrea, who like me were seasoned from climbing Mount Washington, with its harsh weather conditions. And to a small titanium pot for melting snow to drink, which for a few days was the only thing keeping us alive.

Though by now I was seriously into racing triathlons and had raced Ironman, I still had an itch to climb the big mountains. Denali, in Alaska, had long been in my sights. At 20,310 feet, it's the highest mountain peak in North America. Brett and Andrea had been wanting to go too, so we teamed up. We flew into Anchorage and caught a shuttle bus for the two-hour drive north to Talkeetna, a busy little village nestled at the base of Denali.

After flying in a bush plane to Kahiltna Glacier, we began the arduous days it took to reach fourteen thousand feet, just below high camp. When we finally arrived, a park ranger shared the unwelcome news that some weather was coming across the Arctic and would likely hit us in the next few days. That's the game of high-altitude mountaineering. It's a crap shoot, and the wrong call can cost you your life. Given we had come so far, we decided to take our chances and go up to high camp anyway. That turned out to be the wrong call.

* * *

We were at high camp, 17,200 feet up, when the storm arrived. And by storm, I mean blizzard. We recognized immediately we were in trouble. The wind gusts had strengthened to over 100 miles per hour; I knew that because even on Mount Washington, known for its ferocious winds, I was big enough that I could still walk upright until the winds got north of 100. Once they exceeded 100, I'd get knocked down by gusts. And I was starting to get knocked down. It was freezing cold. And with snow blowing everywhere, visibility was degrading toward zero. I thought to myself, "I could die on this mountain."

I was in a single-man tent, next to Brett and Andrea's tent. Peering through the blowing ice and snow, I could see people had lashed climbing ropes over the top of their tents in a spiderweb fashion, using ice axes to stake down the ropes to try to keep the tent from ripping off the mountain. But the tent fabric itself was starting to shred. You would see light coming through little pinholes where the weave of the fabric was opening up. The tents would literally get flattened on top of you by the gusts and then lift up and then get flattened again. They clearly weren't sustainable.

As extraordinarily good luck would have it, the last thing Brett had watched before he left New Hampshire was a video of some climbers on Denali who'd been caught in a huge storm. Building a snow cave had saved their lives. As conditions grew nastier, he stuck his head in my tent and started yelling to be heard over the wind. "This is just like in the video!" he shouted. "This is the same as that storm was. We need to build a snow cave!"

We then crawled on our hands and knees over to the tent next to us to check on a group of commercially guided climbers whom we'd befriended going up the mountain. By then the wind was blowing so hard it sounded like jet engines on the runway at Boston's Logan Airport. The guide and his clients were inside with their backs against the windward side to brace the tent.

Once I identified the leader, I cupped my hands around his head through the tent wall and shouted with my face pressed against his ear, "We're going to dig a snow cave! Do you guys want to stay here or come help us?"

He yelled back, "I think it's going to be OK and our tent will survive!"

I doubted it. Looking around, I could already see tents shredded and gone. Fabric was blowing in the wind where tents used to be; those climbers had all gone into other people's tents. So there were a few four-man tents with eight people crammed inside. "All right," I said to Brett. "Let's start digging."

Once we'd dug the entrance, we excavated the interior, with Andrea digging out the inside and pushing snow toward the door. Brett would scoop the snow up and throw it out the door to me. I would then pull it out of the entryway and toss it into the wind. Brett and Andrea had the shovels, so I was using our titanium pot to scoop up the snow. At one point I noticed Brett staring at me, his eyes wide. I reached up to my face, and it was completely encased in ice. The conditions were otherworldly.

If Brett hadn't seen that video before we went, I don't know that we'd have gone to that as our first solution. But because we did, when our tents got destroyed, we had a relatively safe place to go. That was my first time on a mountain where all our backup plans and strategies and resources were pretty much gone with the wind. We'd lost our tent. We were running out of food. Worst of all, we had limited fuel to melt snow for water.

Without water we would begin to succumb to the high altitude and frostbite. We were already making plans to dig up caches of fuel and food from expeditions that had turned back before us. And then, in maybe the most horrifying moment, our titanium pot for boiling water almost blew away.

We were moving our gear from our tents into the snow cave when a gust hit and blew the pot out of the vestibule of Brett and Andrea's tent. If it disappeared off the side of the mountain, we'd have no way to drink water. That would have been a nonrecoverable event. Fast as a cheetah—which would normally be the last word I'd use to describe somebody whose stature matched mine—Brett dove on top of it and tackled it like a football. He then carried that precious tin pot into the snow cave like it was the crown jewels. There's no question Brett earned our Most Valuable Player award that day.

* * *

Because we were in a whiteout, we couldn't descend for three days. To fight boredom, we added shelves to our cave and a side tunnel that served as a bathroom. Then we tried to sing songs for which we could remember all the lyrics. That activity lost its appeal once we realized we really didn't know any songs. The only one I remembered fully was "The Gambler" by Kenny Rogers, because my dad used to play it on an 8-track during his dreaded car talks. We'd try to ignore him by listening to that song about making the best of the hand you're dealt.

There was a moment, sitting in that snow cave, where it struck me how stupid it would be to fly all the way here, hike all the way up this mountain, just to sit here in this storm and die. The singing and introspection were interrupted—mercifully—at the end of the second day, when one of the climbing guides came over and asked if we could dig out another section of our snow cave for their climbing group, several of whom had developed frostbite, which we did. Then we melted large quantities of snow for water to hydrate them.

Finally, on the third day, a national park ranger on Denali came around with a weather update. "Hey, we just got the forecast, and there's a break in the weather," she said. "We'll still have the high wind, but there's no precipitation for the next ten hours or so. Then more weather is coming."

Everybody immediately started bailing out of high camp. "We need to get out of here," I said to Brett and Andrea. "Now's the only time to go. Get your stuff." We cleared out our snow cave and rapidly packed up. It was a lot easier to hike down the mountain given that both of our tents had blown away during the blizzard; we were carrying a lighter load. Fortunately, we had another tent down at our lower camp.

The winds were still so powerful that climbers were holding on to the rock face, calling out for aid as we passed by: "Help me! Can I tie onto your rope?" And we couldn't take them. We couldn't help other people because it was all we could do to get down ourselves. We were just trying to survive. That was a powerful moment. It added to my growing awareness that activities like this at some point become unhealthy—that taken to an extreme, they can be destructive. The entire sport of climbing involves making trade-offs based on risk and trying to mitigate risk. There's a point at which you can no longer manage it, and we found that place on Denali.

* * *

Nobody died in that blizzard, but there was a lot of frostbite, some so severe that folks had to be carried out on helicopters. We'd skied in, and we skied back out, and skiing out, every time I'd kick off with my skis, my frostbitten toes would jam into the front of my climbing boots, causing excruciating pain. The days were endless, so we could keep going well into the night. We kept trudging forward to get down to low base camp in time to fly out the next morning. My toes were absolutely killing me.

We finally got down to the glacier where planes land, and early the next day, we flew back to Talkeetna Airport. The minute we got to our hotel, I went to my room, turned on the bathroom sink, and drank and drank the cool water until I felt satiated. I remember looking at the little metal pot we'd boiled water in, the one Brett had tackled during the worst of the blizzard so it didn't blow off the mountain. Here in my hotel room, it was useless. But just eighteen hours earlier, it was the only thing keeping us alive.

It seemed like all my life had been a fight to survive: to make it through a seriously troubled childhood, to recover from dangerous addictions, to live through perilous climbs. Now, more than anything, I wanted to find a way to truly thrive and to help others like me do the same.

CHAPTER THIRTY-ONE

COLORADO BOUND

Before climbing Denali, I'd signed up and trained for Ironman Lake Placid. I decided to climb Denali instead. But when I returned, a bunch of my friends were racing. I figured since I'd been climbing uphill for the last month carrying a huge backpack, an intensive workout, maybe I'd just jump in. So I raced Ironman three weeks after returning, July 25, 2004—still with frostbite on my toes.

It was time for a new chapter. In February I'd turned thirty-one. Mark and Leo had both met the women they were going to marry. And I had started feeling more alien in the city. I'd go up to the White Mountains to climb and come back with a backpack with ice axes attached to it. Walking from my car to my apartment, people would be looking at me like, "Who the heck is this guy?" And I'd think, "I need to live somewhere else, where these kinds of adventures are the norm."

I'd done a few trips out West, to Boulder and Moab and Red Rock Canyon outside of Vegas, and I had fallen more in love with it each time. I knew there was still something missing in my life, and I figured out there I might find it. I'd developed my passions and gotten good at them. But I still didn't feel whole. What I was still seeking was purpose.

But also, there were a lot of ghosts in Boston. The final apartment I lived in was just a couple doors down from The Last Drop. I could look out my front bay window, on the top floor of my building, and watch people going in and out. I knew how easy it would be to go down and join them.

It was a big deal to leave a place I'd lived for so long, starting in high school with the Watermark Program. But my friend Jacki encouraged me to do it. She was about to start grad school at Boston College. She said, "You love Boulder. Have more adventures. You've been telling me how much it would fill your heart to find a way to help others. Now's your chance to go do it."

I think Jacki and Leo knew, even before I did, that once I got to Colorado, I wouldn't be coming back. Leo and I had dinner shortly before I hit the road. "I've always known our time together would have an expiration date," he told me. "You have an appetite for life and experiences that are much bigger than mine. I'm grateful for everything I've learned. I wouldn't be the person I am now if I'd never met you. You're a born teacher."

And that stuck with me. I told Leo that thanks to our friendship, I'd grown too. We'd done things and learned things and overcome things together we couldn't have done on our own. To this day I am profoundly grateful that when I asked Leo to be my climbing partner, he said yes.

So I loaded my pickup truck with all my climbing gear, tents, triathlon bike, and mountain bike. Then I locked up my apartment and programmed my early version of GPS for Boulder. On my way out of town, I stopped at an ATM near the on-ramp to the Massachusetts Turnpike. A friend of mine happened to be there too. Spying my loaded-down truck, he said, "Hey, what are you doing?"

I said, "I'm heading west for a bit."

And he said, "Cool, man. Have a nice trip."

It was a simple exchange. But as I drove out of the city, I caught sight of Boston in my rearview mirror. And I knew deep in my gut it would be a long time before I'd be back. I was tired of just chasing the next high, whether through drugs or on mountaintops. I needed to add meaning to my life. Not that long ago, I would have felt like I was running from something. But now I was running toward something. I felt deep in my heart that I could use my eclectic life experiences to help others who were in pain. It was time to make it happen.

A word to the reader: If you notice a slight shift in tone in the stories and reflections that follow, it's because at this point in my life, I had fundamentally changed. That's how I know self-transformation is possible. Before, I was someone focused on my own personal journey. Now I'm someone trying to help as many people as possible connect to the principles and contribution mindset that helped me overcome my challenges.

Moving to Colorado was a turning point for me. It was here that I began the quest to use my gifts and life experiences to help others improve their lives. That mission has been, by turns, every bit as daunting, disappointing, enlightening, exhausting, and exhilarating as my journey into and out of addiction.

The payoff, of course, is incalculable. We can count—just like seeds in an apple—how many people make a long-term commitment to recovery at The Phoenix. But it's impossible to know how many lives—be it the lives of friends, loved ones, or others struggling with addiction—each Phoenix member touches as a result, and how that will positively impact generations to come.

PART IV

COLORADO

You can count how many seeds are in an apple.
But it's impossible to know how many apples are in one seed.

ANONYMOUS

CHAPTER THIRTY-TWO

THE KEYS ARE IN THE MAIL

rriving in Boulder, Colorado, on a hot summer afternoon in late August 2003, with a front seat full of empty Starbucks coffee cups and partially eaten bags of Fritos and Swedish Fish, I was struck as always by the glory of the seven-thousand-foot reddish rock formations on the west side of town. Known as the Flatirons, they are Boulder's most famous landmark. For many they symbolize freedom and openness and nature. For me, they symbolize stability: the rocks that formed into five striking vertical slabs on the east slope of Green Mountain nearly sixty million years ago are themselves nearly three hundred million years old.

My time on Earth felt minuscule in comparison, which was oddly comforting. In the shadows of the Flatirons, my challenges seemed relatively insignificant. At the same time, they made me want to leave as big a footprint as I could. Driving from town to town, considering where to settle, the lyrics to John Denver's "Rocky Mountain High" kept running through my head: "Born in the summer of my twenty-seventh year, going home to a place I've never been before. Yesterday's behind me." This was my thirty-first year. And this felt like a fresh start. Eventually I decided to make Boulder my home base.

When I first got to Colorado, I crashed as needed at the Broadway Inn, near the University of Colorado's Boulder campus, and spent a bunch of weeks living a nomadic, climbing-bum life, stacking up friends back-to-back who would take vacation days and meet me out West. My friend Robert flew out to climb Red Rock Canyon outside of Las Vegas and then Joshua Tree. I dropped him off at the Vegas airport, and Jacki flew in.

158

We drove from Vegas to Moab and then down to climb in Grand Junction, Colorado. I dropped her off at the Grand Junction airport and picked up my friend Steve, and we started climbing and mountain biking our way back toward Moab and Vegas.

I was still living a uniquely privileged lifestyle that most people my age couldn't afford, and I knew it. But I was no longer doing it just for fun or to stay sober. Internally I was still searching, seeking, trying to find and pursue that thing that would add meaning to my life. I was spending most of my time thinking and talking to my friends, especially Jacki, about how to help people struggling with addiction.

I couldn't do it with each foot on opposite sides of the country, I knew that. So I called a realtor friend in Boston and asked him to list my apartment. I FedExed him my keys, hired a moving company to pack everything up and ship it out, and that was it. I was a resident of Colorado. The state motto seemed fitting: "Nil Sine Numine," translated by *Merriam-Webster* as "Nothing Without Divine Will." I'm not super religious, but that resonated. I just felt in my gut that I'd find my calling here.

As it turned out, I found it within weeks of rumbling into Boulder, in a totally unexpected setting, at the Lakeshore Athletic Club in Broomfield, Colorado, between Boulder and Denver. I didn't go in seeking meaning; I went in seeking a paycheck. I was driving through the outskirts of Boulder one day and spotted a gym with a climbing wall inside a health club with a big swimming pool. I thought, "Maybe I can train for triathlon here and work at the gym and make a few bucks." And that's when divine providence showed up, in the tall, lean, powerful form of the climbing wall manager, Ben Cort.

Given that I had at least ten years on a lot of the kids working there, Ben was curious as to why I wanted the job. After hearing a little about my background he asked, "So are you here because you want to climb?" He seemed puzzled.

"Actually, I can't climb right now because I've got some frostbite on my feet. I was on Denali."

That caught his attention. "You were on Denali?" This gave me some cred. It began to sink in that I wasn't a novice.

Ben offered me a bottled water and a smoothie from the snack bar, which I took as a good sign. As we kept talking, I discovered that like me, Ben's wife Christy is also from Pennsylvania. More importantly, Ben and I were both sober. I think the frostbite got me the job. But being in recovery led to a deeper friendship, and we became climbing partners. It was on those climbs with Ben that the idea of starting a sober active community began to crystallize.

∗ ∗ ∗

Since the dawn of civilization, humans have tried to improve aspects of society that aren't working. Or they've wished somebody else would. The most successful solutions have generally come from people closest to the problem, the ones actually living it. Ben and I spent some cold winter months early in 2005 ice climbing in Rocky Mountain National Park, talking about that in earnest.

We agreed the glue that binds society was weakening. With people becoming increasingly disconnected from each other, the addiction epidemic was accelerating. There needed to be a different way to approach it. America's decades-long War on Drugs, launched in 1971 by President Nixon, wasn't working. In many ways, it was making things worse.

In 2005, according to the Agency for Healthcare Research and Quality (AHRQ), some 19.7 million Americans age twelve or older reported they had abused drugs within the past month, with a large number reporting they had abused prescription medications. Most prescription drug misuse involved legally prescribed pain relievers, which are often opiate-based, such as oxycodone (OxyContin) and hydrocodone (Vicodin). At the same time, people of color were being disproportionately targeted for harsh drug sentences that did nothing to support recovery and rehabilitation.

Ben and I agreed with a growing number of experts who saw drug use as a public health issue rather than a criminal justice problem. We were trying to get people sober by arresting them or sending them to treatment, with high relapse rates for both groups. That's because most people coming out of treatment—or worse yet, those emerging from incarceration, having had little or no support—were falling off a cliff, without a robust safety net of resources to catch them. Often it was just "Good luck!" and a pat on the back. And then "Here's a list of 12-step meetings."

I have nothing against 12-step meetings; as noted earlier, I've worked the program myself. But it seemed that for folks in recovery, AA and its spinoffs, like NA (Narcotics Anonymous), were the only games in town. Which was useful for some—both Ben and my brother Mark credit the 12-step community with being instrumental to their long-term sobriety—but not for others. I couldn't help but notice that Ben and I would return windburned and exhausted from ice climbing and wake up eager to jump into life, because life had gotten so much bigger. We reinforced each other's dreams of what was possible in sobriety. Meanwhile, many of our friends were white-knuckling it to stay sober.

"What if we could bring more people along to share this experience?" I wondered aloud one day as Ben and I were coiling our ropes after ice climbing in Rocky Mountain National Park.

He thought about this for a few minutes. "There's a really big difference between climbing and taking somebody climbing," he said. "But it would be really cool to create a healthy culture where people could come together and support each other in recovery." We spent the whole hike back to the car throwing out ideas of what this could look like.

Ben and I had different but complementary backgrounds. He had grown up on public assistance, living the first twelve years of his life in Colorado. His father was a youth pastor with a passion for the outdoors who'd take the kids in his youth groups on lots of adventure-based trips. Those became a big part of Ben's life. Later his dad moved the family to

Washington, D.C., to become a pastor in a very poor, inner-city community. So Ben had plenty of firsthand knowledge of how to lead experiential programs, and he also understood the unique challenges of people from different backgrounds.

I of course had a long and eclectic résumé of experiences, from working with disadvantaged youth on boats to being an EMT to guiding and coaching endurance athletes. That unique collection of adventures had prepared me for a job that didn't exist before but that I could now see clearly.

The third leg of the stool, of course, was Jacki, whose experience as a clinical social worker gave her a real-life perspective on the most effective ways to inspire behavioral change, as well as insights into our country's flawed system for treating addiction. "It has become more and more clear to me that mainstreaming healing through community has to be the way forward, because formal treatment isn't cutting it," she told Ben and me as we began to put shape to what would become The Phoenix.

Again and again, Jacki saw parents being sent away due to trauma-induced addiction, to psychiatric hospitals or into treatment, losing custody of their kids, and fighting an uphill battle to regain the trust of child welfare.

"I see the resilience in so many of these folks," Jacki said. "If they just had a path forward and a community to support them, life could be entirely different. But they must be able to heal from their trauma, and they need something outside of the system because the system isn't there to help them." The three of us agreed the addiction crisis was taking lives at such a fast rate we couldn't wait for so-called experts or policymakers to fix it.

Simultaneous to these brainstorming sessions, I'd been recruiting more and more people who wanted to have exciting, substance-free adventures. And this is something I say about The Phoenix all the time: here you surround yourself with people who'd rather get up at five in the morning to climb a mountain or ride a bike or do yoga and watch a sunrise than stay out partying until five in the morning. In fact, I had already started to build my Phoenix community. It just didn't have a name yet.

CHAPTER THIRTY-THREE

CREATING A "CONTAINER OF SAFETY"

One frosty winter night not too long after returning from the Rockies, Ben and I rounded up all our sober friends in Boulder, along with a few people who weren't in recovery but who had big hearts and wanted to help, to eat pizza and talk turkey about how to formally create a sober version of Mercury Multisport. Our vision was to build a nurturing community of people looking to support each other in our recovery journeys by sharing fitness activities and adventures and inspiring each other along the way. It would be free to join; the only cost of membership would be forty-eight hours of sobriety. I suggested we call it Phoenix Multisport, inspired by the mythical phoenix rising from the ashes.

An eclectic group of eleven people showed up—our early brain trust. The gathering included my massage therapist, Dawn Taylor, who'd worked with me during Ironman training and became a friend and our first Phoenix employee, and Ben's wife, Christy, whose bookkeeping and design skills came in handy in those early days. My roommate, Jess Morgan, whom I'd met at the finish line of Ironman Lake Placid, also attended.

Jess was moving to Boulder around the same time I was and needed a place to live for a while. So when I bought my first house there, with proceeds from the house I sold in Boston, she moved in. Jess was an overachiever with a heart of gold who went on to get two master's degrees and a law degree. She later became The Phoenix's chief legal counsel for a while.

Everyone scrambled to find space to sit on my cluttered couch and the floor. Then I laid out the new approach to recovery that Ben, Jacki, and

I had spent months talking about. "What we have to do to make Phoenix Multisport special is create a container of psychological and physical safety," I said. "In that container, people will try things they never imagined they could, like climbing to the top of a cliff, or riding a mountain bike, or trying yoga for the first time. It doesn't have to be extreme."

Ben jumped in: "And because there's an ethos that creates the safe container, people will be willing to shed their armor and expose their wounds. And that will let them begin to heal." He paused to let that sink in.

"But how is it different from 12-step?" someone asked. "All treatment programs would consider themselves safe spaces, wouldn't they?" It was a fair question.

"It doesn't have to be an either/or," Ben responded. "People in recovery need to find the path to sobriety that works best for them, so the more options the better. We need more tools in the toolbox."

"Yes, true, but there *is* a big difference," I said. "Traditionally society has viewed people with substance use disorder as a problem to be managed rather than viewing it as an opportunity: we're talking about a massive group of people with untapped potential to do great things. Even within the 12-step community, people identify first as their disease: 'I'm Scott, and I'm an alcoholic and an addict.' At Phoenix Multisport, we'll bond around our future goals as opposed to tying our whole identity to our addiction."

Ben, Jacki, and I believed deeply in the intrinsic strength in all people. And I wanted to create a safe space where that strength could flourish. "We will be there to lift each other up, not pull each other down," I said, feeling rocked by a surge of emotion. "It will be a group of people who support and believe in each other, even if we don't yet believe in ourselves."

* * *

It was a noisy, spirited gathering, punctuated by an earnest debate over how to divvy up the Hawaiian and meat-lover's pizzas. But everyone who was there that night contributed in some way to what Phoenix Multisport could be. At one point I showed the group my hideous sketch of a phoenix, which looked more like a burning, screaming chicken. Once we got past the loud guffaws and brief roast of my graphic design skills, the team voted yes to the name Phoenix Multisport, with the caveat that "Scott will definitely need help from a graphic designer for the logo."

(Several years later we shortened our name to The Phoenix, to acknowledge we'd become so much more than just fitness activities; I use the names interchangeably in this book.)

The first graphic artist we hired to create a logo did indeed outdo me with his design. "I'm stoked!" I told him when I saw it. Then I shared it with my friend Cam Brensinger, founder of Nemo Outdoor Equipment—the engineer who'd built the killer sled ramp at my New Hampshire cabin—who shot back a link to the city of Phoenix, Arizona. The design we loved was already in use—by the City of Phoenix! The artist had simply clipped Phoenix's logo and sent it to us. It was a good early business lesson in how not to get hustled.

The second designer we hired, Kristofer Henry, researched images of beautiful Native American birds for inspiration. He created the distinctive logo we use to this day. It's come to mean so much to members of our community that many now sport Phoenix tattoos.

At the end of the night, the general consensus from the group was, "We think your idea is great. You should do it." Which left Ben and I feeling extremely pumped. We were going to make this happen. Though it was late, I called Jacki to fill her in as I collected the empty pizza boxes. As we talked, it occurred to me we had a chance to disrupt health care in a way that was more far-reaching than anything I could have done as a physician's assistant, a dream of mine in my EMT days that had gone unfulfilled.

I couldn't help but think back fifteen years to when I was a teenager working on the *Te Vega*, the first place where I felt I was treated with dignity and respect, as a contributing member of the crew. That marked the beginning of my journey toward self-actualization, a journey I was still on, to find and develop my unique gifts and leverage them in a way that would help others. I wanted to realize my full potential by helping other people like me realize theirs—the principle of mutual benefit. Now, I finally had a chance to do it.

That inspiring thought was followed by another, more sobering one: "OK. *Now what?*"

CHAPTER THIRTY-FOUR

JUST A GUY WITH A BIKE

alling back on the well-worn aphorism "Fake it until you make it," I figured we could start acting like an official organization before we actually were one. In that spirit, with our first donation—$20,000 from my mom—I bought Phoenix T-shirts and gave them out to all my sober friends to build the appearance that The Phoenix was bigger than it was.

Then I flew to Las Vegas with a box full of T-shirts and a sales pitch to drum up sponsorship at Interbike, a national conference of bicycle manufacturers. I was convinced some bike company would agree to sponsor us and give us a bunch of money and a bunch of bikes. That didn't happen. Instead, I just ended up giving away a handful of T-shirts. I talked to one person who pointed out what should have been obvious: "That sounds interesting. But you really don't have anything yet that we can partner with."

I flew back feeling defeated. But we all buoyed each other up. My mom was a big early backer, mentor, and cheerleader. She asked lots of good questions and offered advice to help get us started. With some pro bono help from a lawyer friend, we applied for our nonprofit status. Meanwhile, Ben, Jacki, and I were spending hours coming up with policies and procedures, which we then sent to someone who knew business. They in turn deleted twenty-four pages of what we'd written because it was useless. We were just kind of making it up as we went.

* * *

It was a lonely process to recruit new members in the early days. I'd buy thirty passes to a local climbing gym, then ride around Boulder putting ads on bulletin boards in supermarkets and coffee shops: "Free climbing Friday night at the Boulder Rock Club for anyone who's forty-eight-hours sober. With Phoenix Multisport, a sober active community." Then I'd go there and wait for people to show up. And no one did. I must have looked pretty forlorn standing by the climbing wall in my Phoenix T-shirt with my harness and no takers.

But I didn't lose heart. I had a deep conviction that the Phoenix community we were creating was special and the way we were approaching the addiction issue was unique. At the core of our culture was the principle of empowerment—the belief in the dignity and potential of *every* individual to thrive. Rather than defining ourselves by our past mistakes and how many days or years we had sober, we were bonding over shared goals and challenges and aspirations. Substance use disorder was just a small piece of who we were.

I knew we faced a steep uphill climb—on par with scaling Mount Everest—to break through the jumble and build awareness and credibility in the crowded treatment industry. But I felt strongly the system was so inherently broken, as evidenced by the seemingly intractable addiction epidemic, that if we just persevered, we would eventually reach a group of people who shared our vision of a better way.

So I kept at it. My other recruiting strategy was to post flyers promoting Phoenix bike rides. Then I'd sit with my bike outside of a coffee shop in North Boulder, wearing what had become my Phoenix uniform—a Phoenix Multisport T-shirt (I had a whole box of them at home) and biking or athletic shorts—and wait for people to show up. I drank a lot of coffee, and ate a lot of coffee cake, sitting by my bike, waiting for someone to stop by. Usually I'd just end up riding alone.

Then, one night, at the Boulder Rock Club, a guy showed up. Our first bona fide Phoenix member, outside of my eleven-person brain trust. His name was Barry. I'd met him a few days earlier at an AA meeting. I hadn't gone to AA much prior to that. But I'd started going to get more integrated into the recovery community in Boulder.

One night a guy was sharing about road rage and said he was now riding a bike after losing his license due to repeated DUIs. After the meeting I approached him. "So you like to ride?" I asked.

"Not really," he said. "I ride because I don't have a license." He was a tad grumpy.

"Well, do you want to go on a bike ride?" I asked. "I'm a triathlete and a cyclist, and I'm starting a sober active group called Phoenix Multisport. We also climb on Fridays at the Boulder Rock Club."

That caught his attention. "I don't know if I'd come to ride, but I'll check out the climbing," he said.

And sure enough, on the following Friday, he showed up at the rock wall. "Hi," I said with a big smile. "And welcome to The Phoenix."

* * *

At first, nobody could believe Phoenix membership was free, with no strings attached beyond a commitment to sobriety. They figured there must have been some angle we were hiding. Barry in particular was suspicious.

One day after we'd been climbing at the Rock Club, I took him to the Walnut Café around the corner. As we pulled into the parking lot, Barry spied a U.S. Marines recruiting office right next door. "I knew it, dude!" he said. "This is a hustle! You're trying to get me to join the marines."

I couldn't help but chuckle. "Barry, the marines don't want a couple of recovering addicts," I told him. "We're just headed to the diner to get pancakes."

To this day, people in recovery are skeptical they can use a Phoenix gym with nothing else expected in return. "So no hidden agenda? Or stipulations or fees in the fine print? It's totally free?" they'll ask.

"Yes," I assure them. "That's always been the case with The Phoenix. You can pay it forward by sharing the strength and support you get from The Phoenix with someone else who needs it."

* * *

I wish I could say Barry's story had a happy ending. Sadly, he died from his addiction. But he never gave up trying to get sober, and over the course of half a dozen years, The Phoenix never stopped supporting him through half a dozen relapses. We became good friends.

Barry didn't die of an overdose; he died when a tractor trailer ran over him backing into a loading dock, where he'd gone to escape the cold and passed out. He'd relapsed again after eighteen months clean. Those kinds of deaths don't get included in substance use–related fatalities, but they should.

Over the course of those years, some people would look at Barry as a lost cause and ask, "How many times do we get him into treatment?"

And I'd say, "Every time he calls."

Then they'd ask, "Why do you go back to help him every time? Is there one time that will be too many?"

And I'd say, "Every time he has the courage to reach out and ask for help, I will say yes, because that might be the time when it sticks. And even if he doesn't ultimately get it, imagine the joy he had in the years we were with him."

* * *

I had trouble sleeping in the early days of Phoenix Multisport because when Phoenix members like Barry struggled, all I could do was think about how I could help them. It wasn't completely altruistic; I was still trying to fill a void in my own heart, and I thought by rescuing others, I could somehow rescue myself. But in some ways, it was having the opposite effect. There were hundreds of Phoenix members whose lives were being transformed by being part of this beautiful thing we were building. Yet I couldn't help but focus on the ones who weren't doing well, to the point it was starting to erode me.

A therapist I went to told me, "If there are people drowning in a well, you don't jump in the well to save them. You pull out as many people as you can. Then you eat and sleep and get enough strength to come back the next day and get more people out. But if you jump in the well, no one will be saved." I realized I was emotionally jumping in the well with everybody, trying to get them out. That was a big moment for me, and I approached my relationship with The Phoenix differently after that.

It hearkened back to what I'd learned in my years as an EMT, that it's enough to make everyone's life we touch a little bit better, even if we can't ultimately control all the outcomes. It helped me realize that although Barry did ultimately die from his addiction, some of the brightest years he had in his adult life were as part of the Phoenix community. And that in itself was something special.

CHAPTER THIRTY-FIVE

WHAT'S OUR HEDGEHOG?

Not long after the pizza meeting at my house, Jacki drew up a mission statement and we filed our articles of incorporation, along with an application for nonprofit status. The first was relatively pro forma; the second was a bigger deal because it would allow us to start soliciting actual donations. By fall 2006, Phoenix Multisport was officially a corporation. Ben and Jacki were our first board members, along with a couple of friends of mine. Shortly after that, we took our first trip as Phoenix Multisport, to Moab, Utah.

At that time we still had only around a dozen members. One of them was my sponsor, Michael, the big-hearted guy I mentioned earlier who'd worked the steps with me. Though I'd met him through AA, he was open to other approaches to sobriety. That was in direct contrast to the first person I'd asked to sponsor me, someone I'd met before Michael, who was a 12-step-or-die kind of guy.

This guy had shared something at an AA meeting that struck a chord with me. So I approached him afterward. "Do you take sponsees?" I asked.

"Yeah, I do," he said. "Let's get together so you can tell me your story."

We met for coffee a few days later, and I shared my journey into addiction and my path back out. Unfortunately, from his point of view, that path hadn't included many AA meetings. "So you're tired of being a dry drunk," he said.

"Well, I don't really think I'm a dry drunk," I responded. "I've got decent recovery, and I live a life where I'm very self-reflective about how I treat people."

"But you're tired of white-knuckling it," he said, unconvinced I was solidly sober. "As your sponsor, the first thing I'd tell you to do is start going to more meetings."

I guess that wasn't a surprising response, given his commitment to 12-step. But it was the kind of dogmatic thinking I didn't want at The Phoenix, where we're happy to acknowledge and encourage many pathways to recovery.

* * *

In the spring of 2007, we got the letter we'd been waiting for: our approval to operate as a nonprofit. We were fired up; it was time to start fundraising. That's when things started to get real. At first my only paid staffer was Dawn Taylor, who worked out of the spare bedroom in my house, surrounded by boxes of Phoenix T-shirts, stickers, and cycling gear. (I considered myself staff even though technically I was a volunteer since I didn't take a salary for the first ten years.) Dawn was one of those rare left-brained/right-brained people who are both intuitive and logical. The ideal combination for her dual role—she was running the office and doing all the bookkeeping.

Shortly after hiring Dawn, I brought Mike Britton on as our volunteer coordinator. (He still works for The Phoenix today.) He brought with him experience from working at another nonprofit in Boulder. Ben Williams was our first climbing instructor. When it came to building a new organization from scratch, none of us really knew what we were doing. We learned as we went. And we made use of everybody's unique gifts and talents.

If you were my friend, you probably ended up contributing. I was dating somebody who knew Excel, for example, and she made a spreadsheet for our budget, which was $60,000 per year, barely enough to pay salaries and overhead. For capital investments and to cover any shortfalls, I invested a lot of my own savings.

With the business ramping up, I called Jacki with a big ask. "Hey, any chance you can come out here and help Ben and me get this thing going? We could really use your expertise running nonprofit mental health programs."

She was a year and a half into grad school, and I knew she could work on her dissertation from anywhere. "I have dogs. I have a boyfriend. How long are you thinking?" she asked.

"Three months," I said. "Maybe six months, tops. You can stay with me."

Within a few weeks, Jacki had bought a Volkswagen van and was on the road, headed west. Her then-boyfriend (now husband) Chris stayed behind; the dogs came with. Jacki quickly became immersed in The Phoenix, serving as our first chapter manager and top cheerleader. We had someone who led cycling and others who helped with climbing activities. Among other things, Jacki coordinated all those programs. Once she arrived, we started creating and running as many events as we could.

It quickly became obvious that half a dozen people would be five too many in my small house; we needed more working space. So I sold my cabin in New Hampshire and bought a two-story condo in North Boulder. We used the bottom floor to work, and I rented the upper floor to Molly, a mountain biker in recovery whom we funded and promoted in our athlete sponsorship program.

In a turn of good fortune, she and Griff, another one of the riders we sponsored, placed third in a 24 Hours of Moab event, so we had a Phoenix team on the podium. Seeing them up there in their Phoenix cycling gear was exciting—and moving. We were gaining momentum and addressing stigma in the process. We started to feel like we had the wind at our back.

* * *

When Ben, Jacki, and I wanted to escape midday from the chaos in the office to debrief and talk shop semiprivately, we'd head over to Spruce, a nearby coffee shop that sold a crazy coffee mixture called Spruce Juice. We weren't sure exactly what was in it and we didn't want to know, but we drank a lot of it.

We made an entertaining trio. Ben and I are very tall, and Jacki is only five-foot-three, so walking down the street, we'd catch people doing double takes at the sight of two giant men with a very small woman in between. Finally we had someone on the team who could pronounce the word "philanthropist" and knew what "self-efficacy" meant. (The short answer: believing in your ability to achieve your goals.)

So the three of us would grab a table outside and talk about the various things we were trying to do or what we thought The Phoenix should be doing to help heal as many people as we could in a deep and lasting way. These conversations were mostly in pursuit of answering one key question: *What's our hedgehog?*

Now you're probably wondering what, exactly, was in that Spruce Juice. I don't blame you: prickly, plodding hedgehogs might seem an odd focal point for a working coffee break. But the hedgehog concept, which business writer and consultant Jim Collins developed in his 2001 book *Good to Great: Why Some Companies Make the Leap . . . and Others Don't,* helped guide us in finding our sweet spot.

The hedgehog concept was inspired by a line from Archilochus' ancient Greek parable: "The fox knows many things, but the hedgehog knows one big thing." In the parable, the fox tries many ways to catch the hedgehog. But he never succeeds because the hedgehog knows how to do one "big thing" exceedingly well: roll up in a ball of quills and defend itself. While foxes may be faster and more cunning, hedgehogs are hyperfocused on an overarching vision they can achieve: staying alive.

"What's our one big thing? What's our core value proposition?" Jacki would ask whenever Ben and I started going down rabbit holes. "Are we a climbing organization? Are we going to bring in fitness? Is CrossFit an option?"

We knew from reading *Good to Great* we needed to look at where our passions (our mission), strengths (what set us apart), and the need in the marketplace (find a niche and fill it) all intersected.

We landed on connection and activity as our competitive advantage, in support of our mission to mainstream healing by creating a nurturing community. That's when we decided our hedgehog was going to be a sober active community for people in recovery and anyone choosing a sober lifestyle.

Over the next few years, we broadened our thinking to welcome families, friends, probation officers, and others who provide services like job training and housing for people in the recovery community. Anyone impacted by addiction, even tangentially, is invited to heal along with us. We need everyone to be part of the movement to drive transformational change.

* * *

Beyond hikes and runs and mountain biking and climbing, we spent a lot of our early days rescuing folks. People would call us, and we'd go pick them up and take them to detox or rehab or pick them up from rehab and take them to sober living. We'd retrieve people who were trying to escape from houses where their drug dealer lived. In those days, no matter who called, we just went and did it. It was crazy. We were a community, but we were also helping people one individual at a time.

I'd wrapped my Ford F-250 with Phoenix logos, and I had ten bike racks on top. Before we had lawyers warning us about liability, we hauled gear and Phoenix members all over the place. My truck was a common sight around town. One night my mom and I were going out to dinner; she'd moved to Denver after retiring. That way she could be near me and somewhat centered between Mark, who lives in Napa Valley—so in a region known for its wines, you'll see at least one cyclist proudly wearing a Phoenix jersey out on the road—and Amyla, who'd settled in North Carolina.

While we were stopped at a traffic light, a guy on a bicycle pulled up on my driver's side. He started banging on my window, which was rolled down a bit, and yelling, "Hey, man, you've got to come help me!"

I rolled the window down a little more so he didn't have to shout. "What is it you need?" I asked.

"You've got to come help me!" he said again, pointing to the side of my truck with its Phoenix logo. He'd noticed the words *Sober Active Community*. "My friend needs to go to detox."

I looked at my mom, who gave a supportive nod. "Well, it's not really what I do," I told him. "But I'll see if I can help."

My mom and I followed this guy over to a park, and I told her, "Keep the doors locked and don't get out." I hopped out and talked to the guy, whose friend was indeed in crisis and needed to get to detox. So I called a friend in the sheriff's department, who sent somebody to pick him up. Then the guy on the bike started getting belligerent with the sheriff. "Hey, man, you don't want to do that," I told him. "Just calm down."

The next thing you know, he's on the ground, and more sheriffs show up. At which point I said to one of them, "Are we cool? Can we leave and go to dinner?"

He said, "Oh yeah, you're good to go." So I got back in my truck, and my mom was totally cool with all of it. She loved the work we were doing. She'd always find the folks at The Phoenix who were having the hardest time and get to know them. I'd stop by the office to sign checks or have a meeting and see her on the gym floor talking to the guy with face tattoos or the one with an ankle monitor who had just gotten out of prison. That's just the kind of person she was.

After that night, we all joked that I needed a sober siren that I could flip on and help people get into detox. But it was still eating at me that we couldn't do more. We weren't going to make a dent in the addiction crisis one detox delivery at a time. We needed a way to grow our sober active community beyond Boulder.

Simultaneously, and just as urgently, we needed to start calling attention to what I'd come to believe was the number-one public health crisis in the country, exacerbating the growing addiction epidemic: trauma. I decided the best way to start was to address my own.

CHAPTER THIRTY-SIX

WE'RE ALL IN RECOVERY FROM SOMETHING

I remember after moving to Colorado, even with close to a decade sober, walking home after dinner with friends and passing a bar and looking in the window and seeing everyone inside laughing. And I'd be going home to watch a movie by myself. And I'd think, "I could just go in there and buy a drink, and I'd be right back in it."

That's what's so mercurial about this disease. You can be in a good place and then find yourself going into a bar, and you can't even explain it. This is what is so hard for friends and family to understand. Back then I was still running triathlons, passionately engaged in The Phoenix, and 100 percent committed to my recovery. Yet the idea of entering a bar for a drink still crossed my mind, even if I didn't act on it.

Trauma therapy during Survivor's Week at The Meadows, where Mark had gone earlier, plus the reading I've done since, has helped me a lot. I'm not a clinician, and The Phoenix isn't in the clinical therapy space. But I've gained a lot of valuable wisdom and surprising insights throughout the course of my ongoing recovery. And there's a lot to be said for lived experience. So I thought I'd share a few ideas and resources in this chapter that might provide food for thought to folks struggling with any kind of trauma or substance use disorder and to their loved ones.

* * *

I mentioned earlier giving a TEDxMileHigh talk in Denver in 2016 in which I talked about trauma. It was a momentous evening for me professionally—and one that forever changed my life personally. But that's jumping ahead. For now I want to quote the one line from my talk I most want everybody to remember:

"*We can't talk about healing from addiction unless we also talk about healing from trauma.*"

I know trauma can be a polarizing topic, especially in a country fond of promoting its "pull-yourself-up-by-your-bootstraps" culture. But as Martin Luther King Jr. once said, it would be a cruel jest to say that to a bootless man. The main mission of The Phoenix is to help people step into their empowerment. But trauma denial—the idea that other people have had it worse than you, so you need to just suck it up and deal with it (whatever your "it" is)—can be dangerous too.

It's the nature of the human spirit to seek ways to cope with emotional pain. If we don't find a positive coping mechanism, we will often find an unconstructive one that makes things worse.

As an example, just because one child survives their parents' divorce unscathed doesn't mean the intense, ongoing pain another child feels isn't legitimate. But if others around them treat it dismissively, the urge might be to escape the pain in unhealthy ways rather than address the why behind it. Numerous studies have shown trauma to be a strong risk factor for addiction. Authentically acknowledging the pain helps take the power out of it.

I learned this starting on day one of Survivor's Week, which was basically an intense early childhood trauma workshop. There were twenty-five of us sitting in a room, and we were broken into five groups. Most of the guys in my group were my age. Once we started sharing, it was obvious they were dealing with some pretty serious stuff. I started thinking, "I don't know if I'm supposed to be here. These guys have been through some tough shit."

Back at the hotel, I pulled out the night's homework. I had to read through a list of traumatic events and identify the ones I'd experienced. On the first page, it listed half a dozen severely traumatic events—the kinds of "big *T*" traumas I mentioned in my TEDx Talk, like sexual or physical abuse or witnessing violence or death. No check marks there. On the second page was a list of about thirty-five "little *t*" kinds of traumas—so called because their impact can be more subtle—like emotional abuse, neglect in childhood, food insecurity, experiencing divorce, or getting bullied. Lots of check marks there.

The next day each of the guys in my group had maybe two pages of notes about a "big *T*" trauma they had endured. I had at least six pages of dyslexic scribbles about my "little *t*" traumas. It was the classic "death by a thousand cuts"—maybe others would define them as little cuts, but cumulatively, if you get enough of them, they can kill you.

* * *

One weird moment at Survivor's Week was an exercise they call "Empty Chair Work." You sit next to an empty chair in a room with the lights dimmed and, with the rest of your small group watching in support, confront the person you see as the most significant perpetrator of your trauma. For me, that person was my dad.

By now my father's mental illness had escalated to the point where Mark and I felt the need to start parenting our parent. After getting divorced from Paula, Dad had a depressive episode during which he once again threatened suicide with a firearm and moved in with Nanny and Pop-Pop, who by then were in their late eighties. They wanted to move into a retirement home but couldn't because their fifty-seven-year-old son was in their basement. Worse yet, my aunt called to say, "Your dad's been using your grandmother's credit cards. He's racked up some bills."

"We need to get him out of the equation," I told Mark. He agreed. So we called our father and said, "If you could live anywhere in the country, where would you want to live?"

He was ready with an answer: "I'd love to live in Kalispell, Montana. It's so beautiful." One of his many fantasies over the years had been to live the life of a cowboy out West. So Mark and I flew out there, found a small property, and bought it together. (Our sister had helped our father out on other occasions, but this time it was our turn.) We told him we had an investment property in Montana and asked him if he'd go keep an eye on it. He ended up living in Kalispell for the rest of his life.

We gave Dad a food stipend for use at a local grocery store, which they wouldn't let him spend on booze. It was a small town, so we could communicate with folks. We'd let them know about his mental health struggles, so they kept an eye on him. But it wasn't long before he found someone else to abuse—an elderly woman who was down on her luck and had moved in with him. In return, he insisted she cook and clean and care for him. He would lock her out of the house if she didn't do it. She felt trapped.

She somehow found phone numbers for Mark and me and called. "I want to go, but everything I own is in this house and your dad won't let me leave," she told us. "I don't know what to do." So we lured Dad back East to a family event, and we flew to Kalispell and packed up his house—by now the home of an obsessive-compulsive hoarder, in which we found a horribly abused dog and dog feces everywhere—and sold it. We gave a U-Haul driver two hundred dollars to drive the lady back to her family.

So one of the things I said to that empty chair was "Dad, everything you touch turns into a shit show. Literally. And that crap just flows downhill and washes over the rest of us. And has for years. Yet you selfishly refuse to get help. And so did I, when I was really depressed a while back and would have benefited from treatment, because I was afraid acknowledging I was depressed meant I was just like you. And I don't want to be like you. And frankly, that just stinks."

The memories of moving Dad out of his house in Kalispell were recent and raw. We'd found bottles that Dad had urinated in and not bothered to throw out; it was untreated mental illness run amok. Mark and I would basically shovel stuff into a dumpster all day—there was little of value except a few pieces of furniture and photos of our childhood, which have since disappeared—then go back to a hotel and cry at night and then get up the next day and do it again.

We then staged a mental health intervention to force him into treatment. "All your stuff is in storage," we told him. "We'll still care for you, but only in the context of a structured mental health program where you can live." He agreed. But the day after he checked into the program we'd found in Philadelphia, he signed himself out and returned to Montana. And that's when his life on the streets began.

"Do you know how much it hurts," I asked the empty chair, "to know your own dad is homeless?"

* * *

Spiritual teacher and bestselling author Eckhart Tolle blames something he calls "pain-bodies" for keeping us trapped in a negative, self-destructive mindset. In his bestselling book *A New Earth*, Tolle describes a pain-body as an "energy field of old but still very-much-alive emotion that lives in almost every human being." Carrying around this accumulated pain from the past can control our thinking in very unhealthy ways. After the imaginary conversation with my dad, I felt able to release some of my own pain-body.

The transformational moment came when one of the guys in my group said, "Wow, that must have been really hard." He'd realized I'd tackled some deeply personal stuff I'd never shared before.

"Yeah, it was," I said. "Thanks for giving me a safe space to face those demons." I appreciated his support. But something had changed. In the past, I'd have drawn a sense of value from that conversation. It would have validated how I had always defined myself, as the damaged son of a mentally ill, abusive father. But now I realized, "I'm so much more than this."

And that's a mindset we encourage at The Phoenix that differentiates us from the 12-step community, where people bond primarily around their pain-bodies—being an addict or an alcoholic. In what other instance do you define yourself by your disease? Tolle maintains that when a group bonds around a pain-body, the people in the group can become stuck in that identity.

That's why at The Phoenix we celebrate the accomplishment of individual and shared goals rather than derive our self-worth and group status from our recovery anniversary. Rather than dwell on what we've lost during our active addiction, we focus on what we gain in recovery. On good days and bad, we connect people to hope and their innate value, which is the first step in their self-actualization journey.

In the course of my own quest to become self-actualized (a lofty way of describing my ongoing efforts to find and realize my life's purpose), at Survivor's Week I had to also acknowledge that my mom, whom I'd grown incredibly close to, had contributed significantly to the pain I'd felt since childhood. She could have done more to protect Mark, Amyla, and me from our dad and stepdad and their emotional abuse. But she'd buried herself in her work rather than deal with it.

For years I'd tried to make excuses for that. She eventually apologized. Her "I'm sorry" would have meant more if she hadn't added a "but" at the end. Recognizing that she had failed us in that way as a caregiver was a key part of my healing process.

* * *

One book that has made a profound impact on me is *Deep Survival: Who Lives, Who Dies, and Why,* by Laurence Gonzales. It's about misadventures and survival in the wilderness. But it applies to everyday life as well. It has helped me better understand the interconnection between conscious and subconscious pathways—the "modern" brain (responsible for problem-solving, language, memory, judgment, impulse control, and reasoning) versus the primal brain (survival, drive, and instinct).

The addiction impulses live in the primal part, so keeping them in the conscious part, where you have more agency, is hard. Same thing with trauma. Adverse childhood experiences (ACEs) such as abuse, neglect, parental addiction, mental illness, and divorce can create new neural pathways in a more primal part of your brain. They can actually change our body's biology.

The higher your ACE score—a measure of how many ACEs you've experienced (that doesn't take into account individual differences in resilience)—the greater your risk of chronic illness, suicide attempts, and addiction.

Research cited by Dr. Nadine Burke Harris, author of *The Deepest Well: Healing the Long-Term Effects of Childhood Trauma and Adversity*, shows just how deeply our bodies can be imprinted by ACEs; untreated, the damage can last a lifetime. And you can't un-imprint traumatic moments with the same power with which they were imprinted. You must create new pathways through practice and love and repetition, until the traumatic event loses its strength.

Unfortunately, sometimes this historic pain will trigger an impulsive, visceral response. It could be loneliness, or isolation, or a breakup, or anger about something. If it lands in that old, buried emotional material, your subconscious brain could start making decisions for you.

That's why when somebody relapses, it may be they saw a red car just like the one their drug dealer used to drive. Or it was a summer night that felt like the last night they used. Or something crappy happened at work, and they were triggered by their boss, who is a lot like their dad. And the next thing you know, a person who is weeks, months, or years clean is pulling into a liquor store.

The beauty of The Phoenix, what makes it special, is that it gives you a new outlet for those primal neural pathways. When I'm having a bad day now and need to vent, I want to go work out. My instinct is to just throw on shoes and go for a run or go to a rock-climbing wall. (That was easier before I had kids. Now my wife and I tag team to make sure we each get space to decompress and hit the reset button as needed. If all else fails, we just cuddle on the sofa for fifteen minutes, which is also an effective way to recharge.)

* * *

Under the best of circumstances, life is hard. Few people make it through without experiencing some kind of trauma. That's why at The Phoenix we say, "We're all in recovery from something."

Years after I came out of active addiction, I was still having trouble loving and accepting myself. By doing trauma work, I learned we can all leave the burning building. We can create a whole new environment for ourselves and our kids—the generation that follows. Yet most of us try to find the one room that's not on fire and stay in it. In the moment, that feels safer. But over the long term, we won't survive if we don't get out of the building before the whole structure is consumed.

There's a fairly new framework for addressing mental health issues that is particularly powerful in treating addiction; it's known as CHIME, an acronym that stands for connectedness, hope and optimism, identity, meaning, and empowerment. I like it because it combines the power of community with the elements of self-actualization—The Phoenix in a nutshell. These elements comprise your "recovery capital"—resources you can rely on to sustain your recovery over the long term. The more you have of each, the better.

You'll notice all these elements are grounded in hope for the future rather than fear of the past. That's because at the end of the day, staying sober just because of fear of pain is hard to sustain. To truly thrive, we need meaning and purpose. It's what gets us out of bed in the morning. As Ben Cort has often said, "I got sober because I didn't want to die. I stayed sober because I wanted to live."

I always felt safe with Pop-Pop.

Mom reading to me while trying to keep my busy hands from messing with the pages

A rare photo of Dad and me at Wing Song Farm

Drinking with family at the Tides Inn, age 13

Mark, Amyla, and me at Wing Song Farm with Scuzzy, Dad's Chesapeake Bay retriever

Here I am at 15 with a mohawk and homemade tattoo, looking tougher than I felt.

Enjoying spring break from the Watermark Program. Beer, anyone?

On shark watch during swim call in the Atlantic Ocean on the *Te Vega*

Repairing a mast hoop lashing on the *Spirit of Massachusetts*

Christmas at Nanny and Pop-Pop's. Top row (left to right): half-sister Emily, Dad, Amyla, and Aunt Judy. Front row: me, Nanny, Mark, and Pop-Pop.

Planking the schooner *Alabama* at Fairhaven Shipyard, most likely hungover

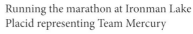

Our three-day drive on unpaved road from Lhasa, Tibet, to Cho Oyu base camp

Running the marathon at Ironman Lake Placid representing Team Mercury

We made it to Camp 2, up 23,100 feet on Cho Oyu, before descending due to weather.

Leo and I on the grounds of Tengboche Monastery with Mount Everest in the background

On the summit of Mount Baker in
Washington State

Testing our human sled jump near my Crawford Notch,
New Hampshire, cabin

The early days of The Phoenix, when we were still called Phoenix
Multisport, on our way to the 24 Hours of Moab mountain bike race

This fitting advice caught
our eye on a Phoenix ice-
climbing trip in Colorado:
Keep off the pipe.

The Phoenix cycling crew
in Boulder

Ben Cort and I at Delicate Arch during the annual Phoenix Moab trip

Last photo of Mom and me, taken at Smith Lake in Washington Park (Denver), 2017

Kait in Maui shortly after everyone on the island received a false incoming missile alert

Ready to race: Kait the day before completing Ironman Lake Placid, July 2018

Throwing the first pitch at Fenway Park for National Recovery Month, April 2019

Jacki speaking to musicians and fans about Phoenix music programs

My West Wing meeting with Gil Kerlikowske, the director of the Office of National Drug Control Policy under President Barack Obama

Jacki delivering her TEDx Talk at the White House

On a trip to Colorado, President George W. Bush met with a group of us to learn more about The Phoenix.

With Anderson Cooper after receiving the CNN Heroes Award

In the midst of COVID-19 and local wildfires, Kait and I wed on October 10, 2020, in Napa, California.

The joy of finally holding my son

Kait and I, now living in Boston, just days away from meeting our firstborn, Magnus

Preparing for our culminating "Gratitude Meeting" at the annual Phoenix Moab trip

Our happy family: Magnus loves being a big brother to his sister, "Baby Alice"

The Phoenix supporting artists back of the house at Telluride Music Festival

Staff and volunteers from across the country dancing at a Phoenix event in Denver

Hanging out with Phoenix Boston's "Mama Bear" Dina at our gym

Tiffany (in the red T-shirt) has impacted at least five thousand lives through her volunteer outreach.

Together again in Moab: From the mountains, we're building a movement.

CHAPTER THIRTY-SEVEN

GROWING PAINS AND GAINS

A s word spread in Boulder about The Phoenix's inclusive, sober active community approach to recovery, our office became a whirlwind of activity, by day and by night. We welcomed anyone, at any fitness level, as long as they met our forty-eight-hours-sober requirement. At the same time we were organizing hikes and bike rides and gym workouts, we were also hosting yoga sessions, sober October Halloween parties, and other community-building activities.

"Connection and activity! That's our hedgehog!" Jacki would proclaim as she bumped into other staffers trying to get to the phone.

Things got so tight on the ground floor of the condo we had to go sit in our cars to make business calls. At one point I went outside to make a call and saw half a dozen other Phoenix staffers in their cars on their cell phones. I finally bit the bullet and asked my upstairs tenant to vacate so we could work in that space as well. But it wasn't long before we'd outgrown the upper level too. At that point we upgraded to a facility with offices and a yoga studio, and we used the Boulder Rock Club for climbing.

In the very early days, I don't think you'd have called us an organization. We were just people in recovery helping people in recovery. Our "hedgehog" kept us laser-focused on our mission and on the need to start building bridges with partners. We knew we couldn't do it all. We reached out to the Boulder mental health community and treatment centers and an organization called Advocates for Recovery, which helped connect people to resources.

If we really wanted to disrupt the way our country approached addiction, though, we needed to go bigger—*much* bigger—and to do that, we needed to grow our donor funding base by orders of magnitude. But how?

That's when someone from the marketing team tossed out the dreaded "G" word. "Hey, Scott," they said, "why don't we throw a gala?" It was courageous of them to suggest it. They knew the idea of wearing a tuxedo, corralling celebrities, and making small talk for an entire evening would be as appealing to me as getting a case of pink eye. Visions of harried waiters carrying trays full of limp shrimp cocktails and mystery meat potstickers danced in my head.

"Have we exhausted all other possibilities?" I asked.

"You know it," they said.

"Would I need to make a speech?" I asked.

"Absolutely," they said.

"Sounds like a terrible idea," I said. "Let's keep thinking."

* * *

On July 17, 2008, we held our first annual gala at the Saint Julian Hotel in downtown Boulder. As gala fundraisers go, it was a fairly relaxed, low-key affair, attended mostly by friends and family, since we didn't know a lot of people with money. It felt more like a celebration of The Phoenix. I actually enjoyed it, except for when I had to go up to the podium and give a speech. I was so nervous I basically blacked out while speaking. I was afraid I was going to throw up on stage. I don't remember anything I said.

The most special part of the night happened during dessert. Just before the peach cobbler was served (Colorado peaches can give Georgia's a run for their money) a Phoenix member joined each table and shared their personal story, then talked about how The Phoenix changed their life. People were so moved by the experience that we continued holding an annual gala for nearly a decade, even though it didn't raise a huge amount of money.

In subsequent years we had some incredibly powerful speakers. The then-mayor of Denver, Michael Hancock, whose sister was in recovery, gave a phenomenal keynote address one year. In 2011, I'd used my own savings to buy a five-thousand-square-foot building in Denver to help The Phoenix expand throughout Colorado. That facility became our first full Phoenix gym. It was on Champa Street, purposely right down the block from a huge encampment of unhoused people, many struggling with addiction. Mayor Hancock had visited a few times and had become a supporter.

We're still on Champa Street today, in the middle of what has become an open drug market, still seeing the potential in all these people society has labeled as irrevocably broken.

Another year Darryl Strawberry spoke, recapping his meteoric rise to baseball superstar followed by his brutal public descent into addiction. (He was suspended by Major League Baseball three times for substance abuse.) He shared about growing up with an alcoholic, physically abusive father and about all the money he'd made playing ball for the Mets, Dodgers, Giants, and Yankees.

He recalled all the houses he'd owned, the fortune he squandered, and how he ended up lying in an alley, left for dead, strung out on drugs and destitute. He's now been sober for twenty years. Darryl had pulled me aside after coming to witness a Phoenix program the afternoon of the gala and said, "You've built something special here. I'll happily cut my speaker fee in half to support what you've done." We were super grateful for that. He also gave us a signed Mets jersey that we still have framed in our offices in Denver.

To anybody who attended our Phoenix galas, one sobering takeaway was that drug and alcohol addiction devastates individuals and families regardless of income, zip code, race, station in life, education level, or any other stratum you can think of. And the pain and heartbreak loved ones feel are the same whether they are rich or poor, a famous celebrity or an everyday Joe, Jordan, or Josephine.

One of the most heart-wrenching gala keynotes of all came from Pat Cashell, son of the former longtime mayor of Reno, Nevada, Bob Cashell. Pat's crippling drug habit had left him living on the streets of the very city his dad was presiding over as mayor. His low point came when his dad found him lying in a parking lot, strung out on meth. "It would be easier for me if you were dead than seeing you like this," Bob told his son.

Those words stuck. Pat got into treatment, and after hearing me talk about my addiction journey and The Phoenix's sober active community approach to recovery on *CNN Heroes* (a show honoring "everyday people who are changing the world"), he moved to Denver and got involved with The Phoenix for several years. He's now got nearly two decades of sobriety and, back home in Reno, helps others struggling with homelessness, mental illness, and addiction.

Pat's story points to another powerful message that ran through all our gala speaker keynotes. It's one that Phoenix staff member Tiffany Foster—who in her darkest days lived on Methadone Mile in Boston and has now helped save thousands of lives as volunteer coordinator for the New England region—quotes regularly: "Where there's breath, there's hope."

* * *

So like the title character in *The Little Engine That Could,* The Phoenix was slowly beginning to gain some steam. The 2012 CNN tribute had certainly helped raise our visibility and credibility within the recovery community. Our phones were ringing off the hook, and enough donations were coming in that we'd increased our yearly budget to $1.6 million. Just five years after getting our nonprofit status, we'd gone from 11 members to 6,200. "We're doing good," Jacki kept telling me. "We're starting to really make a difference."

So why was I still feeling like we weren't? Or at least, not enough? Mainly it was because I still felt responsible for the lives I couldn't save. Like the son of one of our early donors, a young man struggling with addiction whom I never met but whose death I mourn deeply to this day.

We were just starting to figure out how to grow The Phoenix outside of Colorado. We'd started a program for veterans in Colorado Springs, and our gym in Denver was getting lots of traffic. But given the magnitude of the growing addiction epidemic, we were barely melting the tip of the iceberg. So when a current supporter of The Phoenix called and offered us $250,000 to start a chapter in San Diego, where her son lived, it was a big deal.

Her hope, of course, was that we could help her son. And we desperately wanted to. But we couldn't figure out a way to scale that quickly. There was a lot of heated debate over how far and how fast The Phoenix should expand. Ultimately we got bogged down in the quicksand of analysis paralysis. By the time we did launch in Southern California, in Orange County, the donor's son had already lost his life to addiction. Another flickering ember extinguished. I cried when I got that news.

One night around that same time, I was at dinner with my family in North Carolina, visiting Amyla, when I got a call from another distraught mom. Her son David was in the throes of his addiction. "I really think The Phoenix would help him," she said, sounding sad, scared, and desperately in need of hope. "Would you mind giving him a call?" She gave me David's cell phone number, and I promised to reach out to him. "Thank you," she said. "That's such a relief."

My next thought was "I should call him right now." Instead, I went back to dinner with my family, figuring it would be fine to call the next morning.

David died that night. He'd gotten in a car accident that the police attributed to him being under the influence. What they didn't realize was he had sustained a traumatic brain injury. He went home and died in his sleep from that. For months I was plagued with the thought that it was partly my fault. I don't even know whether David would have answered had I called. But I kept asking myself, "What if I had talked to him that night? Maybe I could have helped him in some way."

* * *

Losing two young men whose parents had reached out to me for help back-to-back was a turning point for me and for The Phoenix. It created an urgency and a recognition that we couldn't wait years to figure out how to go bigger. Every day we delayed, another 113 men and women died from a drug overdose. (Today it's double that. And that doesn't count deaths from substance use–related accidents, illnesses, and suicide.)

This galvanized my risk profile for growth at The Phoenix. I bluntly summed up my new attitude about "how far and how fast" we should expand at an internal staff meeting. "The next time we get the opportunity to grow beyond Colorado, we go," I said. "We're not going to overthink it. That approach is costing us lives."

"But it costs money to save lives," Erik, our program manager, said. "How will we afford it? How will we deploy the resources it would take to launch and manage a new Phoenix chapter one thousand miles away without jeopardizing our progress here?"

I thought back to staff retreats and board meetings where similar conversations had taken place. It was starting to sink in that some of our employees and even some board members were values-aligned but not vision-aligned. "We'll figure it out as we go," I said.

For Erik, that was the wrong answer. For me, it was the only answer. As program manager, Erik was erring on the side of caution. I got that. But too much caution came with its own risks. We'd spent a whole bunch of money trying to figure out how to expand, and we were still nowhere but in Colorado. Our close-knit team couldn't move forward if we were rowing in opposite directions. In a heartbreaking moment for all of us, Erik left.

Then the universe stepped in with an added whammy: in May 2012, Ben Cort, who'd been pivotal to the launch and success of The Phoenix to date, announced he was leaving to take care of a family matter. "I know this isn't great timing," he said. "But to take Phoenix to the next level, you need someone to help you run it who shares your vision and can give it 500 percent." We both knew there was only one person for the job.

"I feel another life-changing moment coming on," Jacki said when I told her I had a proposition to make. We'd gone out to the nearby Walnut Café for some eggs Marcos, the staff favorite: scrambled eggs with cream cheese topped with cheddar and two sides of your choice. She no longer lived in Boulder; two years earlier she and Chris had gotten married in a magical "adventure fest" at Whispering Oaks Ranch in Moab, Utah, then headed back East to the suburbs north of Boston so she could finish her PhD dissertation. She managed to juggle all of that while continuing to work full time for The Phoenix. "What's up?"

"How would you feel about becoming my partner in helping take The Phoenix to the next level?" I asked. "We share the same vision and values. You're as passionate as I am about the mission. And with Ben leaving, I need someone to take on the formal role of helping me lead the team. I want you to take on a bigger role in advancing innovation. You're great at it."

Jacki took a bite of her pancakes and considered this. "It's funny. I always assumed I'd end up in a more traditional job. As a social worker, teacher, or researcher. But my favorite part of this job is helping the staff make progress on their innovation journeys." I could see she was tempted. This was her chance to help disrupt, from the inside, a badly broken industry.

"You didn't regret climbing Frankenstein Cliff with me, did you?" I said. "Well, this is just a different kind of mountain we're climbing."

Of course, there was still her personal life to consider. She was newly married, and she and her husband wanted to start a family. But The Phoenix had become more than a job for Jacki; it was her calling. The next day she came to my office bearing treats—Starbucks grande iced lattes, along with a couple slices of cinnamon coffee cake (she knows I've got a weakness for sweets)—and plopped down in a chair. "We're celebrating," she said. "I've decided I'll do it. But I need to stay in Boston."

"You got it," I said. "Now let's go scale this mountain."

CHAPTER THIRTY-EIGHT

FROM FIRE TO THE STARS

In 2010 CBS launched a new reality TV show called *Undercover Boss*. On each episode a top executive spent a week in disguise doing grunt work in different departments of their company. This gave them a close-up view of how things really operated and how employees felt. It was a huge hit, with nearly fifteen million weekly viewers. Luckily for The Phoenix, my brother Mark was one of them.

One night during season two, the undercover executive was Don Fertman, the chief development officer for Subway. During his tenure, Subway went from 166 restaurants to more than 41,000 locations in 105 countries, making it the fastest-growing franchise in the world. Posing as entry-level worker "John Wilson," one of Don's *Undercover* jobs was to make sandwiches, and he was terrible at it.

But what caught Mark's attention as this incognito growth genius clumsily constructed turkey, meatball, and Italian subs was his revelation to a coworker that he was in recovery. Here was this corporate honcho on national TV talking openly about his sobriety.

At the time, Mark was serving as our board chair. "Dude, there's a top Subway exec on TV talking about his recovery. Any problem with me calling him?" he asked.

"Go for it!" I said.

The next day, Mark called Subway headquarters and asked to speak to Don. Surprisingly, they put him through. Mark explained he was on the board of The Phoenix and shared some of his personal story. He and Don hit it off immediately. My brother clearly gave an inspiring pitch because Don agreed to come out to a future board meeting and talk about how to scale a business.

Mark and Don went on to become good friends. And Don became an avid Phoenix supporter and board member—he served as our board chair for more than a decade—who helped unleash our early growth strategy. Before Don's earliest meeting with our board, he, Mark, and I grabbed dinner in Denver and he gave me the best piece of advice I'd received to date.

"So how did you start The Phoenix?" he asked.

"Well, it was just me and a bike," I said. "I would take people on a ride. And sometimes it was me in the climbing gym."

"So you've got to find another guy with a bike somewhere," Don said. "That's it."

It was so simple. And because Don had the résumé to validate his wisdom, for the first time people started listening to that idea. Before he joined our board, he had come to The Phoenix to speak about Subway's growth strategy. Then he turned to ours. "If you started with a guy and a bike, why can't you grow with a guy or a gal and a bike? You find a Scott or a Ben or a Jacki in San Diego or Boston or wherever, and you take it from there."

Don told the group his approach to growth was pretty much "Ready, fire, aim." And I thought, "That is my style. Now I feel like somebody gets me." He validated my feeling that 80 percent of the friction hindering The Phoenix's growth had been internal and that we didn't have the talent we needed to help us scale the way we wanted to.

So we started hiring folks who knew coming in that we had our sights set on the stars and that we expected to encounter a lot of turbulence on the way. And when the next opportunity came along to expand outside of Colorado, we were ready to go. It came in the form of a grant from the Tarsadia Foundation, a family-run nonprofit in Southern California whose mission was "unleashing human potential." They offered us $250,000 to launch a Phoenix chapter in Orange County. We said yes.

"Well, here we go," I told Jacki. "I guess we'd better find a guy or a gal with a bike."

∗ ∗ ∗

Meanwhile, I'd been curious about a new chain of gyms with access to lots of barbells, bikes, lifting belts, and any other equipment you'd need for a high-intensity—but customizable—workout. It was called CrossFit, and it was famous for its fervid followers, though up to this point, I hadn't been one of them. CrossFit's training regimen, which combined elements of gymnastics, weight lifting, and calisthenics, left participants feeling strong and empowered. That got my attention. But its intense culture sounded a little intimidating.

Then we opened our gym in Denver, our first location in an urban center. Rourke, one of our instructors, asked, "What are you going to offer besides boxing and yoga?" It was a good question.

"I don't know," I said. "Maybe Olympic weight lifting." I'd done some of that. But I didn't really have a plan.

That's when a volunteer named Jake, who had helped install our gym floors, said, "You should do CrossFit."

By then I'd gotten certified in a whole bunch of things. I was a climbing guide and wilderness first responder, and I also held certifications in cycling, triathlon, and as a personal trainer. So I decided to get certified in CrossFit to see what I thought of it. Earning certifications is a great way to learn new skills.

It nearly destroyed me. On my first day, the instructor said, "Today, your workout is going to be 'Fran.'"

I said, "All right, sure. What's Fran?"

One of my classmates laughed—an inside-joke kind of laugh. It starts with 21 thrusters, which is where you squat with a 95-pound barbell and then press it overhead as you stand, and 21 pull-ups. Then you do 15 reps of each, followed by 9 reps, as fast as possible. Elite athletes can do Fran in just 5 minutes. There was a 20-minute time cap on it for the class, and I was only halfway through at 20 minutes, dying a slow death while the rest of the class, who'd long since finished, cheered me on. I could barely walk the next day.

But a week later I realized, "OK, wow, I see the magic of it." I could imagine how Phoenix folks would connect to it, because there's a camaraderie in facing this greater adversity together. It's the same as hiking up a mountain. But with CrossFit you fabricate the mountain on a dry-erase board, and you make the mountain as hard as you want it to be.

So that's what led to The Phoenix becoming officially affiliated with CrossFit, as we are to this day. Once we got CrossFit trained, certified, and licensed, we could borrow space at CrossFit gyms for free all over the country to offer fitness workouts, yoga, and other Phoenix programs for folks in recovery, when gym owners had space available.

One additional requirement to becoming a CrossFit affiliate back then was our name: I guess for competitive reasons, our affiliate name couldn't be Phoenix Multisport. "Any ideas?" I asked the team. This question elicited some funny one-liners, but no viable names.

Then I remembered that when we first started The Phoenix, I thought it would be cool to have a Latin slogan that embodied what we were about. A friend who'd worked at the climbing gym where Ben Cort had hired me, Christie French, was a bit of an academic. She'd shared with me a quote about moving through pain to the heavens. I liked it because it evoked emotion. But it wasn't quite right. "We've been through pain in our addiction," I said. "But that's not what it's about."

People so often think of folks with substance use disorder as being broken. But the reality is, despite all the things we've faced, we're still unbroken—like the mythical phoenix, which rose from the ashes of its previous life as a symbol of hope under difficult circumstances.

So I tweaked Christie's idea to say *Per Ignem Ad Astra*: "Through Fire to the Stars." And our affiliate name became Per Ignem, which was unique enough that CrossFit went for it. Eventually they loosened their rules and let us change our CrossFit affiliate name to The Phoenix Cross-Fit. But "Per Ignem Ad Astra" remains our Latin slogan, and a fair number of Phoenix members are walking around sporting tattoos of that phrase to this day.

* * *

For our next growth spurt, we once again found ourselves inspired by Don Fertman's expansion strategy with Subway. Given our budding CrossFit relationship and our trust in Don, when he suggested we call a CrossFitter in Boston named Chris Daggett to help us develop a Phoenix presence there, we were very interested. Instead of a guy and a bike, it was a guy and a barbell.

Chris was a Subway-approved contractor who would build new stores for Subway franchisees. He'd been open with Don about his own recovery, so we gave him a call. He came out to Colorado and spent some time with us in Boulder and Denver, then joined a Phoenix trip to Moab. He immersed himself in The Phoenix. I in turn visited him in Boston a few times, and we began to figure out how we could launch a Phoenix chapter there. We just started carving it out of the wilderness.

The mayor of Boston at the time, Marty Walsh, made no secret of the fact he was in recovery. So I was surprised he didn't do more to help us at the time. He certainly wasn't alone in that regard. I know public officials must juggle a lot of competing constituencies. Nonetheless, they have a major role to play in helping shift the paradigm away from viewing the addiction epidemic as a headache and instead looking at it as a massive untapped human resource opportunity. Just think how many people who could help with the solution are still behind bars, thanks to the draconian legacy of the War on Drugs.

Mayor Walsh eventually connected us to somebody in Boston public health, and they gave us a little old auditorium in a run-down city building. It was still full of desks and chairs that had been used when it was a site for Boston EMTs to take their written exam. (In a weird moment, I realized that's where I'd taken mine.) We didn't have a lot of money to support the Boston program at that time, so we converted that into our first Phoenix facility on the East Coast.

The place wasn't easy to find. Chris used to joke, "All you've got to do to come to The Phoenix is come down to Albany Street, walk into the parking garage, go up the metal ramp, take the elevator up two floors, walk down the hall, then find which little room we're in, and you're there. That's all you've got to do to get sober."

But it was a start, and it allowed us to begin planting more seeds of hope in Boston and eventually throughout New England, with Chris driving the train. He was the one who suggested and then went on to help launch our volunteer-led program by recruiting hundreds of guys and gals with bikes, yoga mats, and barbells. We realized that would be a faster, more realistic way to scale than trying to open brick-and-mortar gyms all over the country.

Chris is about five years ahead of me in recovery, and occasionally when he picks up a recovery chip from AA, he'll give me his old one, which is a special ritual for me. I'll be forever grateful that Don introduced us, both because Chris became a good friend and because he is a perfect example of how anyone who has been touched by the addiction crisis can also become part of the solution.

Many years before we met, Chris had gone to prison for cocaine possession with intent to distribute. Lucky for him, The Phoenix, and a whole bunch of Phoenix members whose lives he helped transform, he was sentenced just before they imposed mandatory minimum sentences. "If I had been arrested just a few years later, I'd have been in jail during the time period Don connected us," Chris said. "Instead, at The Phoenix I found purpose in helping people struggling with addiction find a path of hope. And that strengthened my ability to do the same."

CHAPTER THIRTY-NINE

FALLING HEAD OVER HEELS

When I say I fell head over heels when I first met my wife, Kait, I mean I literally fell head over heels. I met her while we were rolling together at jiu jitsu. She was the only female in an all-male class, very pretty and very tiny, and she showed up one afternoon in November of 2015 with a Groupon, wearing a sports bra and yoga pants. She looked even smaller in the white gi the front desk staff loaned her to wear for the class. During the warm-up, as we did front rolls down the mat, she stood out. A total rookie. So yeah, I noticed her.

Of all the scenarios in which I could have imagined meeting my life partner, that wasn't one of them. Maybe shopping in the produce section at Whole Foods or working out at a CrossFit gym. But not at a Brazilian jiu jitsu class giving her tips on how to better choke me from closed guard.

It certainly wasn't love at first sight. I didn't think much about her after the class ended. And Kait has no memory of rolling with me at all. She made that embarrassingly clear when we unexpectedly ran into each other four months later at the Phoenix gym in Denver. She'd recently broken up with a guy she'd worked out with a lot. "He was my gym partner," she'd told her therapist. "I miss that."

"I have another client who goes to a sober gym," her therapist said. Support for Kait's recovery was something they often discussed. "It's called The Phoenix. Maybe you should try it."

After a string of unhealthy relationships and several relapses, Kait had decided she was going to say yes to every opportunity that had even the slightest chance of breaking her out of this painful cycle. So one cold night in February, she came to The Phoenix and opened what many new Phoenix members refer to as "the thousand-pound door," because you're so scared the first time you walk through it. In early recovery it can be super intimidating to enter an unfamiliar space and try something totally new without a drink or drug in your system. But once Kait found the courage to pull that door open, "I was swept up with kindness," she later told me. "I loved it."

After that, she started regularly attending our Thursday night CrossFit class. I joined the class one night a couple months later, and when I spotted Kait, I thought, "I know her from somewhere." And then it hit me. She'd only come to jiu jitsu that one time, but I remembered her. I'd been terrified of squishing her; I'm sure she was equally terrified of being squished.

On recalling who she was, I walked over and said, "Excuse me, I think I know you." Which admittedly sounds like an overused pickup line. She shut me down, fast—right as the music stopped. So I'm fairly certain everyone in the gym heard her say, "I don't think so." She was so adamant, and the moment so awkward, that I didn't bother to say, "No, really! I think I do."

A few days later, I was giving a group of potential donors a tour of the gym. Kait had just finished a class. "Hey, Coach Brian, who's that guy?" she asked.

"That's Scott," he said. "He started Phoenix."

She was mortified. "Oh, my gosh. I was so rude to him the other night," she said. "I thought he was hitting on me."

Brian shook his head. "I doubt it. Scott's not really like that."

I've since come to learn one of Kait's defining traits is her compassionate heart. "All right," she said. "I need to apologize."

* * *

An encounter with Kait went a little smoother a few weeks later at Phoenix's annual Memorial Day potluck picnic in Washington Park, across the street from my house. People came loaded with burgers, potato salad, cupcakes, and nonalcoholic beverages, along with twenty-pound weight vests. Every year, before some serious chowing down, we'd complete a CrossFit workout called "Murph," in honor of Lieutenant Michael Murphy, a Navy Seal killed in action in Afghanistan.

In the CrossFit community, this is commonly done on Memorial Day not only to honor Lieutenant Murphy but also to acknowledge all military members who have been lost in service to our country. After all-day heats of a strenuous workout, scaled to each person's ability (elite athletes complete 100 pull-ups, 200 push-ups, and 300 squats, sandwiched between a mile run on each end, wearing a 20-pound vest), with many other local CrossFit gyms joining, we fire up the grill for food and fellowship.

Kait approached me and pulled me aside. "I'm really sorry for how rude I was when we first met," she said. "I've been looking for the right time to apologize."

I was struck by how sincere she was. And I was sorry she'd been feeling badly about it. "No apology necessary," I said. "But really, I actually think we've met before."

I could see she was still skeptical. "Where?" she asked, sizing me up.

I really hoped I wasn't wrong. "Did you by any chance train at Easton Brazilian Jiu Jitsu a few months back?"

Her bright blue eyes widened. "Oh my God. We met at jiu jitsu. I'm so sorry. That's crazy," she said. "I had adopted an approach of trying new things," she explained. "And Easton was offering Groupons."

I heard most of what she was saying but admittedly got lost for a moment in her eyes and her beautiful smile.

We walked over to a picnic table so she could show me what she had baked for the picnic: a big fruit pizza (not something I'd ever had before) that looked like an American flag and a cookie decorated with a Phoenix logo and the words "Phoenix Multisport." I really loved that one. "Wow, that's an awesome cookie," I said. "Do you mind if I take a picture of it and post it?" I could only imagine the time she'd put into making that pizza and cookie. I remember the date: May 30, 2016. My life hasn't been the same since.

Kait then went on to talk to other Phoenix members at the picnic. Standing nearby, I could hear her laughter and couldn't help but smile. Seeing how much fun she was having, I could tell she already had a deep love for The Phoenix. That made me want to get to know her even more.

Given how many years I'd spent entering into relationships that were not healthy for me or for them while running from those that were, my therapist had given me some practical advice: "Go into a room and identify all the people you're attracted to, and then talk to everybody else." In other words, he was telling me to manually override my instinct to gravitate to the type of person I had in the past.

I ignored that advice with Kait. She was definitely the one in the room I was attracted to. But this time was different. At this moment in my life, I wasn't putting pressure on myself to search for a relationship. I was more focused on building The Phoenix and spending time with my mom, who had started to experience some challenges we would later learn were related to the onset of Alzheimer's.

Despite the attraction, I tried to view Kait simply as somebody I wanted to get to know better. We went on to spend a lot of time together as friends before we entered into a romance. I had to force myself to let down my guard. I was still frozen in the early steps of just trying to be vulnerable and present.

"At some point you need to really try to commit, or else you're going to miss out on all the gifts that come with a deep relationship with somebody," my therapist had said. So I vowed to give this friendship, or whatever it turned out to be, the gift of time. I told myself, "I'm really going to try. And even if I self-sabotage this relationship, I can self-sabotage it a year from now instead of this month. That's still an option for me. I'm going to take the next step and continue on this journey."

∗ ∗ ∗

One of the first times Kait and I hung out, just she and I, we went to a matinee of *Finding Dory*, the sequel to *Finding Nemo*. (It was a slow week for movie releases.) As she noted later, it would be hard to overstate the innocence of our early relationship. But I was also being mindful of the fact she was still in early recovery.

Shortly after *Finding Dory*, I invited Kait to my house for a barbecue I was throwing for the Phoenix team. This threw her on a couple of levels. One, she was the only one invited who wasn't on staff. Two, she had never been to my house, which was on Franklin Street, right across from Washington Park, where we'd held the Murph picnic. Granted, it looked like too much house for just a single guy. When she pulled up in front, in her little Honda Fit, still outfitted with a breathalyzer, she thought she had the wrong address.

"You live *here*?" she asked when I opened the big wooden doors. "I run around this park imagining which house I'd choose to live in."

As she stepped inside and I started showing her around, I became very aware that, as a single guy, I'd set up my home mainly for function. I kept the thermostat at sixty-five degrees. And damn, it was a little dark. Dark wood floors, dark kitchen, brown couch. "I'm not here a lot because I travel so much for work," I said apologetically. I made a mental note to buy pillows or flowers or *something* to add color and warmth.

"Well, where is everybody for the barbecue?" she asked.

"Oh, they'll be here soon," I said. "I was wondering if you would run over to Whole Foods with me to get some burgers to grill."

Lucky for me—and the folks who showed up with a big appetite—she was willing to help because when we got to the store, it was immediately apparent I hadn't thought through the menu. "You're going to feed ten people just burgers, buns, and cheese?" Kait asked. "What about lettuce, tomatoes, and onions? And you'll want sides. You need lemonade." She paused. "Never mind. I've got this."

To those of you who have always been blessed with self-esteem, this might seem like a small thing. But to anyone struggling with addiction, it won't. Kait told me later she had been at a place in her life where she felt purposeless. And suddenly she thought, "I can do this. I can do this well. I can help Scott." So she sent me off in search of potato salad and a couple cases of LaCroix sparkling water, and she found the condiments and all the other fixings. It felt easy, safe, and comfortable. We could be ourselves with each other, which was refreshing. We were a good little team.

Later, after we'd grilled the burgers and folks were hanging out on the back porch talking, I came into the kitchen to find Kait hacking away at another massive cookie she'd made, on a metal cookie sheet, using one of my favorite kitchen knives. I mention that only to share one unusual means of self-soothing I'd employed since childhood. When I get interested in something—whether it's doing something like climbing or boxing, or buying something, like mountain bikes or kitchen knives—I research the hell out of it first. I become a student of it. It gives me comfort to understand all aspects of something, whatever that something is.

And there Kait was with my extensively researched Shun handcrafted Japanese chef's knife, chopping away at her cookie. I cringed and thought, "She's going to trash that knife." But I couldn't bring myself to say anything to her. She was so pretty and so excited and so happy. I thought, "I don't care if she wrecks the knife."

To this day, when I cut something with that knife, the little nicks in the blade still make me smile.

* * *

I spent most of that summer battling butterflies in my stomach. And not just the fun kind you get when you've met someone you're really attracted to, although I was having a bunch of those too. These were the kind more closely associated with impending doom.

They'd started on the day I'd accepted an invitation to give a TEDx-MileHigh talk. TED is a nonprofit dedicated to sharing "knowledge that matters." They do this by inviting world experts in all kinds of fields to the TED stage to present their big idea in eighteen minutes or less. (TEDx events are locally organized.) The talks are filmed and then made available to viewers online; they're now viewed or listened to more than three billion times a year. My talk was scheduled for August 1, 2016, at the Ellie Caulkins Opera House in Denver. As I noted earlier, it was a big deal for me and The Phoenix.

I had mentioned it to Kait at the Memorial Day picnic. She'd told me she was working in women's retail but that she hoped it was temporary. "I was an art history and philosophy major, and I've always loved writing," she said. "So I'd be happy to help you with your talk if you'd like, or you could practice it with me."

I recognized TED would be a huge opportunity for The Phoenix, so I welcomed all the help I could get. "That's a really nice offer," I said. "If you could give me some tips, I would love that."

We agreed to meet for coffee at Starbucks so Kait could give me some feedback on the current draft of my speech. Looking back, we consider that our first date because of how deep our conversation got that day. But at the time, Kait wasn't sure. She'd gotten dressed up, while I showed up in my usual attire—a black Phoenix T-shirt and workout shorts. That's still my uniform of choice; it makes getting dressed in the morning so much easier.

But it complicated things for Kait. "I saw no change in attire no matter where we went," she joked with me later. "Putting on a polo shirt and cologne—that would be a signal we were dating." With her help, I've since stepped up my game regarding what I wear when we go out.

Waiting for Kait to show up that day, I was in a self-reflective mood. I'd just come from a TEDx prep session where we did some deep work to pull out our inner truth. Kait snapped me out of that for a minute as she walked up. She looked stunning. Then came that killer smile. As she gave me a warm hug, some of the stress I was feeling immediately washed away. To this day, her hugs still have that effect on me.

Once we ordered coffee and sat down, I started sharing some questions from my earlier prep session. Kait remembers me looking at her and asking, "How would you describe your life philosophy in five words?" That was one of the training questions I had been deep in thought about. Kait pondered her answer, then as she shared it, one thought led to another and we ended up talking about our dreams and aspirations and not the TEDx Talk itself.

As it turned out, that TEDx Talk turned out to be a turning point for me personally and professionally. I titled it "Finding Sobriety on a Mountaintop." I'd invited my mom and a bunch of Phoenix people early on, and they had seats in the second row. But as the summer wore on, I thought it would be nice to have Kait there too.

So I bought her a ticket at the last minute, which meant she had to sit near the back, next to two guys who appeared to have been day-drinking. They must have thought this would be an audience full of partiers because they asked Kait to go out for drinks. "Thanks. But I'm here to support the guy who is about to go on stage," she said. "And I'm in recovery." Instant shutdown. They left shortly after I delivered the line that moved her the most: "No one ever dreams they're going to grow up to be an addict."

* * *

Thinking about Kait being out there in the audience and the happy feeling that gave me, there was no denying my feelings had grown into something deeper. After the talk I said, "We're all going to dinner. Why don't you come along?" There were nearly a dozen of us. We all walked over to the EDGE steak house at the Four Seasons to celebrate, and I got a long table. Kait ended up sitting next to my mom, which turned out to be a very relaxing way for them to get to know each other. The dinner invitation was so impromptu that Kait didn't have time to freak out about a potentially scary "meet-the-mom" situation.

And because of my mom's new medical diagnosis, Kait also didn't have to meet her as "this intimidating ambassador to Finland and corporate CEO." Rather, she said, "I met her as an aging, proud mother, full of admiration for her son." She was never Marilyn the Ambassador to Kait. She was "Mimi." They called each other Mimi and Katie.

After dinner I put Mom in an Uber. "See you tomorrow, Mom. Love you." She leaned in and gave me a kiss and said, "I'm proud of you." In recent years she'd made a point of telling me this. But tonight it carried a different weight. I could tell it carried all the pain and worry she'd held inside for so many years that I wouldn't make it through my addiction, lightened by a sense that after this night and the talk and all I had accomplished, maybe she could rest easy knowing that was now all in the past.

Then I turned to Kait. "Hey, do you want to go for a walk? It's such a beautiful summer night."

"Sure," she said. "I was hoping you'd ask."

So we strolled around downtown Denver's convention center area and ended up at the Performing Arts Sculpture Park under two sixty-foot dancing figures we call the "Dancing Aliens." In the beams of their bottom lighting, it felt like we were standing in a spotlight.

Kait was standing on a higher step, so we were face to face. I remember the way her face glowed and her eyes sparkled as she looked at that statue. And I knew that was the moment.

"Do you mind if I give you a kiss?" I asked her.

"I would love that," she said.

So I leaned in and kissed her, in the glow of the Dancing Aliens; I don't remember ever having felt that happy or at peace. And from then on, that became First Kiss Park.

* * *

"So I guess I'm going to have to tell the board we're dating," I said. Kait just smiled; it sounded a little like asking permission from the school principal. But we both knew I had an ethical responsibility to do so. We also knew it would put us in a different sort of spotlight.

As an organization, The Phoenix has always struggled to figure out its policy around people meeting romantic partners, given the inevitability of that happening. We don't have set rules. But we make it clear that The Phoenix isn't a dating club. If you find the love of your life at a Phoenix event, we wish you the best. But if that's your primary purpose for being here, you're in the wrong place; there are apps for that.

We've also grappled with how that policy should apply to staff given that we're not providing a clinical service. Luckily, given the amount of time Kait and I had spent making sure what we had was substantial before embarking on something more serious, the board appreciated our approach and wished us the best. We followed two rules of thumb: One, we couldn't bring any relationship drama to a Phoenix gym or event. And two, *sobriety first*. The onus was on us to be mature and kind to each other if it didn't work out.

With those ground rules in place, for the next few years, we settled into a very low-key, take-it-slow, old-fashioned courtship. The nicest part was the time we spent together with my mom, as her primary caregivers. Every Friday night we'd order pizza and watch TV. Kait and Mom also shared a passion for decorating for the holidays, whether it was a trip to the pumpkin patch to create jack-o'-lanterns for Halloween or both of them directing me where to string the Christmas lights on the front porch. Kait loved getting to know Mom in that way.

For my own part, I felt blessed to have finally met a woman who seemed to be my missing puzzle piece. We had plenty of ups and downs, as most relationships do. But there were more ups than downs. And our broken parts and jagged edges fit together in a way that seemed natural and whole. For the first time in my life, I felt like I could pause, breathe, and exhale, without worrying I had to climb another mountain or run another race or save another life to prove I was worthy.

Little did I know I was about to enter into another equally life-changing relationship—one that would give The Phoenix the funding and management support we needed to create a true paradigm shift in how society views and treats substance use, addiction, and recovery. This would give us a real shot at revolutionizing the addiction treatment industry in a way that would help transform not thousands but millions of lives.

Back in that fateful August of 2016, I couldn't foresee any of that. For once, I was firmly grounded in the moment. And all I knew at that moment was that wherever life led, I hoped that Kait would be by my side.

CHAPTER FORTY

"WE WANT TO BUILD MOVEMENTS."

L ooking back, it was a few months prior to giving my TEDx Talk that all the stars finally started to align for me. But they were doing it in such an unexpected, pell-mell fashion that it felt like I was traveling through space on a rocket ship with a mad scientist handling the navigation, bent on disrupting every corner of my universe.

On the romance front, a remarkable woman had come along who seemed likely to turn my boring bachelor lifestyle topsy-turvy. Further throwing off my equilibrium, just a few months before the Memorial Day picnic where Kait decided to give me a second chance, I'd been invited to join a conference call that would forever change the trajectory of The Phoenix.

A couple of local Phoenix donors had suggested I connect with some folks from a new, community-focused nonprofit I'd never heard of, Stand Together Foundation. It was worth a shot, I figured. What I didn't know at the time was that this foundation was part of a larger community, Stand Together, comprising a unique group of top business leaders and mission-driven donors with the vision and resources to drive transformational change.

Better yet, they shared our values. They believed in the intrinsic strength and dignity in people. They were all about bottom-up empowerment, not top-down government programs. On our first conference call, the foundation's then-CEO, Evan Feinberg, told me they wanted to support social entrepreneurs who were part of the communities they were trying to support—in other words, people who had lived and breathed the problem they were trying to solve.

That was us. A match made in venture philanthropy heaven.

There was just one hitch: the foundation wasn't interested in funding programs—like the gym-based addiction recovery program I was describing—that weren't going to move the needle. "We want to build movements," Evan said. Despite the enthusiastic buildup his team had given me, he was clearly underwhelmed by my vision for the future. In fact, he later told me, he was *this* close to hanging up. "We're looking for big ideas that will get people excited," he told me. Subtext: "You're losing me, fast."

I spent another twenty minutes talking about our goal of trying to recruit thousands of members and how we thought it could be scalable; I also mentioned possibly trying to make Phoenix events reimbursable with medical insurance, along with a few other ideas. I then described various Phoenix specialty programs, like criminal justice and our work with veterans. Finally, Evan broke in. "Scott, just boil it down for me. What is the essence of The Phoenix? What is the core of this thing?"

I thought back to my first conversation with Don Fertman, hoping lightning could strike twice. "I started The Phoenix as just a guy with a bike," I said. "Riding my bike, recovering together with others. I've always had this dream that any guy or gal with a bike could someday start a Phoenix chapter where people could recover together. Then each person's recovery journey would become an asset to help others in theirs."

This was several years before COVID-19 turned office meetings into a series of unending Zoom calls, so I couldn't see Evan's reaction. But I could sense the energy at the other end of the line had changed. "OK, now that's exciting," he said. "Tell me more about the guy with a bike."

* * *

A couple months later, in May, Evan greenlit the launch of the Stand Together Foundation's Catalyst Program, an ambitious initiative that seeks to unlock the potential of America's most disruptive nonprofits. Nine organizations were invited to join a six-month management and leadership development experience that would be an "on-ramp to strategic partnership with Stand Together Foundation." The Phoenix was one of them.

For the next six months, Jacki and I traveled back and forth to Arlington, Virginia, where Evan and his team were based, becoming students again. Underpinning our coursework was Principle Based Management, the framework the Stand Together community uses to empower its employees and succeed long term by creating superior value for others.

Given my arduous academic past, hitting the books again in my forties didn't sound awesome. I conjured visions of unpleasant all-nighters, drinking copious amounts of black coffee and trying to absorb lots of lofty concepts. Luckily, the class was a lot less abstract and a lot more actionable than it sounded.

Basically, we learned how to apply the fundamental ideas and values powering The Phoenix—our belief that all people have something worthwhile to contribute, that in helping others we help ourselves, and that we all have the desire to find purpose and become self-actualized—to build a much stronger internal culture based on principles rather than on rules. Put simply, it was a management philosophy that would empower the people we worked with to empower the people we served.

One of our fellow Catalysts described the tools and skills we picked up during that class as "rocket fuel." That analogy seemed to fit well with the crazy spaceship Jacki and I felt like we were on. "From fire to the stars," Jacki joked when we got our diplomas.

The following year, in spring and summer of 2017, Stand Together Foundation issued its first two donation checks to The Phoenix, totaling $1 million, with the intention to invest twice that amount in 2018 if all went well. (As it turned out, things went well enough that the Foundation granted $2,278,642 to The Phoenix in 2018.) Lots of alcohol-free champagne was popped on those occasions. But we had our work cut out for us.

Our task was to prove we could find lots of guys and gals with bikes who could help us scale The Phoenix from coast to coast. And to incorporate Principle Based Management into our culture in a way that inspired continuous improvement. In other words, we needed to empower all Phoenix members to find new and better ways to turn our revolutionary approach to addiction recovery into a movement. So no pressure there.

At the same time, I was struggling to come to terms with losing a person I loved dearly, admired tremendously, and would miss fiercely—the woman who did her best for me from the day I was born, who didn't give up on me even during the worst days of my addiction, who was The Phoenix's biggest cheerleader, and who helped me become the man I am today.

CHAPTER FORTY-ONE

THE BEST KIND OF GRIEF

I remember listening to my mother's labored breathing as she lay in her darkened hospital room, knowing that each breath could be her last. She was leaving us so much sooner than we'd expected, less than two years after being diagnosed with Alzheimer's. We weren't yet fully prepared.

Staring out the window at the mountains rising up behind the city of Denver—a town with so many memories, where Mom and I had become best friends—I suddenly became aware of the construction cranes across the street, decorated with Christmas lights. Everything had happened so fast, it had barely registered that we were less than two weeks from Christmas. Just seventeen more days, and we'd be starting a new year, with all the promise that held.

I'd envisioned celebrating some major milestones in the years remaining with my mom—taking The Phoenix to the next level of growth, getting married, having kids. In recent months Kait and I, along with my siblings, had started looking for a good care facility for Mom since home care was no longer enough. I hated watching this trailblazing powerhouse of a woman become dependent on others. But I'd hoped to make what time she had left as joyful as possible, filled with noisy visits from her grandchildren—Mark's kids, and I hoped mine as well.

It wasn't to be. Numerous newspapers in D.C., Philadelphia, and Denver published lengthy tributes reporting the news that Ambassador Marilyn Ware—just Mimi to her family—had died on December 14, 2017, at age 74. In the end, it was a blessing Mom passed when she did;

her intestinal tract had stopped working, and eventually she'd have lost the thing she valued most, her dignity.

Kait was with me in the room when Mom died, feeling her own acute sense of loss. Having shared this challenging caregiving experience while still getting to know each other had accelerated our closeness. And even though they'd spent a relatively short period of time together, Kait and my mom had become deeply invested in each other's lives.

Mark, Amyla, and then Kait and I all took shifts sitting with Mom, talking to her, singing to her, recounting stories or simply just brushing her hair back and holding her hand, hoping she could hear us or sense us. Doctors had told us that once she came off life support, the end would likely come quickly. It didn't; she hung on for a few days.

Early on the morning of December 14, Kait and I fell asleep, and when I woke to the first rays of sun bringing a warm glow to the snow-covered Rockies, I looked over and saw Mom wasn't breathing. I knew she was gone. So I just sat with her for a little while before waking Kait. I just wanted to be with her and hold her hand.

An obituary in the *Washington Post* said of my mom, "Her extraordinary ability to connect with people from all walks of life and from every corner of the globe was one of her greatest gifts." The truth of that hit me hard during my first workout at The Phoenix after her passing. We always do a circle-up before our workouts, where we each share something meaningful with the group.

When it was my turn, I talked about how much The Phoenix meant to my mom and how she truly believed people could rise from the ashes of their addiction. She'd seen it happen with Mark and me. "Wherever Mom is now," I said, "I know she will continue to earnestly cheer on every Phoenix member in recovery."

Afterward, as we were doing our warm-up, I noticed several guys were tearing up. These were the ones Mom would stop and talk to when she'd visit the gym—the people others would have written off as the toughest, most hopeless cases. She recognized and acknowledged that every person who entered that gym was so much more than their circumstances. And they loved her for it. My childhood buddies loved her too. Both Danny and Aidan flew in for Mom's celebration of life in Philadelphia, which meant a lot to me.

We see and feel a lot of grief at The Phoenix. I've lost many people I cared deeply about, and it never gets any easier. But I think the grief I felt when my mom died was the best kind of grief, in the sense that it came from sharing so much with her rather than wishing we had shared more. I was sad that I'd no longer be able to add to my wonderful memories of our times together rather than feeling grief that I hadn't had enough moments to experience that joy.

We'd had a bunch of rocky years throughout my adolescence and young adulthood in Pennsylvania and Boston. Ironically, it took coming together in the shadow of the Rockies to finally find our footing as mother and son and best friends. But we also added another dimension to our relationship, as entrepreneurial thinkers who sharpened each other. I'll always be profoundly grateful for that. I just wished she could have hung on a little longer. She would have loved what happened next.

CHAPTER FORTY-TWO

GAME CHANGER!

Inspired by our Catalyst training, Jacki and I had gone into high gear. She was bringing the team up to speed on the principles we'd learned, while I spent a couple years living on airplanes, meeting with potential donors, recruiting dozens of new volunteers, and helping the team build Phoenix's New England presence. At the same time, we were expanding the programs in our Colorado and California locations.

In my nonexistent free time, I was trying to figure out how to take The Phoenix to scale to meet the growing need for an empowerment approach to addiction recovery. Then in early December 2018, I got a call from Tommy Fijacko, Stand Together Foundation's investment manager for The Phoenix. He was hoping I could find time in my schedule to discuss something important. "Let's do it," I said.

I've always had trouble treating time as a finite resource. Being someone who's very relational, it's important to me to spend time with people in an authentic way. And having not spent too much time studying the principles of physics, I tend to view time as endlessly expandable. My schedulers take a slightly more structured approach.

"Scott's calendar is basically full for the next month," my besieged senior executive assistant, Renee White, told Tommy. Renee, who'd come to me from the state capitol, functioned more like my chief of staff, helping me prioritize my competing work and personal obligations. "He does have a brief layover in Dallas next week," she added helpfully.

"I'll take it," Tommy said.

Renee told me Tommy would meet me on December 11 in the lobby of the airport Hyatt Regency hotel for thirty minutes before my connecting flight back to Denver. I was glad we were both going to be in Dallas at the same time; that mitigated one scheduling headache.

"Hey, Tommy," I said when I saw him. "What brings you to Dallas?"

"I'm here just to see you," Tommy said.

This caught me by surprise. "You flew all the way to Dallas just to have a thirty-minute meeting with me?" I said. I wasn't sure whether to feel flattered or apprehensive. Could they fire Catalyst partners, I wondered?

Tommy got right to the point. In the gentlest, most encouraging way possible, he told me the vision and goals we had for The Phoenix were extraordinary. But our management culture—best characterized as "we'll figure it out as we go"—was never going to get us there. We were spending too much time putting out management fires. It was one thing to learn about best practices in a classroom; we needed to start applying them. That stung a little, but it had the ring of truth.

"Scott, we deeply believe in what you're building at The Phoenix," Tommy said. "You see the potential in people—*all* people—in the same way we do. We want to help you grow that."

I nodded. Jacki and I had long dreamed of the day we'd meet up with a group of people who truly understood the magic of The Phoenix and supported our unique approach to addiction recovery. I was now surer than ever that Stand Together Foundation was that group.

Tommy liked to talk in terms of "mental models." For tonight's lesson he needed an especially good one to compete with the distracting aroma of Texas tacos and an unending string of airline gate announcements. He chose the Rosetta Stone. The most famous piece of rock in the world, this inscribed slab of granite became the key that unlocked the mysterious hieroglyphic script of ancient Egypt.

The Rosetta Stone that would unlock the value in our partnership with Stand Together Foundation, he said, was right under our noses; it lay in realizing the full potential of all our people. Jacki and I had a tight grip on the organization; we were overly protective of it. We needed to start trusting everyone who worked at The Phoenix in the same way we believed in our members. And we needed to start really leaning into Principle Based Management.

In terms of my ability to become fully self-actualized and achieve my goal of helping millions of others in recovery do the same, this was a textbook "teachable moment." How many start-ups with ingenious ideas to change the world have fizzled out for lack of good leadership? I didn't want The Phoenix to be one of them.

In Catalyst training we'd learned that organizations are like mini societies. Working in concert, the population is much smarter than any one individual. In an open, collaborative environment, where every person is empowered to bring their best to the table, the group accomplishes things together that any one of them could not have accomplished on their own.

"What I'm saying is that the beliefs that inform how you see and engage with members of The Phoenix can be applied in a management context," Tommy explained. "It can help you transform the inner workings of The Phoenix—not into some totally different thing, but into a powerful expression of the very beliefs you already hold. I think going all in on Principle Based Management is the game changer you and I have been looking for, the one that will help many more people find recovery, strength, and hope through you. It can supercharge your work."

"All right," I said. "All right, Tommy. Let's do this. I'm all in."

* * *

It seemed like some of the best ideas I got from my mentors at Stand Together came informally and unexpectedly, whether it was during a hastily arranged conversation at an airport gate or while chatting casually with colleagues during a meeting break.

Like the day back in 2017 when Evan Feinberg pulled me aside during one of my visits to his office in Arlington. "Hey, did you ever see that movie about Facebook?" he asked. "It's called *The Social Network*." I had.

"In it there's a moment when Sean Parker, who started Napster, tells Mark Zuckerberg, who founded Facebook, 'Instead of calling it The Facebook, you should drop the "The" and just be Facebook.'" Evan then said to me, "I have that moment for you right now. Instead of Phoenix Multisport, just *add* a 'The' and drop the 'Multisport.' That would signal to the recovery community you don't need to be an athlete to join. And it would differentiate you from the city of Phoenix." In September 2017 we officially became The Phoenix.

The airport conversation I had with Tommy a year later was the gateway to more substantial conversations, however, and thus a turning point. We needed to break free of the traditional nonprofit programmatic mindset. We weren't a gym-based, fitness-only recovery program. In fact, we didn't think of The Phoenix as a program at all. We were building a strength-based recovery movement.

We wanted to disrupt the prevailing paradigm—the one that writes off people with substance use disorders as a drag on society. Instead, let's unleash their enormous untapped potential. How? By treating them with dignity. By focusing on their future instead of their past. By bonding over shared goals. By believing in them before they believe in themselves.

* * *

All that might sound Pollyannaish. But I know it works. I've seen countless individuals from all walks of life, from rich to poor, people who live in tent cities in open drug markets, men and women of all ages and backgrounds, whom society views as hopeless cases—"*those* people"—come to The Phoenix and turn their lives around.

People like Tiffany Foster, our volunteer manager for the New England region. From the time Tiffany was seven to seventeen, her dad was in prison and her mom was in and out of recovery. She was pretty much raised by a bunch of "uncles" who worked in the barroom where her mom drank. One day one of those uncles gave Tiffany a pain pill for a toothache. The relief it brought felt like a "big, warm hug." Tiffany, who was just sixteen, spent the next decade chasing that nice warm hug. The drug? OxyContin.

While in prison, Tiffany's dad had gotten sober and had earned a degree as a paralegal. The plan was for her to live with him when he got out and then go to college. But with no support services upon reentry, Tiffany's dad relapsed. He came to her high school graduation in June; in July Tiffany's mom called to tell her he'd overdosed and died. "My life got very dark after that," she told me.

Through her mom's drug dealers, Tiffany got wrapped up in "escorting," a euphemism for human trafficking, which got her access to more drugs. But the drugs stopped working because the things she had to do to get them were so painful. The stigma and shame that came with sex work were even worse than the stigma and shame of addiction. Tiffany now shares about it so others don't have to suffer in silence.

To escape the pain, she started using drugs to the point it was a full-time job just to keep her conscious—she was given a "Section 35" (court-ordered treatment) fifteen times. "If I wasn't in a hotel room, I was either in detox, jail, a Section 35 facility, or on the streets," she says. "I made myself discardable." Until one day she woke up in a wooded park in Boston, on a dirty mattress, covered with frost, next to a guy she thought was dead. And in that moment, she says, "I realized I didn't want to die."

Tiffany called her mom, who by then had gotten sober. She returned home to New Bedford, got into treatment, and began a remarkable recovery journey. (She and others share their stories at thephoenix.org.) Since finding her way to The Phoenix, Tiffany has, through her outreach, impacted at least five thousand lives. And they, in turn, now impact thousands more lives. That's how I know there is enormous potential in every one of what society dismisses as "those people." And that's how we build a movement.

Once we trained our staff to start thinking big like that and helped them develop the capabilities to advance that vision, we were all off and running. At The Phoenix, that's not a cliché. We mean it literally.

* * *

On the evening of June 6, 2019, Jacki and I checked into the Hilton Garden Inn in Arlington, by now our home away from home, across the street from Stand Together's headquarters. We'd been invited to join Evan, Tommy, and a few others on their team for a two-day Phoenix brainstorming retreat beginning the next day.

Evan and Tommy were ready to go big with The Phoenix—really big—and they wanted our boldest, best, most audacious ideas for how we were going to get there. To get our neurons firing, they'd catered in breakfast from the nearby Corner Bakery. Jacki loaded up on coffee while I gulped down a sausage, egg, and cheese croissant. "That's going to put you to sleep," Jacki whispered.

"Nope," I assured her. "My adrenaline is pumping."

I got the ball rolling by throwing out some numbers we considered our Phoenix stretch goals. "We have a multiyear strategy to get to forty thousand members within five years," I told the group. "We've grown to seven thousand members in just two years, thanks to your investments. We think we can increase that by as much as 500 percent by 2024."

I looked around at the group expectantly. I saw Jacki trying to read the room as well. If we were anticipating murmurs of approval and enthusiastic high-fives, we didn't get them. If anything, Evan looked frustrated, maybe even a little exasperated. "Just think about it," he said. "You have the opportunity to change addiction recovery in America. To be the leader of a movement. To totally change the way the country thinks about this."

He let that sink in. And it did, deeply. Then he continued, "Recognizing the enormity of the problem and having learned from all you've done so far with The Phoenix, if you could start again today with no constraints on your thinking, what kind of impact could you make? Instead of thinking about forty thousand, how would you approach this differently if your goal was four hundred thousand?"

I glanced at Jacki, who had written "400,000" on her notepad and was now staring at it. I started doing some fast math in my head (fast math for me being the ultimate oxymoron). Everybody else in the room was silent, intrigued to see where this was going.

The question Evan asked next made it clear he saw four hundred thousand as just the tip of the iceberg: "Do you want to be a 10 percent organization or a 10X organization?"

As he explained it, 10 percent thinking drives slow, safe, incremental change. Do what's always been done, just do it a little better. That's the route most companies take. By contrast, 10X thinking—in our case, coming up with revolutionary ways to integrate 10 times as many members into the Phoenix community (and we consider friends, loved ones, and advocates part of our community) instead of just 10 percent more—can accelerate change by orders of magnitude. But that would mean adopting a more aggressive risk profile.

The funny thing was, I thought we *already* had an aggressive risk profile. But Evan had just lobbed a mental grenade that blew up all our traditional thinking. To achieve our vision at that scale would require a truly disruptive approach.

Equally important, it meant tying our stretch goals to *impact* rather than *effort*. (In the sixties, NASA's mission was to walk on the moon. Training astronauts and building new rockets were just part of the effort to achieve it.) So what did we actually want to accomplish, and what would it take to make that happen? The 10X concept, introduced by sales expert Grant Cardone in his book *The 10X Rule: The Only Difference Between Success and Failure*, was catalytic for me.

I started riffing out loud. "Well, to get to four hundred thousand, we'd need to transition to a largely volunteer-driven model." Our staff, who historically ran Phoenix programs themselves, would need to go from being changemakers to changemaker-makers. If we could inspire more entrepreneurial volunteers, based on some experimentation we'd done, each one of them could impact one hundred people. "That would mean we'd need to recruit four thousand volunteers all over the country to lead local Phoenix teams. That's what it would take to get to that number."

"Well, that sounds doable," Evan said. "That sounds like something you could tackle." Jacki agreed with me that it probably was. "Now if you can prove that you can make progress on that, then I think we could get excited about the kind of major numbers that could actually get us down that path," Evan said.

Jacki and I were still wrapping our minds around the idea of growing the Phoenix community to 400,000 members—a more than 50X increase. I considered that "major." Now Tommy jumped up and took on the aura of an auctioneer, opening our minds to bolder possibilities. "If you can get to 400,000, what about 500,000?" he asked.

"Yeah, we could do that," we said.

"What about 750,000?" With enough support, sure. Tommy's theatrics were working. "So," he asked, pausing for dramatic effect, "could The Phoenix commit to reaching a million people in the next five years?"

My mind was spinning. But this was no time to think small. "We probably could."

"Great," Tommy said. "I know one million seems like a powerful number. But it represents just a fraction of the millions of Americans who currently identify as struggling with substance use. That seems reachable enough. It's a good moonshot goal to aspire to. Forget the incremental one hundred thousand people. We want to reach millions."

Evan brought it back to impact. "Stand Together Foundation isn't trying to be a more effective philanthropy," he said. "We want to change the very paradigms on which philanthropy is built. There are tens of millions of Americans experiencing addiction. No matter how many we reach directly, it will never be enough to change the life of each person who is suffering. But if every friend, family member, and ally out there starts taking a strengths-based empowerment approach to help people overcome their addiction, it will extend our reach exponentially. That's the paradigm shift we want to achieve through our partnership with The Phoenix."

* * *

We spent the next day and a half figuring out what we'd need to do to take the Phoenix model and mindset—one based on the inherent value of every human being, no matter how dire their circumstances—and turn it into a movement. It was an animated, interactive conversation, with everyone in the room jumping up and adding big ideas to sticky notes that were plastered all over the walls. What capabilities did we need to add? What key institutions and industries could be barriers or boosters to a new approach to recovery? The legal system? Education? Music?

By the end of the two days, our meeting room looked like a scene from *A Beautiful Mind,* the film about the brilliant but delusional mathematician John Nash, who scribbled incomprehensible equations all over his office windows. Unlike Nash, we weren't destined to win a Nobel Prize. But we weren't delusional, either. We knew we were onto something that would make a big difference in the world.

It crossed my mind that what was working for The Phoenix, a community of people who lifted each other up rather than pushed each other down, could work for our increasingly polarized nation as well. But that was a mission for another day. By the time Jacki and I walked back to our hotel, late on June 7, we were too mentally wiped out to even have dinner together.

We both went to our rooms, ordered room service, then texted back and forth for a little while—I think mine said something to the effect of

"What the hell just happened? Did we just agree to what I think we did?" We'd arrived with ambitious plans to grow The Phoenix to forty thousand members in the next few years. We were leaving having committed to serving a million people as our first target and eventually adding an *s* to the end of that.

"Yep. Crazy, right?" Jacki texted back. "Can we do this?"

"I hope so," I replied. "If we really want to change the way the whole country thinks about addiction, crazy is probably the only way to get there."

Jacki wrote right back, "At least Stand Together is our kind of crazy. But what we're really talking about is creative destruction." That's a phrase economist Joseph Schumpeter coined back in 1942 to describe industry's need to constantly destroy paradigms, methods, and tools that worked in the past in order to create better alternatives. This process applies to the nonprofit world as well.

I thought about Jacki's last text as I lay in bed staring at the ceiling all night, my mind swimming with the urgent opportunities and daunting challenges that lay ahead—and the $64,000 question: Are we up to the task? Can we really do this? I finally fell asleep with the words of civil rights activist John Lewis crowding out all other thoughts: "If not us, then who?"

CHAPTER FORTY-THREE

LOCKDOWN

On January 16, 2020, Stand Together Foundation issued a press release announcing its commitment of up to $50 million to help The Phoenix reach one million people impacted by addiction by 2025. It also highlighted our intention to transform how the country thinks about and approaches people struggling with addiction—away from top-down efforts that see them as broken and deficient and toward a bottom-up approach grounded in human resiliency.

The new decade was off to a promising start.

Jacki and I thought a winter retreat in a quiet locale would be the best way to coalesce the entire staff around our bold new vision. So we booked the Stanley Hotel in Estes Park, Colorado—why, I'm not sure, since it happened to be the inspiration for Stephen King's *The Shining*. "Hey, Jacki," I joked, "are we sure this is the vibe we're going for?"

We had pretty much the whole hotel to ourselves; not many people stay there in February. It's located at the edge of Rocky Mountain National Park. The isolation and emptiness added to the eeriness of it. (At the time, we couldn't have anticipated how unnatural the year ahead would prove to be.) So we had some fun with it. We had a treasure hunt throughout the hotel with clues like "What's the number of the most haunted room in the hotel?" (The answer: Room 217.) And naturally, being a sober active community, we ended the retreat with a hike in the park.

But the focus of the retreat was to ground the whole staff—which back then numbered around sixty, half the size we are now—in the guiding principles that make The Phoenix special. That way everyone would leave the Stanley and return to their own communities aligned on vision and values.

They'd flown in from all over the country with a mixture of anticipation and trepidation. Growth was good, they agreed, although our hockey stick growth vision would prove harder for some than others. Reaching more people who needed our help was essential. At that point we had brick-and-mortar facilities in just three states. And volunteer-led activities and the use of CrossFit gyms in twenty-two more.

The way forward, I told them, just as I'd told Evan and Tommy, was to go from being changemakers to changemaker-makers. In other words, to find people all over the country who shared our vision and values and train them how to create their own local Phoenix communities.

This scared some people. "Can volunteers lead Phoenix as impactfully as staff can?" someone asked, voicing a broadly shared concern.

"I'm worried it will dilute the Phoenix experience," a colleague chimed in.

"But wait a minute," I said. "I was a Phoenix volunteer for ten years. Have I led impactful Phoenix events?" They agreed that I had. "So I can point to one volunteer who has been deeply committed. I'm sure there's more out there."

Jacki pointed to another compelling reason to adopt a more flexible growth model. "Our need is so great as a nation, we're losing so many loved ones, and this issue is causing so much despair that people everywhere are reaching out to us for help," she said. "So if a 70 percent version of The Phoenix everywhere allows us to answer that call, isn't that a bet worth taking? And isn't that better than having a 100 percent version of The Phoenix in just a few places?"

Not everyone agreed; we lost three key employees because of the stress and tension this new scale model created. (We would later learn that volunteer-led programs created equally successful outcomes as programs led by staff.)

There were also concerns about performance. If you're in charge of helping The Phoenix expand into new markets, and we're going from two new markets a year to two new markets a month, that's a much different tempo. And if you're trying to raise money, everything has to more than double. So everything got amped up. I was feeling pretty stressed out myself; there were times I wasn't sure we could make it to the next evolution.

I found there comes a painful moment when people begin feeling overstretched and start losing their inspiration relative to the vision. I could feel a bit of that at the Stanley Hotel. That's when you need to stay the course, knowing if you can get through this storm, the port is there. You must have faith.

We had little nuggets of proof that it was possible—and necessary. On my Instagram and Facebook pages and through emails, texts, and phone calls, there was always somebody reaching out saying, "I have a loved one who's dying or suffering or struggling. If The Phoenix were here, I think it could help them." That's when I started thinking, "Instead of us trying to get there to help them, how can we empower them to be the help that they're looking for?"

That was an idea most members of the team got excited about. "We've held The Phoenix close enough for all these years that we know what is important to protect. We want to be tight on vision and culture. We can be looser on the other stuff. Let's get out of the way of the people who want to help us scale The Phoenix."

We'd changed our name from Phoenix Multisport to The Phoenix because we are more than just fitness. We're a book club, we have painting, and art night, and socials, and Halloween parties. Gingerbread cookie making and decorating around the holidays. It was becoming so much more because every volunteer who raised their hand had their own unique gifts. But to give them a place to express those gifts, we had to be flexible enough to change what we thought The Phoenix was into what we thought The Phoenix could be.

And through all of that, we just kept reminding ourselves, "We won't achieve extraordinary 10X results with conventional 10 percent thinking."

* * *

So we said goodbye to our rooms at the haunted hotel and headed back to our respective homes and offices, revved up and ready to save the world. Stand Together Foundation was about to process its next payment to The Phoenix. We were all systems go.

Little more than a month later, on March 13, the White House declared the novel coronavirus (COVID-19) a national emergency. Shortly thereafter, the nation went into lockdown.

It was to become, as we know, a global pandemic with tragic consequences. Many communities suffered devastating tolls. But my first thought was for the millions of people struggling with substance use disorders. I knew they'd be among the hardest hit, because social isolation is fertile ground for addiction to take hold.

I got on the phone immediately with my board and leadership team to figure out what to do. The verdict was unanimous: "We've got to pivot to virtual *now*. We need to do it today." Zoom and Microsoft Teams were around but were far from the household words they are today. So I called Tommy at Stand Together Foundation and said, "Hey, given the direction I think the pandemic's going to go, and what we're hearing about all these shutdowns, are you guys still down for this movement-of-millions idea and the fifty-million-dollar pledge?"

I was thinking, "No way are they going to send us the next five million bucks now. Everybody's going to be thinking, 'How many on staff must we fire? Which vendor contracts can we cancel?'" Not to mention Stand Together's donor community had their own businesses to run. Those companies were going to be in turmoil.

"Nothing changes for us," Tommy told me. "We're in."

We weren't on Zoom, so he couldn't see me tearing up. I couldn't believe they were sticking with us through this. "We want to go 100 percent virtual, immediately," I told him.

"That makes total sense," Tommy said. "Let's keep this going. Keep your foot on the gas."

* * *

Just forty-eight hours after the declaration of a national emergency, we held our first virtual event. We'd quickly revised our calendar of activities and posted it on our Facebook pages. That Sunday I did a coffee social on Zoom from my house. I love coffee, so I thought it would be fun to teach people how to make pour-over coffee, which you do by manually pouring hot water over coffee grounds. I taught the folks who joined how to prep the filter and grind the beans and prewarm the mug.

"At a time when life might feel like it's spiraling out of our control," I said with a hint of a smile, "it's nice to know we can control all the variables in the coffee brewing process." That got some laughs. Then I just sat and drank coffee with them and talked about recovery. We'd never done anything like that before, and a lot of Phoenix members hadn't spent much time with me, so it was cool.

We had to come up with standard operating procedures for Zoom programs and teach people about their cameras and how to stay on mute. We also had to point out that just because they were on mute didn't mean their camera was off. We'd be wrapping up a workout, and someone would start changing their shirt on camera. Or someone would be in their bedroom, and their husband would walk through getting ready to take a shower. It was all the Zoom mistakes everyone was making in the early days (and some to this day) of the pandemic.

I did my Zoom coffee meetup three weeks in a row. We then started adding a whole bunch of stuff, like meditation and yoga and CrossFit workouts. For the latter, we had a "Find Your Heavy Object" segment so people could turn household items into free weights. Somebody used their cast-iron skillet as their heavy object, and somebody else used a sandbag. One mom grabbed a diaper bag and stuffed it with heavy books while their two-year-old ran around in the background.

It was insane. We were learning on the fly. But the fabric that bound The Phoenix remained intact. We were a community, and we were all in this together.

Now, five years later, we've run many thousands of virtual events; they've been so successful in broadening access we've kept them going. Best of all, we were surprised and pleased to discover that our virtual programming impact numbers, based on self-reported life transformation scores from the people on our virtual platform, are almost the same as they are for in-person programming. Our virtual pivot was a literal lifesaver.

We also took advantage of the early days of the pandemic to drive forward our talent acquisition plans so that when we emerged from lock-down, we'd have teams ready to go in multiple markets to start driving the Phoenix movement.

We knew the social isolation COVID-19 imposed would have a com-pounding effect on the deaths of despair—in particular, as it turned out, overdose deaths—that were robbing families and the nation at large of so much human potential. More than anything, we wanted to be there when people emerged so we could grab their hand.

CHAPTER FORTY-FOUR

AT LONG LAST, "I DO!"

For a couple years after Mom passed, Kait and I spent more time together focusing on our relationship. She joined me on many Phoenix work trips, which we'd sometimes extend into short mini vacations. Given the sobering work of The Phoenix, that was about as carefree as we got.

We enjoyed one particularly happy West Coast weekend in Huntington Beach, California, where we'd traveled to check in on The Phoenix's Orange County program. Afterward we squeezed in some surfing and road cruiser bike rides along the Huntington Beach bicycle trail, which borders the Pacific Ocean.

We also took a week and went to Maui. Before that I'd taken a full week off just once since starting The Phoenix twelve years earlier. It was Kait's first time in Hawaii. We snorkeled with sea turtles and sat in the sand together watching sunsets over neighboring Lanai.

On our last day in paradise, as we sat on the beach dreading our return to real life, we got an emergency alert: "Ballistic missile threat inbound to Hawaii. Seek immediate shelter." The second part of the message scared the hell out of us: "This is not a drill." There are very few things as effective at snapping you out of your laid-back island vibe as a ballistic missile threat.

After a frantic ten minutes in survival mode grabbing water bottles and trying to find a concrete stairwell or somewhere else safe to hide, Kait and I decided the wisest course of action was to sit on the beach and enjoy our final sunset in Maui—and possibly on Earth. Under the circumstances, what else could we do? By the time we saw on CNN that it had been a false alarm, vendors in town were already selling T-shirts that said, "I survived the ballistic missile threat."

Over the next couple years, we also made several trips to Boston, which was now The Phoenix's East Coast headquarters. We loved trying new restaurants in the North End, Boston's Little Italy, although that marked the beginning of a longstanding argument with Kait: our debate about Modern's cannoli versus Mike's continues to this day. Of course, Modern's are better. (When Kait writes her book, she can make a plug for Mike's.)

As we started to dream about all the adventures we could share together, our lives began to get much bigger. But while I was consumed with building The Phoenix, a passion Kait shared, I could sense she was longing for something that was more her own.

On a rare rainy afternoon in Denver, in August 2017, Kait came into my study and joined me on the small sofa. I could tell she was contemplating something big. I was right. "Do you think I could race an Ironman?" she asked.

I didn't even have to think about it. "Of course!" I answered. "You are a strong runner and so athletic overall. You would have no problem with it. You would just have to train in a focused way."

Kait flipped open her laptop. Staring at the registration page for Ironman Lake Placid, she paused. "This is crazy. I don't even know how to swim a lap. Should I really do it?" she asked again.

"Absolutely," I encouraged her. "You have the determination. The discipline. You can do this."

With a few keystrokes and a click of the mouse, she signed up to race her first Ironman, in just 11 months' time. It was a 2.4-mile swim, a 112-mile bike ride, and a 26.2-mile run. Kait had never raced a triathlon or run a marathon. She had to YouTube how to put on a swim cap. And her most serious cycling had been biking back and forth from the store with groceries hanging from her handlebars because she had lost her license for a DUI. But I believed in her.

I put her in touch with my old triathlon coach, and Kait worked her ass off. That's the only way to say it. She adopted the mindset of a professional athlete and treated it like it was her full-time job. Her coach signed her up for a series of smaller races leading up to the main event—a sprint triathlon in San Diego (the first time Kait ever wore a wetsuit) followed by an Olympic distance race, and then a Half Ironman in Raleigh, North Carolina. She did so well in Raleigh that she qualified for the Half Ironman World Championships in South Africa in September 2018.

In July 2018, Kait accomplished her stretch goal, the one she'd nearly dismissed as inconceivable a year earlier, competing in Lake Placid Ironman. Watching her cross the finish line, wearing her Phoenix triathlon suit, I was overcome with emotion. "You did it," I said. I'd posted photos on The Phoenix's Facebook page, and the congratulatory messages were flooding in. "We're all so proud of you."

The heartfelt hug I gave Kait at the finish line nearly crushed her. But the moment was bittersweet. Lake Placid had been my first Ironman as well. And my mom had been standing in this same spot, waiting for me at the end. I knew somewhere up there Mom was smiling ear to ear and yelling down, "You go, Katie!"

Kait took a short break, trained some more, and in September we flew to South Africa for the Half Ironman World Championships. She placed, as she put it, "smack dab in the middle," which was damn impressive given she was racing against the fastest women in the world, with less than a year's experience. Kait was once again wearing a Phoenix triathlon suit, and I had my Phoenix T-shirt on, as always. It was our way of publicly sharing what's so special about The Phoenix: we replace shame in addiction with pride in sobriety.

* * *

For anyone who's feeling dubious that two people in long-term recovery, both with significant emotional baggage, could end up in what sounds like a fantastical, happy-ever-after Hallmark-movie romance, let me put your mind at ease: we weren't that couple.

Throughout our relationship, Kait and I have worked through some dramatic highs and lows; our diametrically different emotional ranges and styles of dealing with conflict, and the trauma we'd both experienced, could come out in some pretty ugly ways that brought us to the precipice of a breakup more than once. Grace, sobriety, love, and a commitment not to give up on each other are what got us through.

* * *

By 2019, after all we'd gone through with my mom and with each other, I'd gotten to a point where I couldn't envision my life without Kait in it. We balanced each other out. I brought the calming energy, and she brought the fire energy. At least, that's how Kait put it. And we both felt safe being vulnerable with one another, which was a first for both of us. There was something really special about that.

Now I just had to come up with the perfect time and place to pop the question. We had a vacation to Bora Bora planned for July. That seemed like a contender. I figured as engagement spots go, we could do a lot worse than a romantic Polynesian paradise. I wasn't positive I'd propose there, but I bought a ring knowing what was in my heart.

When you're living with somebody and packing for a trip overseas, it's hard to hide stuff. I was worrying, "Where am I going to hide this ring?" I like photography as a hobby, so I decided to hide it in my camera bag with all my camera stuff. Then I started agonizing about leaving it unattended because now my camera bag had more than doubled in value. Luckily the bag and the ring made it safely to Bora Bora, though I think Kait questioned the wisdom of filling up our small room safe with my camera bag.

Shortly after checking in, we had an argument. "Oh no," I thought. "This is not the best start to a trip where I'm thinking about proposing." But then I thought, "This is just life. We will have ups and downs and peaks and valleys, and some of the most meaningful experiences we've had involved helping each other climb out of the valleys."

So we started enjoying ourselves and taking in the spectacular scenery. Under the guise of having a new camera, I took a ton of pictures of Kait, but in reality I was scouting for a beautiful spot for the proposal. I wanted to record the big moment, so she was my excuse for putting my camera on a tripod. Unfortunately, every time I had the camera set up, ready to record, a group of tourists would stroll by, or some other hotel guests would drag their beach towels right into the frame, or some kids would run by with a Frisbee.

I finally found a more secluded spot. We were sitting on the beach, and I was a little jittery because I knew it was now or never. By this point, Kait was over my sudden obsession with photographing her. "All right, I'm good," she said. "I'm done with photos for the day."

I think I had 350 photos at that point. Meanwhile, I was just waiting and waiting for the world's slowest paddle boarder to paddle out of the frame. I was going nuts, thinking, "Oh my God, this guy's so slow." It was like a sitcom, with him paddling in slow motion out of the shot.

Finally, I said, "OK, one more. Turn around. Now look out to sea." I walked up behind her and got down on one knee. She turned around and—in a reaction she jokes she'll regret for the rest of her life—she said, loudly, "Shut up!" She was blown away. But she did say yes. And we have all of that on video. So it turned out to be really special.

About an hour later, she started having doubts. "Is this really what we want to do? What if it's wrong and we're not right for each other?" I wasn't entirely surprised. It was the first mature, healthy relationship Kait and I had ever had, and she was still learning to trust the normalness of it. I fell back on what Kait had said to me earlier when my love-avoidance tendencies kicked in: "Well, let's just try, and if it doesn't work, then it doesn't work. But let's just try and see where it leads us."

* * *

We planned to get married at the Boston Public Library in January 2020. It was going to be a black-tie affair with 350 guests. We had the invitations stamped and ready to go. Caterer, photographer, and florist arranged. Such an exciting occasion. So why weren't we happy and excited?

Kait was the one who pulled the plug. "Scott, I can't do this," she said, sitting in front of the box of wedding invitations. "I can't put these in the mail. It doesn't feel right." I couldn't wait to be Kait's husband. I'd been looking forward to this day. But I knew what she meant. We were both very private people, and the wedding planning had taken on a life of its own. It didn't feel like ours anymore.

"It's fine," I said. "We'll get married when and how we want to. We'll consider our deposit a donation to the library." She was grateful to me for being so understanding. But I knew it would happen when the time was right.

Plan B was to elope in the spring. We figured we'd invite only our families and rent a villa on the Amalfi Coast. This time it was fate, not Kait, that stepped in. We'd just returned from the staff retreat at the Stanley Hotel when we started hearing more about some new virus in China, not long after the first case had been reported in the Pacific Northwest. "Maybe we should try to plan this trip sooner rather than later," I told Kait. "It sounds like travel could get weird." Within weeks, Italy had joined China as ground zero for COVID-19.

Being the designated "slow, calm, giant comfort creature" in the relationship (again, Kait's words), I took it in stride. "Let's just see what happens," I said. "Maybe this will blow over."

By summer, we were both struggling. We'd been living together since soon after we met. But Kait wasn't used to having me underfoot 24-7, nor was I used to being so stationary. I'd spent a lifetime on boats, planes, and mountains. I knew I had it better than most. But I was driving us both crazy. For Kait's sanity and my own, I needed a project away from the house.

The solution, I decided, was to take up gardening. So I set about building a cedar garden box in the backyard. It soon became apparent that my woodworking skills far surpassed my gardening skills. "I can't stop this zucchini plant from spitting out zucchinis and, every now and then, a tomato," I told Kait in frustration. "But I can't get anything else to grow."

I took a brief work trip in July, and when I returned, Kait asked me to go out back. "There's this crazy blue thing in the garden, and I don't know what it is."

"What do you mean?" I asked.

"You've just got to check it out," she said. "It's near the tomato plant."

So I went out to look. There, under the tomato plant, she had hidden a pregnancy test, with the blue strip showing it was positive. She'd stashed her phone in the bushes so she could get a little video—of me in tears, as usual. "Congratulations," she said, with the sweetest, most joyful smile. "You're going to be a dad."

* * *

On October 10, 2020, more than a year after I'd proposed in Bora Bora, Kait and I finally got married in a small ceremony in a vineyard in Napa Valley, California, with a dozen members of our immediate family with us to celebrate. My brother Mark was there with his wife, Lisa, and his four daughters. Kait's parents and brothers had flown in, along with her sister and her young children, including a newborn. As if we hadn't faced enough hurdles already, it was wildfire season, and two of the places in Napa where we'd planned to get married burned down.

But in the end, everything came together. Even Kait's wedding dress. With the help of two pairs of Spanx, she was able to fit into the one she'd bought for the ceremony we'd planned for January, despite being fourteen weeks pregnant. Which nobody was aware of—until the reception. In our toast, we said, "Thank you all for coming, and braving the fires, and braving the pandemic, and flying cross-country with newborns." Then we paused and smiled, and Kait's hand moved reflexively to her stomach. "The *three* of us are just so happy you're all here."

* * *

Kait and I had decided we wanted our baby to be born in Boston. Our plan was to move back there for a year, then return to Denver and move back into our house, which was being renovated. We spent our honeymoon in Maui; we were on the very first plane to land in Hawaii once lockdown restrictions started easing up. A week later we flew back to Denver, got our stuff, and Kait caught a flight to Boston. I drove back east in my truck, pulling her car behind.

It felt surreal, making the return trip cross-country, thinking of how my life had changed since the day I'd said goodbye to my pal at the ATM machine before getting on the Massachusetts Turnpike and heading west. I'd left Boston sixteen years earlier as a young man in recovery, still searching for the thing that would fill the void within. I was pretty sure it involved helping others with substance use disorder rise, recover, and thrive.

Now I was returning as a husband and soon-to-be-father, in recovery for nearly twenty-four years. Best of all, the Phoenix community was poised to reach a million people with addiction issues over the next five years, empowering them and their loved ones to find joy in sobriety. "Not a bad payoff for an unplanned solo road trip," I thought to myself as I took the exit and headed into the heart of the city. But I had to wonder: "What new and unexpected challenges and opportunities would this next chapter hold?"

PART V

BACK TO BOSTON

We as humans naturally gravitate to places where we feel accepted and loved. For people with substance use disorders, The Phoenix is one such place. But it's not just people with addictions who need nurturing and support. Imagine if as a society we could help give that to each other. That sounds like a lofty goal, but I don't think it is.

SCOTT STRODE

CHAPTER FORTY-FIVE

"LET'S ALL GO TO FRANCE."

I had my last conversation with my dad, the charismatic, creative, emotionally erratic, all-too-human Jack Strode, on December 9, 2020. That afternoon a nurse called from Montana to tell me he was in hospice so if there were any last things I wanted to tell him, now was the time.

The news caught me off guard; I knew Dad was in declining health, but I was less worried about him than I had been in years. He was finally in a stable living situation where he was safe and had access to food, shelter, and health care, which was a profound relief.

Thanks to the ever-resourceful Renee, who managed all aspects of my life, and to Montana's Department of Social Services, instead of living on the streets, Dad was now living in a good eldercare facility that had a program for "complex" patients.

Prior to that, I'd spent a year paying for him to live in a series of hotel rooms. He would eventually destroy each room and get kicked out, until we ran out of hotels in Kalispell that would allow him to stay.

I'll forever be grateful to the Lakeview Care Center in Big Fork, Montana, for providing a stable living environment for Dad in his final months.

After listening to the Lakeview voice message, I called him immediately, sitting in my parked truck outside our new house in Boston. I wanted to be alone when we spoke. It struck me as ironic, and it made me very sad, that this would be our final car talk. I hoped this one would bring some measure of closure for us both.

Dad was now seventy-nine; I was closing in on forty-eight. But listening to his fantastical rambles on the phone that day, I could have been sitting in the back seat of his car forty years earlier, hurtling through the Lancaster countryside, wondering what was coming next.

On this day, though, I had nothing to fear. He told me how much he loved all his kids and how proud he was of us and how he wanted to go do something with all of us. He had just the place. "Let's all go to France together," he said. "I've heard it's so beautiful. When I'm feeling better, we should go."

I had to smile; that was my father, fashioning his own reality right up to the very end. "Yeah, that sounds good, Dad," I said. "We'll do that."

And then I said something else. Years earlier, after struggling through the "empty chair" exercise at The Meadows, in which I told the chair how much it hurts to know your dad is homeless, the therapist stopped me from returning to my seat. "Is there anything else you want to tell your father?" she asked. I was hit with so many emotions it was hard to get the words out. "I love you," I whispered.

Since then I'd spent years burdened with the fear my dad would die on the streets, alone and unacknowledged, as if he'd never existed. I felt the empty chair would be my only chance to say goodbye, that I'd never get to say it for real.

Now I was getting that chance. "Wait, Dad, there's one more thing," I said as I sat in my car, choking back tears. I was overcome with gratitude that I was getting this moment—the gift of being able to say goodbye. I cleared my throat so he could hear my words very plainly. "I just want you to know I love you."

* * *

Dad died two days later. He'd never met my wife; he would never meet my kids. He'd never been to a Phoenix gym. Which was sad on many levels. But out of self-preservation, I'd had to create boundaries so I could heal. I so badly wanted to be the husband and father he couldn't be.

I never stopped loving my dad or wanting to feel truly loved and accepted by him. He's one of the reasons I find solace in nature. I'll always remember him as the dad who would sit with us at the crest of the hill in the dwindling light of day looking across the field at our farmhouse, teaching us how you could tell where the pheasants were roosting for the night by their call and the sound of their wings. That's who he really was, under his dark cloak of pain and mental illness.

I kept thinking about the transmission of pain from generation to generation "until somebody is willing to feel it." Faced with the prospect of dying on my bathroom floor twenty-four years earlier, I had finally let myself feel it. Now, just months away from becoming a first-time father, I hoped the trauma and recovery work I'd done on myself, within the nurturing environment of the Phoenix community and through my relationship with Kait, would prevent me from passing my pain onto my kids. I told myself with hope and a prayer in my heart, "My kids' story will be different."

CHAPTER FORTY-SIX

"WOW, DADA!"

had my first conversation with my son, Magnus Alexander Strode, on March 19, 2021. Well, it wasn't actually a conversation. It was more along the lines of "I love you. It's so good to meet you. I was getting a little worried; it took you a while to get here. But you hung in there. You are just as tough as your mom." It was clear to me from his robust newborn wails that this was a spirited and precocious kid who understood every word I was saying.

Kait's labor had made her Ironman competitions look like a casual jog. She was pushing hard, unmedicated, for at least six hours, not making enough progress in the opinion of the delivery team. So I was worried about her and the baby. I could see Kait was overcome with fatigue. "We're concerned because she's been pushing for so long," the attending physician told us. The doctor's rough examination techniques on top of her terrible bedside manner heightened the anxiety and agitation in the room. "We're going to come back at midnight. If we haven't made any progress, we may have to do an intervention."

At that point my wife somehow found this moment of composure and grace in the middle of labor and said, "All right, guys. Calm down. Let's make this happen." And she did, with Magnus entering the world just after midnight. Kait held him skin to skin for a few moments as he nursed, and then I got to hold him. I had waited so long to meet this little guy, so feeling his sweet, warm body against my chest was just beautiful.

* * *

With all the red-eye flights I had been taking between Denver and Boston while still living out West, Kait and I had thought about investing in a crash pad near the new Boston-based gym The Phoenix had purchased. Another reason we decided to move to Boston while our home in Denver was being renovated, in addition to wanting Magnus to be born there, was so I could spend more time helping build The Phoenix's East Coast presence.

Add to that, Kait had always dreamed about spending more time in the Boston area, where she'd attended the College of the Holy Cross. But we had no intention of staying for good. "Don't worry!" we told our Colorado friends and coworkers as we packed up all our stuff. "We'll be back in no time." A year later, we put our house in Denver up for sale.

Over the course of those twelve months, Kait and I had both fallen in love with Boston—she for the first time and I through a new set of eyes. Before leaving Denver, we'd found a cozy, two-story brownstone nestled in Boston's South End, next to a small neighborhood park. The first floor is up one level from the street, and we added windows to get light on three sides, so in spring and summer, we're surrounded by leafy trees. We don't even have to close the blinds in the summer. We call it the Tree House because that's how it feels to be in it.

A couple years after moving in, we developed an even deeper connection to Boston: our daughter Alice—or "Baby Alice," as her brother still calls her—joined us in the Tree House.

In many ways it felt like a culminating moment of self-actualization. I'd brought The Phoenix home to Boston, where years earlier my addiction had only deepened the gaping void within me. I'd started The Phoenix to help fill that void—to help myself by helping others. Now The Phoenix was poised to help countless other people like me transform their own lives.

On the personal front, through our sobriety and recovery, Kait and I would get to raise our kids in a home where trauma wouldn't be present the way it was for me. We had no illusions we'd be perfect parents; it's so easy to create an impossible expectation of yourself in that role. Where

Kait and I landed was that we'd do our best and try to be aware enough to apologize when we didn't do it perfectly and hope that would make a difference for our kids.

I created my template for what good parenting should be by watching my brother. In the same way he taught me how to shave, he showed me how to be a dad. Mark and I taught each other how to be men in the world because, other than Pop-Pop, we didn't have any strong, sober, nurturing men in the family to model ourselves after. Prime example: When Mark loses his temper or yells at his kids, he always says he's sorry. I don't remember the adults in our lives ever apologizing for anything.

* * *

No matter what kind of day I'm having, no matter how frustrating or depressing or stressful, two words can turn it around: "Wow, Dada." I'll be in the park with Magnus, and he'll squat down and notice an army of ants crawling in procession across a rock and study them, fascinated. "Wow, Dada." And I'll squat down next to him and realize that, wow, nature does have this inherent beauty and magic to it that we overlook or take for granted in the grind of daily life.

One day recently, Magnus and I got up even earlier than usual and I opened the blinds in our living room to a spectacular sunrise. The morning sky was a watercolor painting of vivid pinks and reds. This delighted my son. "Wow, Dada!" I was delighted too. Because wow, it is pretty wild that this thing is coming up over the horizon and brightening our kitchen from more than ninety million miles away.

But as I knelt down next to Magnus, the "wow" I echoed back came from a deeper place. What engulfed me in that moment was the peace and serenity of knowing here I was with my sweet son, watching a new day begin, while my wife and daughter were upstairs safely sleeping. I was filled with joy at the thought of having more of these moments, and I just felt so profoundly grateful.

CHAPTER FORTY-SEVEN

TIME TO HEED THE CANARIES

While I was busy getting married and starting a family—at the same time I was working with increasing urgency to grow the Phoenix movement—the pandemic was taking a devastating toll on the addiction community. In 2020 alone there were an estimated 93,655 drug overdose deaths in the U.S., according to the Centers for Disease Control and Prevention—a 30 percent increase from 2019. The overdose rate had begun accelerating at the beginning of the lockdown in March of that year. In 2021 the number spiked again, to 107,622. No surprise there. For folks battling addiction, isolation is a killer.

Demand for live, virtual Phoenix events—everything from coffee pours to Pilates workouts to weight lifting, yoga workshops, and meditation—started surging from the day we first announced them on our social media channels and remains strong to this day. Our ability to ramp up our online programming overnight enabled us to help eighty-seven thousand people all over America stay safe, sober, and connected during a time when they were at their most vulnerable.

One of those people was a Colorado firefighter named Kara. She shared with some Phoenix donors that we became her lifeline during COVID-19. Facing the unwelcome reality of quarantining alone, most likely drinking every day, she said, "I had to get sober in that moment." To do that, she attended The Phoenix online classes all day long. It was a game changer for her to be able to sign on to her computer and find the support she needed.

Likewise, Samantha, a military vet, joined The Phoenix to get sober during the pandemic and discovered the power of community—she came for the physical fitness but stayed for the camaraderie. Plus, she says, she could afford the cost of membership—just forty-eight hours of sobriety. "It's changed my life."

These stories warmed my heart. But as always, I continued to be plagued by thoughts of the millions of people we *weren't* reaching. In the time it's taken me to write this book, another one hundred thousand people have died of drug- or alcohol-related causes. Many of these fall under the category of "deaths of despair."

This of course coincides with a period of increased political and social polarization in our country. Everybody pointing a finger or slinging a slur or directing a punch at somebody else. Red versus blue. Rural versus urban. Environmentalists versus climate change deniers. Pro-life versus abortion rights. Gun control advocates versus gun rights supporters. Tough on drugs and crime versus smart on drugs and crime.

But instead of gathering and collaborating to find common ground, rather than coming together as neighbors and fellow Americans with a shared love of our country's founding principles, we're vilifying and "othering" each other, focusing on what divides us rather than what unites us. It has started to feel like the fabric of our nation is unraveling—literally fraying at the seams—as we all pull apart.

* * *

Interesting fact: one-sixth of Boston—some five thousand acres—is built on landfill. That's more than in any other American city. Boston was originally a tiny 789-acre peninsula, connected to Massachusetts by a narrow spit of land known as the "Neck." In the 1800s, for a whole bunch of reasons, a vigorous stretch of man-made land-making began. That's why Boston is no longer a peninsula.

There is a bit of irony in the result. Today, residents of some of Boston's seemingly most enduring neighborhoods—such as the South End, where I live, and affluent Back Bay—live and work on surprisingly shaky ground. On the surface, these centuries-old homes and buildings look solid, strong, untouchable. Below ground, though, they are supported by thirty- to forty-foot-long wood pilings that extend down through the landfill to a harder layer of clay. If the water table gets too low, the pilings can be attacked by dry-air microbes that can cause them to rot and crumble. We can't see it, but the danger is always there.

And not just for Bostonians. If you think about it, the pillars upon which America was built—our founding principles, starting with equality and respect for human rights—are just as susceptible to gradual erosion and decay. For these principles to endure, they must support everyone and inform every decision we make as a country in solving complex issues like addiction. If these pillars collapse, so does America as we know it.

To fortify these foundational pillars of our society, we can start by building more inclusive communities that recognize the value in everyone. We need to stop thinking in terms of "us" versus "them." This is the magic that happens at The Phoenix. I've seen it work, so I know it's possible.

* * *

Where I live, and maybe where you do too, it's easy to think of our city as separate neighborhoods instead of one whole. My safe, warm home is located just six blocks from an area of Boston famously known as Methadone Mile. Locals call it "Mass and Cass" because it's where Massachusetts Avenue connects with Melnea Cass Boulevard. You can't miss it; it's right by one of the major I-93 off-ramps. It's a sad, squalid, open drug market, like the Tenderloin in San Francisco or Skid Row in Los Angeles.

The open drug use in Boston is heartbreaking. On a typical night, I'll see a dozen people shooting dope on my way home from work. (The Phoenix is purposely located right down the block.) I regularly stop to see if someone on the ground needs Narcan, the overdose reversal drug, and have had to use it. The area was long referred to as Tent City because of all the makeshift plastic shelters that stretched down several city blocks.

(Late in 2023, with violence at an "untenable" level, our mayor, Michelle Wu, banned the tents. But the drug use and dealing remain rampant.) My family and I live so close that I've found needles in the little park my kids play in next to our house.

The people camped out at Mass and Cass are perhaps the most obvious examples of the canaries among us—the people who are susceptible sooner to societal toxins, whose troubles and vulnerabilities are on public display for all the world to see. And, sometimes, to scorn.

But here's the reality: We're all in the coal mine together. Some of us may have succumbed to the toxic environment first—we see it tragically on our streets in homelessness and poverty and active addiction. And in our shelters and treatment centers and emergency rooms and prisons.

These unhappy places are full of people the outside world views as inherently broken, flawed individuals because they have not coped well with unfortunate circumstances. But we at The Phoenix see it differently. We see that they are us and we are them. These are people with enormous potential. They might be your child or your sister or your friend. They might be you. Just think of how society would benefit if all that human potential could be unleashed.

Instead, we lock them up or hide them on side streets and hope the problem will go away, not considering that *what sickened them is beginning to sicken the rest of us too.* Meanwhile, deaths of despair keep trending upward, robbing families of their loved ones, and communities of precious human assets, at an alarming rate. The message seems clear. The canaries are dying. So why aren't we paying attention?

* * *

I sometimes attend Phoenix events at a CrossFit gym in a rural community in Western Massachusetts. If ever there were a vivid cross-section of American society, this is it. On any given night, in the parking lot I'll see a Trump or Biden/Harris bumper sticker on a pickup truck or SUV next to a car with a pro-choice sticker on it, while inside someone wearing a Pride T-shirt will be talking to someone drinking coffee from a "Live Green" mug. Pick your passion, persuasion, or political preference, and you'll likely find it here.

What you won't find is people divided by their differences.

If not for their shared recovery journey, these are people who might not otherwise have crossed paths. Or, if they did, they might have assumed they had nothing in common. Or that they'd dislike each other. Yet no matter how diverse the group, the Phoenix ethos is always the same. Some people introduce themselves with their pronouns, others don't, nobody passes judgment, and at the end of the workout, everyone is fist-bumping and high-fiving each other—lifting each other up instead of tearing each other down.

Is there a lesson here for broader society? I believe so. The people who show up at The Phoenix have a resilience we could all learn from. What if they have found something special in this safe, supportive, sober active community that we all could benefit from? If it can heal them, maybe it can heal us all.

At The Phoenix, I watch healing happening daily. Folks with ankle monitors, with tattoos on their faces, men and women who'd been asking for money on the street corners of our cities, living under blue tarps and cardboard boxes pieced together, come together and build a nurturing community. One where people see the best in each other, regardless of their differences. Isn't that what we've lost in America and what we're hoping to find?

These folks—and I'm one of them—may be more susceptible to pain and the fear of isolation and the adverse effects of trauma than the average person. We have admittedly adopted unhealthy, hurtful ways to self-medicate and cope. But our illness also puts us ahead of the learning curve on how to recover. It starts with giving each other some grace. Whether in a family unit or a community or in society at-large, the principles and ideals that are the bedrock of The Phoenix culture can be the glue that binds people.

At The Phoenix, we believe in the inherent worth of all individuals. We help ourselves by helping others. We empower people to self-actualize—to find purpose and realize their potential. These principles transcend addiction. They are invaluable in helping us build healthy relationships and fulfilling lives. And isn't that what we all want? Doesn't that feel better than unfriending a family member on Facebook because we disagree with them about climate change?

So instead of getting worked up over all the social media memes and talking heads and media headlines that emphasize our differences and encourage us to pull each other down, I'd like to propose taking some time to learn how this unique group of people within the Phoenix community is using connection and a nurturing spirit to help each other rise again.

CHAPTER FORTY-EIGHT

RISE. RECOVER. LIVE.

The first time you make your way to The Phoenix's two-story, eleven-thousand-square-foot gym at 54 Newmarket Square, located in Boston's Wholesale Food Terminal—a seemingly random location but immediately adjacent to the intersection of Mass and Cass—you might get salty with your GPS. You might also hear your stomach start to growl. Delivery trucks and warehouses in all directions advertise Pig Rock Sausages, Boston Brine and Smoke, Seafood Kingdom, Chinese Spaghetti Factory, Lighthouse Soups and Chowder Company, and much more.

If you hang in there, behind all the food warehouses and aggressive truck drivers will emerge a large red and white building with our trademark Phoenix logo. (Thanks to the greater Boston donor community, we were able to raise the deposit on the building and secure a commercial mortgage.)

I wish we had better food to offer our visitors, given our nearby competition; I'm afraid the best we can offer in the way of cuisine is my famous pour-over coffee along with some leftovers from the potluck social the night before or a takeout menu from Victoria's Diner around the corner, where several of the waitstaff are also in recovery. But if it's emotional nourishment you're seeking, you've come to the right place.

When you enter—through front doors that will be heavier the first time you walk through them than they ever will be again—you'll be welcomed by somebody at our ever-popular coffee counter.

That person might be Alex, a gregarious Phoenix volunteer coordinator with an infectious smile who got sober in March of 2020. Five years ago, instead of being at the gym at 7:30 a.m., he'd likely have been strung out looking for his next bag of methamphetamine. Now he's at our morning circle-up, sharing a little bit of his story and telling newcomers, "At The Phoenix we can do something better with our lives that we can't do alone." Alex has now mentored dozens of volunteers who are in turn reaching hundreds of Phoenix members.

Or you might be greeted by Dina, our resident "Mama Bear," a survivor of childhood sexual abuse who's in recovery from a long-term heroin addiction: Dina did heroin from age twenty-nine to fifty. Before that she'd worked steadily at a bank. Then something happened to open the floodgates, and all the pain she'd stuffed for years rose to the surface.

Over the next twenty years her life became unmanageable, as she lost jobs and resorted to petty crimes to feed her addiction, leading to jail time. On her last day of using, Dina tried to commit suicide and her daughter saved her life. "That was unconditional support right there," Dina says. "The next day I went to detox, and that was it."

Dina is fortunate that her husband and kids—she also has a son—stuck with her. "Families do recover," she says. "My family didn't turn their backs on me because they knew who I was. They just couldn't help me unless I could tell them where it hurt. Nobody signs up for addiction," she adds. "No one says, 'Give me that pen; I want to ruin the next twenty years of my life.'"

A few weeks into her recovery, Dina's recovery facilitator introduced her to The Phoenix. She's been coming ever since. On February 28, 2019, she became a Phoenix staff member. Currently, her title is community champion. She does outreach in prisons, runs sober socials, provides packets of recovery resources for anyone who comes to The Phoenix, and she is a trained recovery coach who wants to become an advocate for women in the penal system. "It's amazing what we can do once we know our worth," she says. "And that's what we do here at The Phoenix. We help one another."

* * *

Once you make it past Alex or Dina, whose warmth and cheer invite you to hang out indefinitely, if a workout is in progress, music will be booming. You'll see an enormous rock-climbing wall, lots of weights, and high above the gym floor, a banner with these words: "Rise. Recover. Live."

Those are the goals all of us in the Phoenix community share and inspire each other to achieve. We help each other rise from the ashes of our addiction. We support each other in our recovery. And when we say "live," we mean more than survive. We empower each other to thrive.

This, in a nutshell, is The Phoenix culture. And culture drives movements. In our case, it's a strong sober active community culture, which I talk about in this chapter. But also digital culture and pop culture, which I talk about in the next. Our vision now is to employ all three to change how society views and treats addiction. And in so doing, to turn our empowerment-based approach to thriving in sobriety into a movement of millions.

That's not a pipe dream. After years of adding members one bike ride or hike or climb at a time, our new member outreach is firing on all cylinders—we're now adding as many new members each month as we used to reach in a year. That's partly due to the volunteer-led strategy I proposed in that fateful meeting with Stand Together Foundation in June 2019. Since 2021, when we launched our volunteer program, we've built a legion of trained volunteers who lead roughly two-thirds of all Phoenix programs in the fifty states.

In addition, our online workouts, yoga sessions, dance fitness, strength building, meditation, crafting, and more continue to connect thousands of Phoenix members nationwide. And our generous, committed donors—some of whom have battled addiction themselves or have loved ones who are still struggling or are in recovery—have allowed us to open popular brick-and-mortar chapters in several states beyond Colorado; we're now also in California, Florida, Nevada, Pennsylvania, Kansas, and Massachusetts.

All these new initiatives, most of which have happened in the past five years, have put us on track to reach the million-member mark by 2025. From there, we'll start working on adding an *s* to the end of the word "million." At our current growth rate, we intend to reach ten million people by 2030 and twenty million over the next decade.

* * *

Our volunteer strategy has not come without its challenges and crazy moments. I first started testing it several years back, pre-COVID-19, while working closely with Chris Daggett to launch our Boston chapter. At that point, we had already expanded to Orange County, California, thinking the only way to scale was to open gyms everywhere.

That meant we'd need millions of dollars to fund a Phoenix chapter in any new market we entered. Even under our most optimistic scenarios, that was not sustainable. Jacki had calculated that to serve the number of people in need with our current brick-and-mortar model would mean hiring a thousand new employees in California alone.

"Am I reading the tea leaves wrong, or does it seem insanely undoable to hang our growth strategy on building a coast-to-coast chain of Phoenix gyms?" I asked Chris one day after we finished a Phoenix workout together. "I'm thinking we need a new approach."

It must have taken him a whole two seconds to say, "Yeah, truth! I agree." Turns out he'd been thinking about this as well.

That's when Chris shared an idea about how we could empower volunteers—people in recovery who shared our vision and values—to run Phoenix programs in willing CrossFit gyms. To protect ourselves, we decided to launch the test initiative as an off-brand Phoenix spin-off we called Human Strength. That way if things didn't go well, it wouldn't reflect poorly on the Phoenix brand.

We knew the appetite for people to volunteer was there because so many had been deeply impacted by addiction. For example, a gym owner who'd previously given us space to launch in Orange County had lost his business partner, a co-owner of their gym, to addiction. Another gym owner, who'd given us a space in his CrossFit gym in Philadelphia, was himself in recovery.

We activated those early adopters along with a few other locations with amazing success. And because those sites shared the Phoenix ethos and our guiding principles, the culture at Human Strength events replicated the Phoenix culture, led and inspired by volunteers. It was so popular we realized we had to move it on brand quickly.

So we added an "Initiate" tab on our website, calling for volunteer cohorts interested in starting a Phoenix chapter in their community. We figured we'd be lucky to get a couple dozen serious applicants. Instead, all those people who had reached out over the previous decade wanting The Phoenix in their community came out of the woodwork. In the space of a few months, we had seven hundred cohorts apply, from cities all over the country.

Applicants included individuals in recovery who had unique gifts they wanted to share in supporting others; this group included cycling coaches, yoga teachers, and fitness instructors. Not surprisingly, we heard from an overwhelming number of family members, loved ones, and friends of someone struggling who they were trying to help. An unexpected bunch of responses came from EMTs and probation officers who wanted to do more to assist the people they served. We even heard from individuals who were civic-minded and simply wanted to make their communities better.

Granted, some applicants didn't exactly qualify as a cohort, like a guy with a bike, who I of course had a soft spot for, but who was only two weeks sober. But we also got some really strong ones, like the parent of someone who'd struggled with addiction in Boise, Idaho, who was closely connected to that community and got us started there. That's where I learned an invaluable movement-building lesson: if you want to make something happen, find a motivated mom to help.

So with more applications coming in than we could handle, we took the "Initiate" tab down and activated the top thirty. But not before the groundswell of interest from folks closest to the problem caught the attention of our new funding partners at Stand Together, who believe deeply in bottom-up solutions to society's most intractable challenges.

What was dawning on all of us was the idea that everyone who's been touched by addiction has, through their own intrinsic strength, the ability to be part of the solution. That led us to start asking: What if we'd been able to activate all seven hundred applicants? So we started opening up our thinking about what The Phoenix could be and empowered our volunteers to add a broad spectrum of activities to The Phoenix's calendar.

A funny thing happened a few years later. I went to a volunteer-led workout at one of the original sites, and the people there did a double take when they saw the Phoenix logo on my shirt. "That's just like the Human Strength logo!" somebody said.

"I know." I laughed. "That's because it's the same thing."

"Yeah, right" was the look I got back. The brand loyalty had grown quickly because of the impact Human Strength had made on people's lives. It had taken on a life of its own. I'm sure they still think I was just a guy who'd ripped off their logo.

* * *

One hot summer day after juggling three very rewarding but clearly competing sets of demands—helping (I hope) my wife take care of our two energetic toddlers; leading and supporting Phoenix team members in their growth initiatives; and writing this book—I took a break and headed downstairs from my Phoenix office to the gym to join a workout.

Not just any workout, though. This one was full of what society would classify as the most "broken" people. Some straight out of prison, a half dozen with ankle monitors on. Lots of crooked noses earned the hard way. People whose bags held all their worldly possessions, who were staying in temporary housing as they climbed their way out of homelessness. Yet in comparison to what I was seeing on my twenty-four-hour news and social media feeds, they were the most supportive group of people I'd been exposed to in quite some time.

At the Boston Phoenix, in collaboration with the Boston Police Department, we have an aged wellness program, in which older people living in lower-income senior facilities come in once a week for a coffee social. Most of the individuals in this program have been impacted by substance use either personally or through a loved one. Realizing there's power in multigenerational mentorships, we started inviting people living in nearby sober homes to join the social.

It's a way of bringing together older folks who don't have as many people in their lives anymore with younger guys in their thirties and forties. The rewards are two-fold: the folks in the aged wellness program feel a greater sense of purpose, and these younger guys get some love, respect, and admiration they might not currently get from their own families. This is a classic case of mutual benefit—both the senior citizens and the guys reentering society end up helping themselves by helping each other. It's nice to watch it happening in real time.

Similarly, we give local firefighters and EMTs free access to our Boston gym for training exercises and workouts. This helps reduce the stigma and stereotyping that goes with addiction. These firefighters and paramedics are out on the streets saving lives—occasionally by administering Narcan to someone in danger of dying from an opioid overdose. When they realize their healthy, helpful greeter at The Phoenix is a person whose life Narcan saved, it helps change their preconceived notions of addiction.

These Phoenix gatherings look like a mosaic of people from all different backgrounds. I find it remarkable that the most nurturing places

I'm exposed to in communities throughout America are the Phoenix events I attend. This diverse group of individuals coming together to help lift each other up comprises people who are viewed as being on the fringes of our society. Yet it seems to me that people all over America are thirsting for what folks in recovery are finding at The Phoenix.

Label us as "on the fringe" or "hopeless case" or whatever. But we've found a way to build a nurturing community grounded in ideals, principles, and an ethos that all start with believing in each other. There's something for everyone to learn from that—and it transcends addiction.

CHAPTER FORTY-NINE

CULTURE BUILDS MOVEMENTS

When you think about music festivals, what images come to mind? For me, it's big crowds, my favorite bands, overpriced merchandise—and lots of drugs and alcohol. That's what you sign up for when you buy your tickets, right? It's just generally accepted concert culture. The result: many people in recovery just stay home. Given the transformative power of music to heal and inspire, that's deeply unfortunate.

So we've decided to turn that challenge into an opportunity. In partnership with Stand Together Music, The Phoenix is working with the music community—including Live Nation Entertainment, which owns the majority of the top U.S.-based amphitheaters—to help destigmatize addiction, support recovery, and create a more inclusive environment in which all music fans feel safe and welcome. We're calling this campaign "1 Million Strong."

We know culture campaigns can shift paradigms. Think about a few that became movements: Tobacco-Free Kids. Earth Day. #MeToo. Black Lives Matter. So we asked ourselves: "What if we built on The Phoenix's organic, grassroots campaign to reach a million people struggling with substance use by 2025 by leveraging the power of pop culture—starting with music—to reach this goal, and surpass it, even sooner?"

Many top players in the music industry didn't need a lot of convincing. When we started talking about ideas like creating sober spaces at concerts, selling mocktails, and having musicians spread the word that sober concerts are cool, they said, "Hell, yes. We're ready, because we're losing too many artists and others we care about."

So in 2023, for the first time, The Phoenix hosted a sober kickoff party before the New Orleans Jazz and Heritage Festival. Over the course of two weekends, we saw around twenty-five hundred people come through the 1 Million Strong sober tent, in the middle of the Fair Grounds Race Course where the festival is held. The Phoenix members, volunteers, and staff were on hand to meet with concertgoers and talk about our sober active community.

It was so popular we did it again in 2024, early enough to promote our sober events in the Jazz Fest marketing material. The crowd favorite was the mocktail truck parked outside the sober tent, which tapped up to twelve kegs of mocktails nightly—beverages included the Gin Fizz, Grapefruit Spritz, and Libre Refresher—based on Phoenix-curated recipes.

This year we had a presence for the third year in a row at Bourbon and Beyond in Louisville, Kentucky, and that's a big deal in the recovery space. People say, "Oh, you guys are back. OK, I can depend on you." And this time they bring their dad or their brother or their best friend. The next weekend in Louisville we were at Louder Than Life. Throughout summer and fall of 2024, we connected with roughly twenty thousand people within the sober spaces we created at a variety of music festivals around the country.

Eventually we want to develop a model for others to adopt if they want to create their own sober spaces at concerts and to offer sponsorship opportunities—for example, a 1 Million Strong Wellness Retreat sponsored by a local hospital, where people can go to recharge before going back out into the festival space.

But the bigger idea is for The Phoenix's inclusive, supportive ethos to spread beyond the sober tent to the concert venue as a whole—so even though The Phoenix and 1 Million Strong will not always be at a festival, the spirit is there because the festival is using our blueprint to bring it to life.

To that end, Live Nation is committed to helping its employees incorporate sober culture into its concert venues. As a start, given the enormity of that goal, they're giving their staff the tools they need to live a sober lifestyle themselves. They call the initiative "Sober Nation." As part of that, a newly created internal group of Live Nation employees can connect with their colleagues who are in recovery as well as with outside resources.

But I'm saving the best for last. Given that concert promoters and managers frequently travel, Live Nation employees can now find the Phoenix community wherever they go. That's because part of what powers Sober Nation is The Phoenix's revolutionary new digital app, which we've been developing since September 2020—based in part on Jacki's suggestion we create an online "Community for Good" to elevate hope over fear—and rolled out in 2021.

The Phoenix app will eventually be the gateway to a whole online ecosystem for people in recovery and their loved ones to connect with limitless sources of help and with each other. If culture builds movements, then digital culture has enormous potential to help build a sober movement of millions. So, I told the team, "The logical next step in The Phoenix's evolution is to transform how we build community through technology." I can't overstate how excited I am about the progress we're making to do just that.

* * *

Jacki's passion to expand our digital community grew out of watching the pandemic turn us into a nation of social media users. At the same time, Zach Sloan, a tech expert we hired during the pandemic to help The Phoenix pivot to live-stream programming (and who is now also our chief operating officer), was really locked in on the fact that deaths of despair had become the fastest-growing category of cause of mortality in the U.S., in tandem with the well-documented epidemic of loneliness.

"We're having all these mental health and substance use issues at the same time we're seeing high rates of loneliness," Zach noted at a meeting during the height of the pandemic. "Could there be some correlation there?" That led us to take a deeper look at the power of human connection and ask, "Even in this world where we're more digitally connected than ever, are we more socially disconnected than ever?" This question resonated with all of us.

"Well," I said, "who better to solve for that than The Phoenix?" Zach was super motivated to lead that effort.

It started as just a calendar function, so you could find Phoenix events near you. But early on, a Stand Together adviser, Ski Ahmad, who had experience helping the YMCA in Wichita develop a similar app, asked, "Hey, what is so unique about Phoenix in-person events?"

Jacki immediately responded, "It's the authentic, genuine connections that are being made in person that help fortify sustained recovery and long-term community."

Spending time with Ski is like plugging yourself into an electrical outlet. If someone could bottle his positive energy and sell it, they'd get rich quick. His eyes lit up. "Well, then that right there has to be the core design tenet of this technology," he said. "We don't want to build this as an efficiency engine. We want this to be an extension of what we do in person."

That led to a whole host of ideas, including the need for a Team Up function that lets Phoenix volunteers connect with each other and self-organize to deepen and expand Phoenix programs within their communities; a quality control function that allows users of the platform to rate The Phoenix or partner activities in a format similar to a Yelp review; and a plan to bring partners on board from the treatment, recovery, and mental health communities to provide resources and a portal to their own community space.

If you work in the food service industry, for instance, there's a group called Ben's Friends, a nonprofit that hosts recovery support meetings for restaurant workers, on our app. In future updates, members of the treatment community will be able to set up private groups for their alumni to stay connected and to help support their recovery journey by connecting them to other partner resources on the platform.

You can also join The Phoenix live in-person or online events, as well as on-demand virtual events. If you don't want a live event, you can do a ten-minute gratitude meditation or a five-minute practice for restful relaxation. If you're feeling more energetic, you can do twenty minutes of exercise, building strength for handstands and push-ups. Those are on demand at any time.

Community support is always just one click away. One of our virtual fitness instructors, Melissa DeStefano, overcame a heroin addiction following a traumatic childhood to become a personal trainer, and now the daily online ThePhoenix.org workout group she leads has become like a family. "I don't have a lot of friends in recovery in my hometown," one of the members of that group, Ellis, told us. "Melissa is my best sober friend in the world. And seeing her every day, I know that it matters to her, that I matter to her."

* * *

What's amazing is that in just four years, we've come close to adding much of the functionality we envisioned in those early brainstorming meetings and we're already coming up with additional features to make the Phoenix app smarter and more interactive.

For example, we recently added an exciting new feature called Moments. It allows users to capture special moments—something as exhilarating as climbing a rock face or as peaceful as savoring their sobriety at a coffee shop—and upload them to the Phoenix home feed. You become the hero of your own journey. If you're a new member hitting that home feed, you'll be comforted and inspired by lots of real-life reels of people thriving in sobriety.

And as the app gets smarter, it can be used to support and track your own individualized self-actualization dashboard. Once you're at the point in your recovery journey where you're starting to think about a meaningful career path, for instance, your dashboard will add workforce development events to your calendar, along with opportunities to clean up your résumé and learn computer programming skills or whatever is relevant to your goals and interests.

Or maybe, like me, you get to a contemplative place where you're ready to do some trauma work to address the underlying *Why?* of your addiction. At that point, "Seek Healing" would start showing up in your feed.

As is the case with our in-person community, the whole purpose of our technology platform is to help you learn and grow. It won't be about accumulating more followers or likes or about selling you products, and this is what sets it apart. Today most social media and technology apps exist to monetize users and their data. Yet the sole purpose of the Phoenix app is to empower the people who use it by helping them knock down barriers that are keeping them from reaching their full potential.

If you've seen the Oscar-winning docudrama *The Social Dilemma*, you'll recall it depicts social media as a monetizing, capitalizing, extorting universe that plays to the darkest elements of our soul. But what if we could use the power of technology and social media to do just the opposite? What if we could use it to lift, support, connect, and empower all our members toward self-actualization? To create, as Jacki proposed (after watching *The Social Dilemma*), a digital community for good?

Just imagine every swipe, click, and morsel of content you consume moving you closer to meaningful connection with others. The Phoenix app has the potential to do that at scale, and in fact is already helping hundreds of thousands of people. It will offer a wide array of resources far beyond what The Phoenix alone can offer. This is another example of how we're using culture, in this case digital culture, to help grow a movement.

CHAPTER FIFTY

FROM IRONMAN TO FLOWER MAN

One of the most invaluable and enduring gifts my mother gave to me, back in 2012, was an introduction to a remarkable human being whose support, advice, and friendship I've come to rely on more than she knows. Her name is Renee White, and I mentioned her earlier—she is my senior executive assistant at The Phoenix, and she has figured out how to fit forty-eight hours of meetings and commitments into twenty-four-hour days while keeping everyone happy in the process.

But she's so much more than that. In some ways Renee, who has a son just a little younger than me and calls me "one of her boys," helped fill a piece of the large gap my mother left behind. They'd met in the spring of 2011 while Renee was working as chief of staff for Colorado's Senate Minority Office and my mom was being honored for her work as U.S. ambassador to Finland by the State Senate. She and Renee got to talking in Senate Minority Leader Mike Kopp's office, and they hit it off.

A year later Mom's assistant, Evelyn Lim, invited Renee for coffee. "I don't know if Marilyn told you her son Scott has a nonprofit called Phoenix Multisport," she said. Renee had never heard of it. "It's starting to grow, and Scott needs someone who can wear many hats. They'd like to have you come work for him." Mom had thoroughly vetted Renee, and I trusted her instincts when it came to judging people. Renee sounded like just what I needed, albeit maybe a little overqualified. So we agreed a lunch was in order.

We all met at our location on Champa Street. Renee arrived from the splendor of Denver's brass and marble capitol to find The Phoenix building situated in a run-down neighborhood, with unhoused people out front. But once she met me and learned more about The Phoenix mission, she later told me, "That was a done deal for me. I never looked back." Coming to work for The Phoenix was the best decision she could have made, she said, because she was "in recovery from politics." And she was only half joking.

Renee also benefited from The Phoenix as a person with several loved ones who'd struggled with addiction. That includes her son, who is in long-term recovery from an OxyContin addiction following two back surgeries twenty years ago, and her ex-husband, who died of alcohol-related causes. AA had not worked for him. Renee believes that if The Phoenix had existed then, he may still be with us.

Renee's father, a World War II veteran, also suffered from alcoholism; he drank to stuff the pain he'd felt growing up an orphan, followed by the trauma of war. Because of her work with The Phoenix, Renee developed insights about trauma and addiction that brought closure in a conversation with her dad before he died. "Now I get it, Dad," she told him. "I don't know how you got through it all. I'm sorry I didn't understand your pain. But now I do."

* * *

Renee turned out to be a gift from my mom that kept on giving. One day, just before Christmas of 2012, she walked into my office with a festively wrapped package.

I opened it to find a remarkable wordless picture book called *The Flower Man* by a local author and artist named Mark Ludy who lives in Windsor, Colorado. It's about this little old man who arrives in a dreary, run-down, black-and-white town and buys a shabby house. He paints it and plants lots of flowers, which he starts giving out to the townspeople, who are amazed at his colorful house.

Each page of the book gets happier and more colorful as the Flower Man spreads friendship, love, and joy throughout the town. Until the last page, which returns to black and white, as the Flower Man begins again in the next town.

Renee gave me the book because, she said, "Yeah, you're an Ironman. But you're also the Flower Man. [She also knew that being dyslexic, I liked wordless books!] It's exactly what you're doing, going into communities that might be dark and bringing some light. You start by helping one person, and that keeps going like a ripple in a pond. That's The Phoenix—it keeps going and going. It can change so many lives."

And yes, of course, I did what? I cried.

Mark holds little art fairs once in a while. After attending one, Renee surprised me with signed, framed prints based on the book. In one the Flower Man is drinking a cup of coffee, and on the back, she'd written, "Your drink of choice is now coffee." That it is, and how grateful I am for that. In another, a little bird sits on the Flower Man's shoulder. Renee said, "That's me, the little bird. So if you ever feel alone in this daunting work, just know I'm always right there with you."

I'll never forget how much Renee has helped me, in both my professional and personal life. I'm endlessly touched—and motivated—by her faith in me and her kind words comparing me to the Flower Man. But the message that resonated with me most of all from the book was on the final page, back to black and white: just like the Flower Man's, our work here at The Phoenix is never done.

CHAPTER FIFTY-ONE

JUST A GUY ON A TRAM

So now you've heard my life story. One day soon I'd like to hear yours. Because if you're reading this book—whether you're in recovery (and as I said earlier, I think we're all in recovery from something) or are still struggling with some type of addiction—you're someone who is no stranger to trauma and suffering. You have your war stories, and some might be truly terrible. Yet here you are, still in the fight. That ember inside you is still burning. And whether you know it or not, your courageous inner self is quietly seeking a nurturing place where that ember can get the air it needs to catch fire.

If a supportive sober community is what you or your loved one is looking for, The Phoenix is here for you. No questions asked. The only cost of admission is forty-eight hours of sobriety.

Not into gyms, rock climbing, and barbells? Don't worry; neither were lots of Phoenix members when they first walked through our doors. Many still aren't. In fact, my boxing and mountain climbing journey to sobriety is not the norm for 99 percent of Phoenix members. That's why we have yoga, art, nature walks, and low-intensity workouts. And we are excited to add new activities that our entrepreneurial volunteers suggest. After all, it's their movement as much as it is mine.

We're a sober active community, yes. What do we mean by "active"? It starts with the act of taking that first step.

At The Phoenix, we're here to lift each other up, not pull each other down. That's our ethos. Our culture is guided by principles rather than rules. Those principles are grounded in a deep belief in the dignity, worth, and limitless potential of *all* people, regardless of their circumstances. That's why when you enter a Phoenix gym or participate in a Phoenix activity, you'll feel the warmth of lots of embers burning brightly all around you. Before you know it, you'll be part of a nationwide Phoenix bonfire, glowing from coast to coast with brilliant, previously untapped human potential that has been unleashed.

* * *

In retracing my personal journey to sobriety while writing this book, I kept thinking back to the night on the lower field on my dad's farm, where Mark, Amyla, and I had sat with him watching the sunset. It occurred to me that the sober empowerment movement we're building is not unlike the flocks of geese we'd heard flying overhead to land on the lake below. One lone goose flying overhead might go unnoticed. But in concert they are hard to ignore.

Here's something you might not know about geese: they are very loyal and emotional. They mate for life and mourn the loss of their mates and eggs. They fly as a flock, in a V-formation, because they can get farther faster. Why is that? Because each bird behind the leader takes advantage of the updraft of air coming from the wing tips of the bird in front. *They literally lift each other up.* That's how they preserve energy and build momentum to reach their destination.

And just as a flock starts with one bird or small group of birds, a movement starts small and grows as more members join the formation and we begin to lift each other. That is the wing song that could lift us all. I think back to the early days, just waiting at the gym, hoping somebody would show up after spending all day sticking flyers on corkboards in supermarkets. And eventually somebody did, and then more and more showed up, until our numbers were increasing exponentially. And I thought, "Now this is becoming a movement."

Then one day I was traveling through Denver International Airport. At fifty-three square miles, it's the biggest airport in the U.S. and the second largest in the world (behind Beijing). I was wearing my Phoenix T-shirt, and I'd jumped on the tram to get to the main terminal. I noticed the guy next to me eyeing my T-shirt.

"Oh, man, you go to The Phoenix too?" he asked.

"I do," I answered with a smile. We always remind our members that when we're wearing The Phoenix apparel, we're serving as ambassadors in the community. We might be the first person somebody meets on their path to recovery. So we go out of our way to always be thoughtful.

"Yeah, me too, man. What's your favorite event?" he asked.

I said, "Oh, I love all of them. I try to go to as many things as I can."

"Yeah, same here. I really dig it. Where do you go to The Phoenix?" he asked.

"In Boston, mostly," I said. What about you?"

"I go in Wichita," he replied.

And that's when it really hit me. I'd started in Boulder back in 2006 as just a guy and a bike, with a simple vision. I wanted to build a nurturing community of people who would support and empower each other in recovery by bonding over shared goals and experiences, and believing in each other, rather than identifying first as our disease. I'd hoped this new approach, based on the innate strength and dignity of *all* people, regardless of circumstance, might change the way loved ones, treatment industry experts, government officials, and society at large view and treat addiction.

As these ideas took hold, it struck me that Phoenix events had become a microcosm of America, with people at all stages of the addiction spectrum, from people struggling with alcohol to opioid overdose survivors, doing squats next to the cops and first responders. With people of all ages and beliefs—liberals, conservatives, and members of all faiths, sexual preferences, and gender identities—fist-bumping and listening and learning from each other. Plenty of loved ones and supporters show up too.

And I thought, "Wouldn't it be great if the Phoenix ethos could permeate society more broadly?"

And now that movement had spread to the point where here I was, just a guy on a tram, one of a couple hundred thousand people passing through the airport that day, standing next to a guy who was a proud member of the Phoenix community in Wichita. He didn't know who I was, and it didn't matter. I was wearing a Phoenix T-shirt, so I was his friend. And he was mine.

To me, he was the walking embodiment of how far we'd come. A guy who personified pride in sobriety rather than shame in addiction. A guy who could have been any Phoenix member anywhere, eager to connect, ask how I'm doing, and tell me he's doing OK. And to let me know where I could find him. And one day I knew I would.

"Well, keep it up, man," I said. "Maybe I'll see you there."

DISCOVER MORE RESOURCES ONLINE

Dear Reader,

Thank you for joining me on my journey of recovery and finding freedom in sobriety.

As we navigate this path together, I want to offer you additional resources to improve your experience and support your journey or that of your loved one.

On The Phoenix website, you'll find:

1. **A Guide to Combatting Stigma:** Learn how to discuss addiction and recovery in a compassionate and stigma-free manner, fostering understanding and empathy for individuals impacted by addiction. (You may have noticed that over the course of the book, my language shifts as a reflection of how my understanding of this changed over the years.)

2. **The Phoenix Ethos and Values:** Explore the principles that guide our community and inspire positive transformation in the lives of individuals overcoming addiction, as well as those supporting them. We believe these principles can be applied in all aspects of our life to build more nurturing and empowering communities throughout our country.

3. **Actionable Guides and Resources:** Gain access to practical resources and actionable guides to aid your personal recovery journey, provide support to loved ones, or learn how you can help the Phoenix movement grow. It is up to us to be the change we want to see in the world.

Whether you're seeking guidance for your own recovery, offering support to someone you care about, or simply looking to learn more about substance use disorders and related topics, we have valuable tools and information for you.

Simply scan the QR code below or visit **thephoenix.org** to access these resources. You can also join the Phoenix community by downloading our new The Phoenix app at **thephoenix.org/app**.

Together, we can create a movement where everyone is empowered to thrive.

HOW THE PHOENIX WORKS

THE SCIENCE BEHIND SOBER ACTIVE COMMUNITIES

*I*n my story, I tried to show how the basic principles of The Phoenix arose more or less organically. They were, at the start, based on my experience. I knew how powerful shared physical activity was from sailing on the Te Vega, climbing Cho Oyu, and biking with Phoenix Multisport. I saw it quiet the negative forces that drove my addiction. I saw how the accomplishment inherent in shared activity began to build my self-esteem and heal my trauma. I saw how a connection to a sober active community not only supported me in recovery but also gave me space to thrive. The Phoenix's first research experiment, if you want to call it that, was my own life.

Add to that the wisdom of a couple amazing friends who have been instrumental to the launch and growth of The Phoenix. Together, Jacki Hillios (now The Phoenix's deputy executive director), Ben Cort (now the CEO of Union EAP and NRT Behavioral Health), and I instinctively set out to build a community in which people believe in each other no matter what circumstance they are overcoming. This is how the Phoenix ethos got woven into the organization's fabric from the beginning.

From this foundation, Jacki, whose PhD is in social work, integrated theory and science to build our first change model and shape our approach. Early on, for example, the growing science behind the power of peer support solidified our commitment to empowering people to help one another. Research on trauma cemented our belief that creating safe, supportive spaces was essential. At every turn, science has informed our strategic decisions.

281

Today, we rigorously track the impact our program has on our members. We do this not only because we always want to know how to improve but also because we know that producing new insights about The Phoenix's success will help persuade others to bring our approach to their work too. This is how The Phoenix became more than a community. It became a movement.

In this appendix, I want to share some of what we've learned. Over the last several years, Jacki has been able to grow the team to include world-class research scientists such as our director of research and evaluation, Dr. Beth Collinson, and senior researcher Dr. Katie Heinrich. I'll let them take it from here.

* * *

From its earliest days, The Phoenix's approach has centered on a simple hypothesis: when people affected by addiction or mental health challenges have access to a sober social network and engage in meaningful activities in a safe, supportive environment, their odds of staying sober and thriving

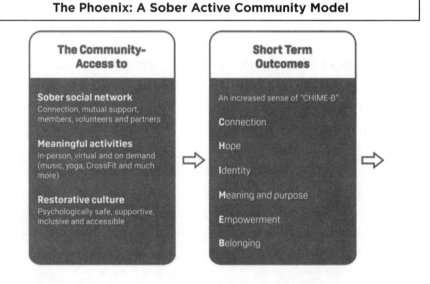

in the long run get dramatically better. That's the thesis driving our sober active communities, which we capture graphically in the model below.

A few key factors have shaped the model, including the experience of people in recovery, as well as theory and research from a variety of disciplines. The model continues to evolve, and we stand ready to revise the model in light of new research and our own evaluation of our members' well-being.

HOW HAS THE PHOENIX MODEL WORKED SO FAR?

To measure improvements experienced by members, we rely on standard surveys widely accepted among researchers in the field, such as the Brief INSPIRE-O,[1] BARC-10 questionnaires,[2] and the Harvard Flourishing Index.[3] We focus on a few key metrics: CHIME-B (members' feelings of connectedness, hope, identity, meaning and purpose, empowerment, and belonging),[4] recovery capital (our members' access to personal, social, and community resources aiding recovery), and flourishing (an experience of whole-life satisfaction, including measurements of mental and physical health, economic security, and stable family life). Researchers in the field have linked all three to sustained recovery and long-term well-being.

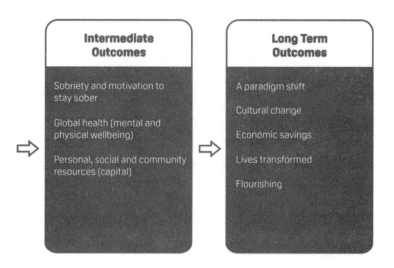

By these measures, surveys of The Phoenix members so far have emphatically supported the effectiveness of our model.

Phoenix members report significantly higher CHIME scores after three months. In our research, members who were new to recovery started their journey at The Phoenix with lower scores on all five parts of the CHIME scale. Within three months, their average score rose 39 percent to a level comparable to the averages of other members. Members who have been in recovery longer—and even members who never had wrestled with substance abuse—also showed improvement in average CHIME scores.

Improvements in CHIME Scores for Phoenix Members by Recovery Status

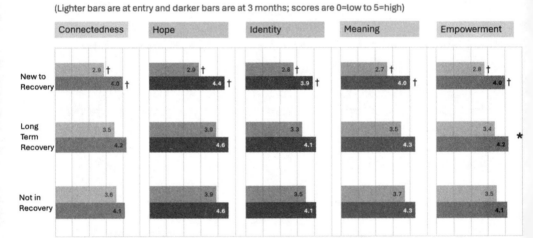

(Lighter bars are at entry and darker bars are at 3 months; scores are 0=low to 5=high)

	Connectedness	Hope	Identity	Meaning	Empowerment
New to Recovery	2.9 † / 4.0 †	2.9 † / 4.4 †	2.8 † / 3.9 †	2.7 † / 4.0 †	2.8 † / 4.0 †
Long Term Recovery	3.5 / 4.2	3.9 / 4.6	3.3 / 4.1	3.5 / 4.3	3.4 / 4.2 *
Not in Recovery	3.6 / 4.1	3.9 / 4.6	3.5 / 4.1	3.7 / 4.3	3.5 / 4.1

† Significantly lower than the other groups; *All groups have significant improvement from entry to 3-months on each part of CHIME

The improvements in CHIME scores are widespread, especially among those new to recovery. Four of every five Phoenix members new to recovery reported an improvement in CHIME scores after three months of membership in The Phoenix. The frequency of reported CHIME improvements was somewhat lower among those who had been in recovery longer or who had not suffered from substance abuse. Even so, more than half the members of those two groups likewise reported higher CHIME scores.

Percent of Members Who Increase CHIME Scores by Recovery Status

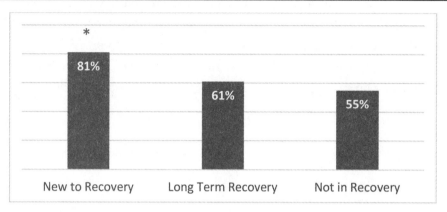

*Significantly greater than the other two groups

Phoenix members also report higher measures of recovery capital after three months. Scores on the BARC-10 measure of recovery capital range from a low of 10 to a high of 60. Overall, the average Phoenix member increased recovery capital by 10 points, while members new to recovery averaged 15-point increases. These increases are around 10 times higher than the 1.3-point increase reported for other recovery community organizations.[5]

Improvements in Recovery Capital Comparing All Members to Those New to Recovery

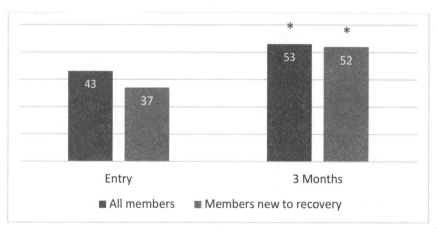

*Significantly greater than the other two groups

Members report that flourishing improves the longer they remain members. Collectively, these changes in CHIME-B and recovery capital increase members' sense of flourishing long-term. Our research shows that Phoenix members' flourishing scores continue to improve with each year of engagement with The Phoenix. Research in the field shows that flourishing protects against substance use and relapse, as well as lessening mental health issues such as suicide, anxiety, and depression.[6,7]

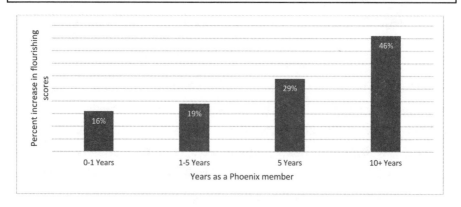

Flourishing Increases by Length of Phoenix Membership

SOME CONSIDERATIONS ABOUT THESE RESULTS

We base our results on the Phoenix members' answers on surveys administered within three months of enrolling with The Phoenix. Biases and recall errors exist in any kind of self-reported data. In addition, The Phoenix is a welcoming organization open to all, encompassing individuals in various recovery stages: actively in treatment, formerly in treatment, spontaneous recovery (never receiving formal treatment), or not in recovery at all (such as family members). Therefore, one should be cautious in making direct comparisons between Phoenix's outcomes and those from other recovery programs.

That said, we are highly encouraged by these results. Because individuals newly embarked on their recovery journey are at the greatest risk of relapse, these indications of significant changes early in their participation with The Phoenix powerfully suggest that they have set a foundation to sustain long-term progress. (To read more detail on The Phoenix results and current research projects, summarized by The Phoenix core research team of Dr. Jacki Hillios, Dr. Beth Collinson, and Dr. Katie Heinrich, please visit thephoenix.org/our-research.)

WHY IS A SOBER ACTIVE COMMUNITY LIKE THE PHOENIX EFFECTIVE?

There are three key factors at play in The Phoenix's success so far: the welcoming nature of our community and the presence of like-minded sober peers, the members' participation in meaningful activities, and a culture that emphasizes psychological safety and a restorative ethos.

THE EMPHASIS ON COMMUNITY SUPPORTS RECOVERY

Community provides a social network of others who are sober: Research highlights the critical role of social support networks in sustaining sobriety.[8,9] However, individuals impacted by addiction may face difficulties finding such networks because of the experiences of trauma, large and small, that led to addiction in the first place. Such scarring experiences can lead to feelings of vulnerability, lack of trust, and a perceived absence of safe environments,[10] which hinder the formation of supportive social connections. The Phoenix addresses this challenge by fostering a safe and inclusive community where members can connect with others in recovery. This shared experience of hard-won sobriety fosters trust and a sense of belonging[11] and provides a supportive environment that empowers members to help each other achieve lasting sobriety.

It encourages volunteering. Many Phoenix members find tremendous meaning and purpose by volunteering. Not only does this strengthen the community, but research has shown volunteering can lead to reduced mortality rates;[12] sustained sobriety;[13] increased connectedness, self-worth, social well-being;[14,15] and improved mental health.[16] In addition to the satisfaction that volunteering provides Phoenix members themselves, it also transforms communities. The meaningful activities hosted by Phoenix members are often held in collaboration with local partners like yoga studios, music festivals, and gyms. This integrates recovery and healing into the fabric of communities—in contrast to the isolation of traditional treatment settings—and allows for exponential growth of the Phoenix movement.

It welcomes partners within local communities. The Phoenix eagerly collaborates with local partners to help members tap into supportive services beyond The Phoenix itself. In 2023, The Phoenix launched a first-of-its-kind online "marketplace" for recovery resources as a way to help members find what they need. When members take part in other recovery resources, there is an added benefit: the interaction allows non-members who are tapping into the same resources to meet members and discover the vibrant Phoenix community.

MEANINGFUL ACTIVITIES ARE A CRITICAL ELEMENT

Even though other recovery strategies rarely involve meaningful activities, the research is unambiguous: engaging in meaningful activities plays a vital role in supporting long-term recovery and well-being.[17,18,19] In the context of The Phoenix, these activities might include not only biking, climbing, and exercise but also, for example, a music jam, yoga, arts and crafts, or a pickleball group. Activities like these provide structure and opportunities for social connection. They also foster a sense of purpose and meaning. Together, these effects help build resilience, reduce relapse risk, and promote personal growth.[20,21] The social nature of these activities further emphasizes the importance of community in recovery, demonstrating that the journey to sustained sobriety is not a solitary endeavor.[22]

PSYCHOLOGICAL SAFETY IS THE THIRD PILLAR OF THE PHOENIX APPROACH

The Phoenix culture prioritizes psychological safety, the condition in which people feel able to take risks and be vulnerable without worrying about negative impacts.[23] This is proving to be essential to the success of The Phoenix model. "The Phoenix is such a comforting, welcoming community," says one member and volunteer. "Even if you mess up . . . you know you'll have the support of the community."

In its training of staff and volunteers, The Phoenix emphasizes that fostering psychological safety is critical.[24] It is, in Scott's phrase, the "magic in the middle." When members participate in The Phoenix and feel psychologically safe, they report having a greater sense of meaning in life, and feeling more connected and more empowered. These factors in turn contribute to increased motivation to stay sober, along with increases in mental and physical health.

How Psychological Safety Facilitates Key Outcomes Within the Phoenix

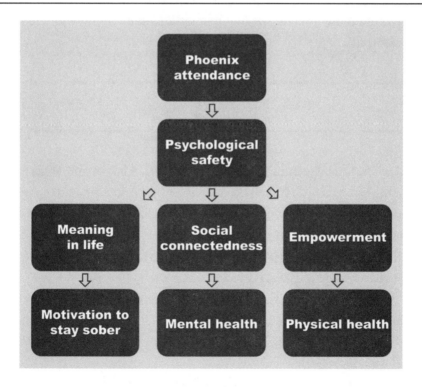

In conclusion: No matter the location of the Phoenix community (in person or virtual), when individuals connect with one another through meaningful activities in psychologically safe, inclusive, and supportive environments, their lives transform for the better. It's important to note as well that the benefits of these substantial individual improvements don't stop with the members. They ripple out to connections around them, such as family, friends, and neighbors. This leads to a more supportive understanding that can interrupt the intergenerational addiction cycle and produce lasting transformation, not just for those in recovery but also for society at large.

One member and volunteer chose these words to sum up the potential of the movement that The Phoenix has ignited: "I'm so happy I found The Phoenix, because that was when I found [a] community that helps me step over the stigma and step into myself. . . . At The Phoenix not only will we step over the stigma, but we will break the stigma. . . . Hopefully, one day, people and children like who I used to be won't need to run to a bottle or to a drug. They can, instead, run into open arms and find friends and community that will help uplift them and help them rise."

To read more on The Phoenix research, please visit thephoenix.org/our-research.

NOTES

1   Moeller, Stine Bjerrum, Pia Veldt Larsen, Stephen Austin, Mike Slade, Ida-Marie T. P. Arendt, Martin Stolpe Andersen, and Sebastian Simonsen. "Scalability, Test–Retest Reliability and Validity of the Brief Inspire-O Measure of Personal Recovery in Psychiatric Services." *Frontiers in Psychiatry*, April 29, 2024. https://doi.org/10.3389/fpsyt.2024.1327020.

2   Vilsaint, Corrie L., John F. Kelly, Brandon G. Bergman, Teodora Groshkova, David Best, and William White. "Development and Validation

of a Brief Assessment of Recovery Capital (BARC-10) for Alcohol and Drug Use Disorder." *Drug and Alcohol Dependence*, 177 (August 2017): 71-76. https://doi.org/10.1016/j. drugalcdep.2017.03.022.

3   Vanderweele, Tyler J. 2017. "On the Promotion of Human Flourishing." *Proceedings of the National Academy of Sciences of the United States of America*. https://doi.org/10.1073/pnas.1702996114.

4   Leamy, Mary, Victoria Bird, Clair Le Boutillier, Julie Williams, and Mike Slade. 2011. "Conceptual Framework for Personal Recovery in Mental Health: Systematic Review and Narrative Synthesis." *British Journal of Psychiatry*. https://doi.org/10.1192/bjp.bp.110.083733.

5   Ashford, Robert D., Austin Brown, Brent Canode, Adam Sledd, Jennifer S. Potter, and Brandon G. Bergman. 2021. "Peer-Based Recovery Support Services Delivered at Recovery Community Organizations: Predictors of Improvements in Individual Recovery Capital." *Addictive Behaviors* 119. https://doi.org/10.1016/j. addbeh.2021.106945.

6   Keyes, Corey L. M. 2007. "Promoting and Protecting Mental Health as Flourishing: A Complementary Strategy for Improving National Mental Health." *American Psychologist* 62 (2). https:// doi.org/10.1037/0003-066X.62.2.95.

7   McGaffin, Breanna Joy, Frank P. Deane, Peter J. Kelly, and Joseph Ciarrochi. 2015. "Flourishing, Languishing and Moderate Mental Health: Prevalence and Change in Mental Health during Recovery from Drug and Alcohol Problems." *Addiction Research and Theory* 23 (5). https://doi.org/10.3109/16066359.2015.1019346.

8   Best, David W., and Dan I. Lubman. 2012. "The Recovery Paradigm: A Model of Hope and Change for Alcohol and Drug Addiction." *Australian Family Physician* 41 (8).

9   Bathish, Ramez, David Best, Michael Savic, Melinda Beckwith, Jock Mackenzie, and Dan I. Lubman. 2017. "'Is It Me or Should My Friends Take the Credit?' The Role of Social Networks and

Social Identity in Recovery from Addiction." *Journal of Applied Social Psychology* 47 (1). https://doi.org/10.1111/jasp.12420.

10 Forbes, David, Emma Lockwood, Andrea Phelps, Darryl Wade, Mark Creamer, Richard A. Bryant, Alexander McFarlane, et al. 2014. "Trauma at the Hands of Another: Distinguishing PTSD Patterns Following Intimate and Nonintimate Interpersonal and Noninterpersonal Trauma in a Nationally Representative Sample." The *Journal of Clinical Psychiatry* 75 (2): 147–53. https://doi.org/10.4088/JCP.13M08374.

11 Landale, Sarah, and Martin Roderick. 2014. "Recovery from Addiction and the Potential Role of Sport: Using a Life-Course Theory to Study Change." *International Review for the Sociology of Sport* 49 (3–4). https://doi.org/10.1177/1012690213507273.

12 Oman, Doug, Carl E. Thoresen, and Kay McMahon. 1999. "Volunteerism and Mortality among the Community-Dwelling Elderly." *Journal of Health Psychology* 4 (3). https://doi.org/10.1177/135910539900400301.

13 Hansen, Mary, Barbara Ganley, and Chris Carlucci. 2008. "Journeys from Addiction to Recovery." *Research and Theory for Nursing Practice* 22 (4): 256–272. https://doi.org/10.1891/1541-6577.22.4.256.

14 Jason, Leonard A., Bradley D. Olson, David G. Mueller, Lisa Walt, and Darrin M. Aase. 2011. "Residential Recovery Homes/Oxford Houses." *In Addiction Recovery Management: Theory, Research and Practice*, edited by John F Kelly and William L White, 143–61. Totowa, NJ: Humana Press. https://doi.org/10.1007/978-1-60327-960-4_9.

15 Sin, Nancy L., Patrick Klaiber, Jin H. Wen, and Anita Delongis. 2021. "Helping Amid the Pandemic: Daily Affective and Social Implications of COVID-19-Related Prosocial Activities." *Gerontologist* 61 (1): 59–70. https://doi.org/10.1093/geront/gnaa140.

16 Jenkinson, Caroline E., Andy P. Dickens, Kerry Jones, Jo Thompson-Coon, Rod S. Taylor, Morwenna Rogers, Clare L.

Bambra, Iain Lang, and Suzanne H. Richards. 2013. "Is Volunteering a Public Health Intervention? A Systematic Review and Meta-Analysis of the Health and Survival of Volunteers." *BMC Public Health.* https://doi.org/10.1186/1471-2458-13-773.

17 Dekkers, Anne, Lore Bellaert, Florien Meulewaeter, Clara De Ruysscher, and Wouter Vanderplasschen. 2021. "Exploring Essential Components of Addiction Recovery: A Qualitative Study across Assisted and Unassisted Recovery Pathways." *Drugs: Education, Prevention and Policy* 28 (5). https://doi.org/10.1080/09687637.2021.1943315.

18 Stokes, Mandy, Peter Schultz, and Assim Alpaslan. 2018. "Narrating the Journey of Sustained Recovery from Substance Use Disorder." *Substance Abuse: Treatment, Prevention, and Policy* 13 (1). https://doi.org/10.1186/s13011-018-0167-0.

19 Best, David, and Charlotte Colman. 2019. "Let's Celebrate Recovery. Inclusive Cities Working Together to Support Social Cohesion." *Addiction Research and Theory* 27 (1). https://doi.org/10.1080/16066359.2018.1520223.

20 Dingle, Genevieve A., Tegan Cruwys, and Daniel Frings. 2015. "Social Identities as Pathways into and out of Addiction." *Frontiers in Psychology* 6 (November 30). https://doi.org/10.3389/FPSYG.2015.01795.

21 Best, David, Jamie Irving, and Kathy Albertson. 2017. "Recovery and Desistance: What the Emerging Recovery Movement in the Alcohol and Drug Area Can Learn from Models of Desistance from Offending." *Addiction Research and Theory* 25 (1). https://doi.org/10.1080/16066359.2016.1185661.

22 Collinson, Beth, and David Best. 2019. "Promoting Recovery from Substance Misuse through Engagement with Community Assets: Asset Based Community Engagement." *Substance Abuse: Research and Treatment* 13. https://doi.org/10.1177/1178221819876575.

23 Schein, Edgar H., and Warren G. Bennis. 1965. *Personal and Organizational Change through Group Methods: The Laboratory Approach.* Wiley.

24 Kahn, William A. 1990. "Psychological Conditions of Personal Engagement and Disengagement at Work." *Academy of Management Journal* 33 (4): 692–724. https://doi.org/10.2307/256287.

ACKNOWLEDGMENTS

I have a long list of individuals I'm deeply grateful for. These are people who have played a role in my own life transformation. Many of these same people have also helped me build the Phoenix movement into what it is today. Here are just a few.

My family members: As you know from the book, my mom Marilyn, sister Amyla, and brother Mark were the touchstones in my life during the ups and downs of my journey through childhood and adulthood, and I'm deeply grateful for them. Intergenerational pain and environmental trauma in our formative years can sometimes cause a ripple of dysfunction among siblings, and for the things I could have handled better over the decades, I am sorry, and I love you.

My wife, Kait, and my children, Magnus and Alice: You are my safe harbor and support system on this daunting and important journey of building the Phoenix movement. Thank you for all you do and the sacrifices you make every day, and for the joy you fill my life with.

Jacki Hillios and Ben Cort: Even though Jacki and Ben are mentioned in the book, I could have written separate books about all the adventures I shared with each of them. Those experiences became the foundation of The Phoenix and all the subsequent adventures we shared together building The Phoenix into what it is today.

Ben—I'm grateful for all our times together, from tying into climbing ropes on Yosemite's pristine granite to swinging ice axes in Smuggler's Notch in Vermont to climbing in Rocky Mountain National Park. I'm also thankful for our conversations on long bike rides and for the days we supported each other through the tough times in life while trying to carve The Phoenix out of the wilderness. And for Alpine starts in the Andes with you and Rourke. And for sharing tears over the Phoenix members who ultimately succumbed to their addiction and pain.

Thank you to Jacki for all the long hours we worked together painstakingly strategizing on the next evolutions of The Phoenix and the constant shared pursuit of creative destruction. And for leading the final pitch on Independence Monument outside of Grand Junction, Colorado. Also for the joy I felt in watching you share your TEDx Talk, "Transcending Addiction and Redefining Recovery," at the White House. And for being there as we looked through our tears after losing our beloved mothers at different times. And most of all just for your friendship.

The Phoenix: First, I would like to thank Katie Waters, who over the years has taken on many of the tasks Renee used to help me with. You have been a blessing in my life and to The Phoenix in building this incredible movement. Also, thank you to every Phoenix staff member, board member, and volunteer. I have learned and grown from my experiences alongside each and every one of you. Special thanks to Dan Jenkins, Dawn Taylor, and Renee White, and to Mike B., Rob B., Michele C., Sean C., Shannon C., Chris D., Todd J., Maggie, Mary Jane, Jo M., Emily Q., Zach S., Tad T., Ben W., and Rourke W.

Shipmates: The *Te Vega* and *Spirit of Massachusetts* crews, Doug and Kristin Atkins, Jim Holmes (Homer), Steve Jacobusse, Burt Rogers, Steve Wedlock, Alex, Amy, James B., Roric B., Shannon C., Jeff and Tara, Kelly S., Niels, James W., and every other crew member I have built boats with or set sail with.

Climbing Teachers and Partners: The EMS Climbing School, Christine Boskoff, Dave Kelly, Matt Mooney, Robert Sagerman, Craig Taylor, Charlie Townsend, Conrad Yeager, John B., and everyone else I've tied into a climbing rope with.

Friends: Team Mercury family, Cam Brensinger, Chris Hillios, and Joe Jingoli (who shares my sobriety birthday but is a few years ahead of me, for your fellowship and friendship in and out of the ring, which did more for me than you may ever know), and to Kim Loeffler from KL Endurance; Leo Martinez; and Dave Sullivan (Sully), Andy C., Galen G., and Kara L. And a special thanks to all the friends I've made along the way who played a key role in this incredible journey.

Mentors and Supporters: Susan Broderick, Jason Crow, Don Fertman, Jamie Horwitz, Charles, Liz, Elizabeth, and Chase Koch, Josh McClellan, Steve Treat, Askia A., Kelly B., Linda C., Katie E., Evan F., Troy and Elizabeth F., Tommy F., Nancy G., Brian H., Lou H., Mary L., Charlie T., and all of our funders, especially those who believed in us early on and those who fueled us in going to scale.

There are so many I didn't mention here, but for all who believed in me, I'll be forever grateful.

ABOUT THE AUTHOR

Scott Strode is the founder of The Phoenix, a national sober active community that has reached more than half a million people impacted by addiction, with the goal of reaching ten million people by 2030.

Born in Pennsylvania to an emotionally abusive father who suffered from untreated mental illness and a distant, workaholic mother, Scott turned to alcohol and cocaine early on as an escape from his tumultuous upbringing.

On April 8, 1997, Scott finally made the life-changing decision to get sober. His strength and resolve came in large part from adopting an active lifestyle that would carry him through his recovery. That lifestyle included boxing, cycling, mountain climbing, triathlons, and almost anything that got him outside.

But it was the connections he formed with others as they bonded over new experiences and shared goals that kept him sober. And this gave him a powerful idea.

Since Scott started The Phoenix in Colorado in 2006 as "just a guy with a bike," this innovative network has expanded across America. It offers a safe, sober active community of peers who support and empower each other every day, fostering healing through all kinds of activities, including concerts, hiking, yoga, lunches, book clubs, meditation, and music jam sessions. As Scott puts it, "We believe in each other even before we believe in ourselves."

He lives in Boston with his wife and two children.